PENGUIN E

VIVEKANANDA

Sankar (Mani Sankar Mukherji), one of Bengal's widely read authors in recent times, is the creator of *Kata Ajanare* (*The Great Unknown*), *Chowringhee*, *Jana Aranya* (*The Middleman*), *Seemabaddha* (*Company Limited*), *Ghorer Madhye Ghar* (*Thackeray Mansion*). *Seemabaddha* and *Jana Aranya* were made into films by Satyajit Ray. Many of Sankar's non-fiction works, including books on Ramakrishna and Vivekananda, have been bestsellers and translated into several languages. Sankar lives and works in Kolkata.

Malati Mukherjee is a writer, translator and editor. She is a storyteller who has published *Nature Songs of Tagore*, a book of songs of Rabindranath Tagore translated from Bengali to English. She has edited (and part-written) a 200-page coffee table book, *The Legendary Fr. E.H. McGrath SJ–Revered Teacher, Inspiring Forever*. She has translated Bitan Chakraborty's novellas *Redundant* and *Collapsed,* which are awaiting publication. Malati runs Words and Space, a writing and editing service. Born in Dakshineswar, Malati now lives in Coonoor, in the Nilgiri hills of South India.

SWAMI VIVEKANANDA

The Feasting, Fasting Monk

SANKAR

Translated from Bengali by
MALATI MUKHERJEE

PENGUIN BOOKS

An imprint of Penguin Random House

PENGUIN BOOKS

USA | Canada | UK | Ireland | Australia
New Zealand | India | South Africa | China

Penguin Books is part of the Penguin Random House group of companies
whose addresses can be found at global.penguinrandomhouse.com

Published by Penguin Random House India Pvt. Ltd
4th Floor, Capital Tower 1, MG Road,
Gurugram 122 002, Haryana, India

Penguin
Random House
India

First published in Bengali as *Ahare Anahare Vivekananda*
By Dey's Publishing, 13 Bankim Chatterjee Street, Kolkata 700 073
First published in Penguin Books by Penguin Random House India 2019

10 9 8 7 6 5 4 3

ISBN 9780143450467

Typeset in Adobe Caslon Pro by Manipal Technologies Limited, Manipal
Printed at Replika Press Pvt. Ltd, India

www.penguin.co.in

Author's Note

Sometimes at a royal banquet served on a golden plate, sometimes sharing a poor man's hunger in a tiny hut and sometimes experiencing the meagre fare of a sanyasi on a pilgrimage through a lonely forest, the last two decades of Swami Vivekananda's years tell an amazing story of a phenomenal life struggle.

Over the last 150 years, a lot of research has been going on, in several countries, on Swamiji's culinary interests. This includes hitherto unknown stories of Swamiji spreading the art of making biryani, pulao and *khichuRi* (khichri—a dish made with rice and lentils), along with his propagation of the Vedas, in the United States of America.

Although today's social philosophers wonder greatly at this world-renounced monk's immense enthusiasm for teaching Indian cooking, it is not quite clear why no complete book about our culinary expert 'Maharaj' Vivekananda has ever been published in any language.

Vivekananda—The Feasting, Fasting Monk is the humble, researched illumination of this thousand-faceted diamond, by me, Sankar.

Translator's Note

My introduction to Sri Mani Sankar Mukherji was through his first book, *Kato Ajanare* (*To So Much That's Unknown*), which I devoured over two days as a schoolgirl. Years later, having begun translating books in earnest, I harboured a desire to one day translate this book.

Last year, when my cousin was to interview Sankar Babu, he asked me half in jest whether I had anything to ask the great author. I replied in the same tone, that he should ask Sankar Babu whether I could translate one of his books to English. I was stunned and elated when the next day my cousin gave me Sankar Babu's response, which was an offer to translate two of his books!

I grew up in Dakshineswar, in my grandfather's home, filled with books, photographs and thoughts of both Sri Ramakrishna Paramahansa and Swami Vivekananda. Occasionally skipping alongside my grandmother on her pre-dawn trips to Kalibari, the famous Kali temple that was Sri Ramakrishna Paramahansa's abode, I was more interested in the trains that thundered over the bridge above the Ganga than in the energy pervading that revered space.

And in all these years, I have never attempted to read a book about either Thakur or Swamiji. Never opened a page of the *Sri Ramakrishna Kathamrita* that sat on my father's bookshelf in a deep blue binding with gilt-lettered titles. Once when a sanyasi in the ochre robes of the order visited my father's home, he urged my father to initiate us children into reading the *Kathamrita*, quoting Thakur as saying that the parrot learnt to speak only if it was taught young. I felt a sense of pride as I heard my father say, 'I would rather they grew up and decided whether to read Thakur's *Kathamrita* or not.'

And as I grew up and moved away from Calcutta, my thoughts veering completely to staying afloat in the world of an English-medium education, I unconsciously decided I would rather not. My grandparents passed on, and Dakshineswar and the temple faded in my memory. Now, while translating this book, those memories have reached out and touched me.

With the convenience of the Internet, I have found myself reading many letters, stories and anecdotes of Swamiji and getting my fill of the writings I have missed out on. It has been an amazing journey, not just of translating the really difficult language, but also breaking off to read about Swamiji as seen through the eyes of his adoring devotees in India, the UK and the US.

This book focuses partly on the 'foodie' aspects of Swamiji, but even more, on his love for cooking and feeding people—feeding his disciples, who could not complain about the red-hot spice and had to eat it up quietly, as well as others he met along life's way and decided, impulsively, to cook for. It speaks of the pain and hurt he felt when he encountered hunger for the first time, and how it changed his perspective forever. Of how he could not bear the anguish of another human being suffering from hunger.

Sankar Babu has meticulously researched through many books to come up with gold nuggets of stories and anecdotes that will thrill the hearts of Vivekananda's admirers. The first part of the book also gives us interesting insights into the history of food and cooking in Bengal. Of how coal came into the state, of the homes before the advent of electricity and how water kept outside overnight turned to ice! It gives us a clear picture of how global warming is slowly turning all our cities warmer by the day.

The second part of the book touches upon the deep relationship that developed between Thakur Ramakrishna Paramahansa and his chief disciple, though young in years. It tells the story of Thakur's last days and how, after his death, the Ramakrishna Mission was set up by twelve young lads, and the untold struggles they went through to discover themselves, and their path.

It also covers Swamiji's travels through India and abroad, and the warmth, love and respect he received almost everywhere he went. Delightful stories abound—on Swamiji's conversations in the US and England and of the opportunities he found to cook his beloved Bengali food for friends and disciples. We owe a huge debt to Swamiji's brother Mahendranath, who in his later life, after Swamiji's death, wielded the expert pen to give us some treasured gems from the life and travels of the Datta family and, in particular, of Swamiji.

The last part speaks of Swamiji's advice to all of Bengal. Having travelled across the world and sampled first hand the food and culture of various countries, he was filled with determination to share the knowledge and advice with the people of his beloved Bengal—on what to eat, how to live and what to practice. Each of these pieces of advice is even truer today than when these books were first published.

This book is the result of deep research into many sources and comes up with stories that may not always be in chronological order. They are delightful anecdotes from each of the three phases of Swamiji's life. They contain pearls of wisdom shared by him with his many disciples in this country and abroad.

An interesting realization for me was that Swamiji did not believe in the concept of vegetarianism for the hardworking poor of our country. He insisted, on several occasions, that while the well-to-do—who do no physical labour and face no real hardships in life—may well indulge in the luxury of vegetarian fare, the poor who have to struggle every day with the hardships life throws at them, need the protein and strength that they can only receive through inexpensive and easily accessible non-vegetarian food.

Through it all, we get a glimpse of Swamiji the person—his abiding love for humanity, his prankish humour and his deep understanding of and belief in the human spirit. Although this is not meant to be a spiritual book, many gleaming truths come through, which help us realize what it means to be a *sadhak* or a seeker.

All translations are demanding. It is very challenging, sometimes impossible, to convey the meaning of the beautifully worded gems of one language in an alien one. This book is even more difficult because of the several words on every page that describe particular items and dishes that do not even exist in other cultures.

On the question of transliteration of the Bengali words in the book, I have used the capital R to emphasis the hard 'r' sound, but for the rest, I have decided to go with whatever is the simplest representation of the actual Bengali sound. For example, the Indian 'barfi' becomes the Bengali '*borfi*'.

My deepest gratitude and pranam to my father, for always urging me to seek the Unknown amidst the known.

My deep gratitude to Sri Mani Sankar Mukherji for the opportunity to immerse myself in the world of Swami Vivekananda and Sri Ramakrishna Paramahansa and for the uplifting experience of getting to understand a little bit of who they were.

My deep gratitude also to my cousin and friend Sri Aditya Chatterjee, through whose intervention this project came into being, but even more, for his painstaking editing and tireless responses to my hundred questions about those aspects of Bengal to which I have had no exposure and for opening my eyes to the context and basis of the hidden nuances that abound in this delightful book.

I am grateful to the editors at Penguin for their thorough and detailed editing and proofreading of the manuscript.

I hope I have been able to convey to the curious non-Bengali reader some understanding of Swami Vivekananda's world, and the joys and sorrows, the elation and the angst that filled his days. Thank you, dear reader, for picking up this book. I hope you will find it fulfilling.

Malati Mukherjee
Coonoor

Dedicated to Dr Sanjiv Goenka, Chairman,
RP-Sanjiv Goenka Group, my three-in-one
employer, student and teacher.

—Sankar

In Gratitude
To my constant companion in all my explorations of
Vivekananda—dear friend, Sri Arunkumar De, whose
ceaseless curiosity, encouragement and affection have
made this book possible.

—Sankar

'He who cannot cook well can never be a genuine sanyasi.'

—Swami Vivekananda

'He stands before you, in so many forms,
where do you search, rejecting them all?
Only he who loves all creatures,
truly serves God.'

—Swami Vivekananda

Author's Preface

To understand the genesis of this book, we must travel back many years, to when the Second World War had occasioned the closure of our Howrah District School in 1942, and I found myself enrolled for a while in Khurut Road's Howrah Vivekananda Institution. Although we were only in the fifth standard, our respected principal Sri Sudhangshu Shekhar Bhattacharya shared many important milestones of Vivekananda's life with us. It was only through his kindness that I had the opportunity to read Vivekananda's letters and biographies—no easy task—at a very early age. A senior school student had informed us that Swamiji loved to eat—and to feed others—from childhood itself. Even more remarkable was the fact that Swamiji himself was an expert in many different cuisines!

When I was a little older, I learnt that very early in life, even before he had bought any books on the Vedas or Vedanta, Swami Vivekananda had already purchased, in easy instalments, an encyclopaedia on French cooking. And with indomitable enthusiasm, long before he established any monastery or mission, he had set up a fancy foodies' club at his Calcutta residence, naming it 'The Greedy Club'.

The same school senior, after extensive research, gathered and gladly shared these exciting snippets of news with us. In later years, he settled abroad, and on his occasional visits to India, continued to supply us with updates about Vivekananda's culinary interests.

Swamiji held that 'God can be attained not just through counting His name with the rosary beads nor through austerities alone. He can be reached through the untrodden path of the flavours of the tongue too.'

Halfway through my life as a writer, I too became keen to learn more about this particular aspect of Vivekananda and initiated attempts to know him well, although I was never brave enough to think of writing a separate book on this difficult subject. In 2014, at the insistence of a friend, I began to wonder how it would be to write something about this amazing sanyasi's food habits along with his long periods of fasting and also to throw some light on his anguish at the world's hungry.

From that audacity arose this quest to discover Maharaj Vivekananda anew ('Maharaj' here is a pun, referring as much to the position of near monarchy he holds among his spiritual followers, as to the term used for erstwhile chefs in the large joint families of India). Readers will be able to surmise from this book why the sanyasi, who had renounced his own home, was so anxious to alleviate the sorrows of the world's famished millions. Why, in rebellious tones, he declared to the world's citizens that there could be no religious practice or indeed any worship at all on an empty stomach.

Quotes

'Keep at it. Keep at it. Don't delay—death approaches ever nearer each day. Don't wait, saying you will do it later—then nothing will happen . . . those who cannot empathize with mankind's sorrows, what kind of humans are they?'

'The history of the world is the history of a few men, who had faith in themselves.'

'Control over self cannot be attained unless control over food is achieved. Overconsumption can cause a lot of harm.'

'People like me are at the culmination of all aggregates. I can eat large quantities of food, or stay without eating at all, smoke continuously or abstain completely. My control over my senses is so strong. Yet, I also willingly experience the senses. Else, where is the value of abstention?'

'*The battles are lost and won, I have bundled my things and am waiting for the great deliverer. Shiva, O Shiva, carry my boat to the other shore.*'*

'One day perhaps, I will throw away this body like an old garment and leave. But I will never give up on service.'

---

* These quotations were originally in English and the actual words spoken by Swamiji himself.

'We Bengalis are very sentimental; that is why there is so much dyspepsia here.'

'Ever since I was conscious, I have never slept for more than four hours in my life.'

'He who does not feed his own mother, how will he ever feed another's mother?'

'Brother, how can the Bengali renounce anything? He could not experience anything; could not earn more than two or three lakh rupees, how will he renounce?'

'When I became a sanyasi, I chose this path knowingly. I knew I would have to go without food. So what? I am, after all, a beggar.'

I am glad I was born, glad I suffered so, glad I did make big blunders, glad to enter peace. I leave none bound, I take no bonds. Whether this body will fall and release me or I enter into freedom in the body, the old man is gone, gone forever, never to come back again. The guide, the guru, the leader, the teacher has passed away; the boy, the student, the servant is left behind.

. . . Behind my work was ambition, behind my love was personality, behind my purity was fear, behind my guidance the thirst of power! Now they are vanishing and I drift. I come! Mother, I come! In thy warm bosom, floating, wheresoever Thou takest me, in the voiceless, in the strange, in the wonderland, I come—a spectator, no more an actor.

Yours faithfully,
Vivekananda

Alameda, California, 18 April 1900
Written to Josephine MacLeod

Having arrived at the evening of my life, I sometimes blame myself for the lack of foresight in my youth and childhood. I remember many conversations about Vivekananda, who is the North Star for people like me. Sometimes in the midst of their detailed interpretation of the textbooks, Howrah's Vivekananda Institution's principal Sudhangshu Shekhar Bhattacharya and his younger brother Himangshu Shekhar, would start to tell us stories about the world-conqueror Narendranath Datta and the significance of his speech at the Chicago's Parliament of World Religions. For the students of standard five, all this was impossible to comprehend. And we would ask, 'What would have happened if Vivekananda had not been able to raise the travel and living expenses for his trip to America?'

Sudhangshu Shekhar would be startled but not bowled out. He would think for a moment and say, 'Our Swamiji is not someone to be stumped so easily. He has acknowledged that it was only his high-spirited boyhood that made it possible for him to travel around the world many times over, even as a penniless adult.'

During school breaks, we were given library books about Swami Vivekananda, like *Karma Yoga* or *Raja Yoga*, which were far too difficult for us. We did read them at the behest of our teachers but could not make anything of them. We often felt that this man Vivekananda was no fun at all! At every opportunity, he spoke incessantly about ignorant Bharat, impoverished Bharat,

Bharat trampled underfoot and suppressed, and yet made no
mention of how we floated on a sea of endless happiness on
our Howrah Khurut Road, Howrah Kali Babu's Bazaar and
Howrah Bangabasi Cinema Hall.

Just when our misunderstandings about sanyasi
Vivekananda had created an insurmountable distance, his
birthday celebrations occasioned huge excitement. There
were tempting preparations of *darbesh* (a Bengali sweet),
khichuRi and oranges being served in every classroom. We
heard, in confidence, that to obtain these special handpicked
Darjeeling oranges, some enthusiastic teachers had crossed
the Ganges to the Chitpur Mechhua Bazaar Fruit Market.
A Muslim devotee of Sri Ramakrishna sold the oranges from
Darjeeling at a special rate. The teachers, all ardent readers
of *Sri Ramakrishna Kathamrita*, believed in and followed the
'Buy a dozen and get one free' principle, as Sri Ramakrishna
had advised his followers to do. Therefore, in accordance
with Thakur Ramakrishna's instructions, they first tasted
the extra and free orange to find out whether they were sour
or sweet, although the fruit seller would say quite clearly
that Darjeeling was Darjeeling—there mango trees yielded
mangoes, not hog plum!

A few days before Vivekananda's birthday, all kinds of
rumours would spread in the school. Rumours that oranges
would be distributed even before the assembly and that for the
mid-day meal there would be Ramakrishna *Math*'s favourite
khichuRi prasad. And in between the two, to keep our hunger
at bay, a 'surprise item' would be served.

There was also once a rumour that we would be served
guavas from the Varanasi wholesale fruit market. The guava
was called '*aamrud*' in Hindi, which for us meant that it was
sure to be as good as the *aam* (the mango).

While the junior boys readily believed the rumour, our well-informed senior, Gaya Da, contested it. 'Impossible!' he said. 'From oranges, we will leap straight to *khichuRi* at 1 p.m.'

Without mentioning his name, I have already said many things about our school senior Gaya Da. In later years, Gaya Da became a non-resident Indian, and at one time, very affectionately supplied me with many little-known facts about Swamiji's life. Gaya Da is not in this world today, so it is necessary to acknowledge my gratitude to him. If he had not taken it upon himself to be our revered guide at school, it would have been impossible for me to dive into the research on Vivekananda at this advanced stage of my life.

To go back to the guava anecdote, disregarding the rumours, Gaya Da had said that mangoes, grapes, apples, pineapples, walnuts, etc., could all be offered at Vivekananda's birthday celebrations, but the guava would never find a place.

Our principal (nicknamed Handu da) told us that Swamiji himself had once revealed that of all the fruits in the world, the one he liked the least was the guava. Our Sanskrit teacher's son Haraprasad, a classmate, often supplied Gaya Da with such interesting bits of information. There is a Hindu ritual that requires participants to permanently give up a fruit of their choice. If Narendranath were to give up any fruit, it would certainly have been the guava! There were, of course, no further discussions about distributing guavas for Swamiji's birthday celebrations.

'Swamiji could not discern the value of a good fruit,' said Gaya Da. We heard that *parabat* or *peyara* (the guava) came to us from across the seas in the first century, during the rule of Kanishka. There is a special mention of this in the ancient Ayurvedic texts of Charaka-Samhita.

I developed a huge respect for Gaya Da. Completely
neglecting the other aspects of Vivekananda's treatise on
samadhi, dhyana, yogasana, etc., he unceasingly and with
with single-minded focus, pursued his attempts to discover
Swamiji anew through the medium of food. His theory
was that researchers had not yet collected much valuable
knowledge about Vivekananda's experiments with food,
fasting and starvation. Gaya Da held that this important
aspect of Vivekananda's stance on all things food-related, had
escaped his world of followers. This audacious sanyasi, who
churned the ocean of the shastras (scriptures), declared to the
travellers on Sri Ramakrishna's path, 'If you cannot cook well,
you cannot be a good sanyasi!' In every era, therefore, there
has been an invisible parallel between a faithful seeker and a
good cook.

Gaya Da always expounded his views on the correlation
between God and food. At every opportunity, he reiterated—
that God could be attained even through food, and this was the
challenge Sri Thakur's dearest disciple Narendranath had left
behind for the world.

Similar to Swamiji's aversion for the guava, devoted followers
have recorded for us many anecdotes from their recollections
about his attitude to various fruits. Without sequencing them
chronologically, I am recording those as received from the book
Vivekananda in the Light of Memory by Swami Poornatmananda.

Let's take the case of his dear disciple Swami Shuddhananda
(1872–1938), who was the head of Ramakrishna Mission for a
short while in 1938. His household name was Sudhir Chandra
Chakraborty. He received his *deeksha* or initiation after Swamiji
had returned from the USA to Belur *Math*, and on the same
day as another of Swamiji's famous householder-disciples,
Sharat Chandra Chakraborty.

After Sharat Chandra's initiation, Swamiji had taken a few litchis (a small, sweet, juicy white fruit with a thin, prickly red skin and a large, maroon egg-shaped seed) from him as *guru-dakshina*. There were some litchis lying in front of Swamiji after Sudhir's initiation as well. He lovingly put them in his disciple's hands and said, 'Give me *guru-dakshina*.'

The chilli cannot be called a fruit, but throughout his childhood, Swami Vivekananda had a tremendous attraction for it. He endorsed it at various times and in various ways. While on his travels, he had told his friend Haripada Mitra, 'A travelling monk receives all kinds of food from various people and water from all sorts of places. That can harm the health. To counter this unhealthy eating and drinking, many monks become addicted to hemp and other intoxicants. I eat chillies for the same reason.'

Once during his travels, hearing that monks should never be stout, he gently objected, saying: 'This is my insurance against famine! Even if I do not get any food for several days, my fat will keep me alive, whereas your vision will be blurred if you do not eat for even a day.'

About exceedingly high expectations from sanyasis, he had said to Haripada Mitra, 'Society thinks that a man becomes *trigunaatita* (one who has conquered all the three *gunas—sattva*, *rajas* and *tamas*) as soon as he takes the monk's vow. You believe he should not eat well, should not have a bed to lie on, so much so that he should not even wear shoes or use an umbrella! Why? Is he not a man like you? Should he not wear saffron robes until he becomes a Paramahansa (a monk of the highest perfection)? That is unfair.'

Swamiji's *gurubhai* (disciple of the same guru) Premananda's younger brother Shantiram Ghosh had jokingly said that Swamiji's favourite fruit was the gulab jamun, not a fruit at all, but a sweetmeat! On Jogeen Maharaj's direction, Shantiram and his wife received initiation from Swamiji on 23 March 1897, after Swamiji returned to Calcutta from the USA. After the initiation, Swamiji said, 'Please bring me some fruit or something.' Shantiram brought a gulab jamun that Swamiji promptly ate. 'He didn't give any further advice.'

Sri Ramakrishna's wife Sarada Devi's disciple and the first pujari (priest) of Belur *Math*'s *Durgotsav* (Durga Puja), Swami Dheerananda has written about another favourite fruit of Swamiji. He (Swamiji) loved to have tender coconut with sugar and ice inside. 'I gave him a tender coconut at Balaram Babu's home. He had it, saying, "Aah! Wonderful! Here, you have some." And then when I was eating it, like a child he said, "Give me some too!" He was not at all concerned about having my leftovers (something inimical to most sanyasis).'

When Swamiji left India for the second time, his South Indian devotees arrived at Madras to see him off on the ship with a few sacks of South India's famous king coconut.

Haricharan Mallik too has reminisced about a meeting with Swamiji at Master Mahendranath Gupta's rented residence in Calcutta's Bhavani Datta Lane. Mahendranath Gupta, often referred to as Mastermoshai, was the author of the seminal book, *Sri Ramakrishna Kathamrita*, the teachings of Sri Ramakrishna. Swami Turiyananda, famous as Hari Maharaj, was also present at the gathering. Swamiji himself had asked Mahendranath in an intimate tone, 'Mastermoshai, can you please arrange for a watermelon or something? Let's have a bite to eat.' It was summertime, and as requested, Mastermoshai arranged for Swamiji's favourite fruit.

Not just the watermelon, there is some reference to the jamun, the Indian blackberry, as well. Towards the end of his life, Swamiji had once rested for a few days in Jagulia at Sister

Mrinalini Basu's home. Naresh Chandra Ghosh has written that when Swamiji left for Belur *Math*, she gave him a basket of fresh jamuns. When they reached the *Math*, Swamiji said, 'First wash all the jamuns well and juice them.' Subsequently, some bottles were washed, filled with the juice and corked tightly. The corks were then secured with strong twine and left in the sun for a week or so. Then, Swamiji asked for the bottles to be transferred to a little dark room next to the Belur *Math* kitchen, under the stairs. One day, when he was having tea, there was a sudden loud burst. He said, 'Run and see—the bottles must be popping.' That was exactly what had happened; the fermented juice had begun to push the corks out and managed to burst out of one of the bottles. Swamiji said, 'This is *sirka* (a kind of cider/vinegar)—very good for digestion. Now it's done to perfection. All of you must have a little daily.'

When we speak of *jaam* (jamun), we cannot forget the *aam* (the mango). Having spent many months at Belur *Math* as a student, Gaur, a lifelong bachelor, has chronicled a few anecdotes from his own life. Among them is the story of Varanasi's Imperial Bank's famous *Lyangda* variety of Mango, then unseasonal, which Swamiji received very happily.

We have already seen Swamiji's partiality to litchis as *guru-dakshina* after initiating his disciples. In the USA, when he enrolled as an art student, Swamiji himself introduced this ancient Indian ritual. American artist Maud Stumm has written about this in great detail.

Miss Stumm was present at the New York harbour to receive Swamiji and Swami Turiyananda in 1899, during Swamiji's second visit to the USA. When he got off the ship, Swamiji had a large bottle with him. He would not part with this valuable bottle at any cost. Apparently, he had brought it all the way from India. Swamiji said it was a very tasty pickle, 'This is for Joe (Josephine MacLeod).'

Miss Stumm writes, '*One day he told me that he wanted to undertake some sort of work that would keep his hands busy and prevent him from thinking of things that fretted him at that time—and would I give him drawing lessons? So materials were produced, and at an appointed hour he came, promptly, bringing to me, with a curious little air of submission, a huge red apple, which he laid in my hands, bowing gravely. I asked him the significance of this gift, and he said, "In token that the lessons may be fruitful."*'

Swamiji's disciple Manmathanath has also written about eating apples in India. When Swamiji first returned from the USA in 1897, Manmathanath took leave from work and joined him. Manmathanath, whose memoirs were published in English in the *Vedanta Keshari Magazine* in 1960, passed away in 1953 at the ripe old age of eighty-six.

In his memoirs, Manmathanath reminisces about one afternoon when he reached Belur *Math* at the time when prasad was normally served. 'I was very anxious to receive prasad from Swamiji but did not say anything. Suddenly, Swamiji went into the storeroom and came out with an apple. Then, borrowing a knife from one of the monks, he himself slowly skinned the apple and, halving it, gave me one half and ate the other himself.'

From the apple stories, let us go back to Gaya Da. He often quoted from the Bhagwad Gita, 'Action is your right, not the fruits thereof.' In other words, the Gods, with immense foresight, continuously endeavour to keep the popularity of fruits within limits!

Let's stay with our childhood seniors, for Gaya Da's stories don't seem to want to end.

After coming under Gaya Da's influence, my initial disinterest towards Sri Ramakrishna and Swamiji turned into heightened curiosity. Gaya Da never disclosed his source for the daily bits of news about his hero's favourite foods. He had heard somewhere that unless one researched Swamiji's childhood thoroughly, it would be impossible to understand where the root of his love for food lay. We had a textbook in school named *Swamiji's Life*, but it only contained descriptions of the world leader Vivekananda's struggles and successes. There were no analyses about what Vivekananda liked to eat at each stage of his life, or why. Gaya Da used to tell us stories during our breaks, like the one that chronicled how, except for the attraction for *rosogollas*, Gadadhar Chatterjee (Sri Ramakrishna's original name) and Narendranath Datta (Vivekananda) would never have met.

Books inform us that Baghbazar's Nobin Chandra Das invented the *rosogolla*, the famous Bengali sweetmeat, in 1868. Here is the interesting anecdote Gaya Da referred to, involving the *rosogolla*, Sri Ramakrishna and Swamiji.

One day, Swamiji's elder cousin and Thakur's great disciple Dr Ramchandra Datta told the young Narendranath, 'Come, let us go to Dakshineswar's Thakur. He feeds visitors with very good *rosogollas*.' Narendranath, who couldn't care less about what he said to anyone, was wary of stepping into a *rosogolla*-trap. So he warned his beloved Ram Da (Dr Ramchandra Datta) that if the sweets did not appear as promised, he would tweak the much-loved pandit (Sri Ramakrishna)'s ears!

Those days, this advance warning about tweaking ears was quite prevalent in Calcutta. We have heard that another contemporary personality, Kailash Chandra Basu, swayed by doubts, had also threatened to twist our Dakshineswar Thakur's ears! But Kailash Chandra was left very embarrassed

by our fun-loving Thakur. While he was waiting for a sight of
Thakur, someone announced, 'Thakur is calling the person who
had said he would twist his ear.' The *rosogolla* did not seem to
have played a role this time. But in the case of Naren, the sweet
rosogolla did play a huge role in transforming his life, a fact that
many people of Calcutta, the pilgrimage for sweet lovers, have
almost forgotten. More on this subject later.

Unfortunately, today's sweet makers do not seem enthused
to find the shop from where this *rosogolla* was procured and
to look at the possibility of whether there can be a resurgence
of that brand name to earn crores of sweet-currency. Our
mischievous seniors at school termed this first meeting between
Sri Ramakrishna and Swami Vivekananda a 'spirituality
grounded on sweets'.

Gaya Da often said, that once we were older, we would need
to undertake serious, ceaseless research on Swamiji's culinary
interests. Our deep desire was that one day when we grew up,
we would all collectively contribute to an authoritative history
of our adventurous endeavours to find spirituality through food,
fasting and starvation.

We believed Gaya Da would be the most competent person
among us to undertake the responsibility of writing this book.
However, due to familial financial demands, Gaya Da joined
aviation and left for England.

In England, Vedanta may have received some recognition
but the Bengali *rosogolla* has not yet received its due. And this
despite some of us reiterating all our lives that our Thakur and
his beloved Narendranath will not be fully understood unless
one reflects on this critical dimension of the spirit and the
palate.

In our school, named after Vivekananda himself, my
deliberations on Swamiji had started at a very young age, as a

fifth-standard student. Needless to say, from the very beginning, our guide was again the exceptional Gaya Da. He would urge us to always look for new paths. We may not otherwise have been able to find our way among the intricate lanes of the Vedas and Vedanta.

Our Vivekananda, however, had taken the difficult route of hunger and thirst and bravely marched forward. He went abroad to preach the greatness of the Vedanta but did not forget his own country's *khichuRi*, pulao and biryani. He has spoken about all this in various ways and in various situations. And yet, the world has not quite been able to understand the philosophic value of those words. However, to understand Vivekananda completely, there is no other way but to also understand this chef—the Vivekananda of the kitchen.

Our principal, Sudhangshu Shekhar Bhattacharya, always maintained that Vivekananda was truly unparalleled. He held that Swamiji was a worshipper of modernity. 'Look for him away from the well-trodden paths. In one body Swamiji had so many forms, that even after so many years of his Mahasamadhi (a state when the Yogi decides to leave his mortal body), we have not been able to understand him fully.'

Vivekananda had wanted to show a new path to the poor of India, devastated by hunger. It was he who had asked people to raise questions: 'Why do we have such frequent droughts in a country that is blessed with *sujalam*, *suphalam* (beautiful streams and wonderful orchards)? Why do the streets of our cities overflow with the stench of garbage and crowds of hungry people? And why does this deplorable situation not awaken the might of the people, of the masses or the government of the time? Why do we—over and over again—move helplessly from one famine to another?' To seek the answer to these difficult questions, Vivekananda spent a large part of the one and a half

decades of his mystic life in various continents. He spoke about
loving all creation:

> 'He stands before you, in so many forms,
> where do you search, rejecting them all?
> Only he who loves all creatures,
> truly serves God.'

In other words, instead of wasting time searching endlessly for
the great energy named God, seek Him through loving all living
beings. Establish a new God of many names in your heart, only
through your love for all creatures.

Some people consider this to be a degradation of the
seeker, while others say that eventually, they have found the
opportunity to serve a new God. Is this thinking a disregard
for the infinite God who has no beginning and no end? Or is it
simply assigning a new name to the same eternal God? Let the
new conch shell now announce, on every path, victory, victory,
victory to thee!

In his various essays and memoirs, Narendranath's brother
Mahendranath, has alluded to his family's immense love for
cooking and feeding the poor. Even in Swamiji's mother's
home, this practice of feeding the poor was a very important
one. If we appreciate these aspects of Swamiji's family, then it
may be easier to understand the Narendranath who loved to
cook.

In this regard, it would be good to first get some information
about Swami Vivekananda's lineage. Mahendranath informs
us that Swamiji's grandfather Durgaprasad Datta was married
according to the practice of the time, at the age of sixteen
or seventeen, to Shyamasundari, daughter of Shyambazar's
Rajeevlochan Ghosh. The couple had a daughter, who died in

infancy. Vishwanath Datta, Swamiji's father, was born at North Calcutta's 3, Gourmohan Mukherjee Street.

When Vishwanath was six or seven months old, during his *annaprashan* (rice feeding ceremony), his father Durgaprasad, then twenty or twenty-two years old, left home to become a sanyasi. Mahendranath tells us that the *annaprashan* of the newborn was not very festive. Later, the ill-fated Vishwanath also lost his mother to cholera, when he was barely twelve years old.

Vishwanath too, was married at the age of seventeen or eighteen to Bhuvaneswari Basu, daughter of Nandalal Basu of Ramtanu Basu Lane in Simulia village, Calcutta. Many forget that Narendranath was not Vishwanath's eldest son but one of ten siblings. Similarly, his famous contemporary Rabindranath Tagore was his father Debendranath's fourteenth child and had another younger brother. An American admirer had told Tagore, 'You alone sir, are sufficient reason why India should not practice family planning.'

Information about Narendranath's other siblings is still not very clear. Based largely on Mahendranath's statements, historian Sailendra Nath Dhar has attempted, in his famous *A Comprehensive Biography of Swami Vivekananda* (a set of three volumes), to bring out some details of the family history.

Vivekananda's father Vishwanath was born in 1835 and passed away at the age of forty-nine. His mother Bhuvaneswari was born in 1841, and was only ten years old when she was married to Vishwanath. She died in 1911, nine years after her beloved son Narendranath's death. Sailendra Nath has written that their first son, whose name is not known, died at eight months. Their next born, a daughter, lived for only two-and-a-half years. The next child, named Haramoni (or maybe Haramohini), lived till the age of twenty-two. The fourth daughter Swarnamayee, also known as Swarnabala, is very well

known. This exceptionally beautiful sister of Swamiji also lived
a part of her seventy-two-year life at 3, Gourmohan Mukherjee
Street. Vishwanath's next child, also a daughter, lived for only
six years, and after that came Narendranath, who was first
known as 'Bilay' and Bireshwar.

According to Sailendra Nath's book, Swamiji's next sister,
Kiranbala, lived till the age of sixteen, although Mahendranath
thinks she may actually have lived till the age of eighteen or
nineteen. The next sister Jogendrabala, according to Sailendra
Nath, lived for twenty-two years, although Mahendranath was
of the view that she lived to be twenty-five. After this came
two sons—Mahendranath (1869–1956) and Bhupendranath
(1880–1961). Swami Vivekananda lived for thirty-nine years,
five months and twenty-eight days. The three claimants to a long
life among the Datta siblings were Swarnamayee (seventy-two
years), Mahendranath (eighty-eight years) and Bhupendranath
(eighty-one years).

Mahim (or Mahendranath), on whom we are hugely
dependant for a reliable description of the intriguing events
in Swamiji's family, was six years younger than Swamiji, and
the youngest, Bhupendranath, was seventeen years younger.
Mahendranath, as uninhibited and adventurous as his elder
brother, was not present in Calcutta at the time of Swamiji's
death, but lived for another fifty-four years and left behind
many precious reminiscences of the Datta family.

Mahendranath has recorded many interesting accounts
from Swamiji's childhood. He informs us, that in both features
and physique, Narendranath bore a strong resemblance to his
grandfather, who for unknown reasons had left his family in an
untimely manner, to become a sanyasi.

Mahendranath also cites a possible reason for Swamiji's
lifelong fondness for tobacco. 'At a very young age,

Narendranath's favourite toy was a dry, flat-bottomed hookah. He always carried it around and sometimes sucked here and there on the shell. This game was a highly entertaining one for him.' The family coachman used to lift the baby onto the horseback and say, 'Bilu Babu, smoke your hookah.'

All the three children of 3, Gourmohan Mukherjee Street's Datta family are famous for their appreciation of food and for feeding others. To understand the diversity of their interests, it is important to know that from their mother's side they are Vaishnavas (followers of Vishnu). Their grandmother, whom they called Jhee-Ma, told them many Vaishnava stories. Mahendranath recalls lying in bed at night, listening to these stories, many of them related to eating and drinking, from his elder brother Bilay. In later years, Swami Vivekananda enthralled devotees in far-off lands with the same stories. Mahendranath too, in later years, reminisced about these stories.

Here is one of those favourite stories of Swamiji—a story of a poor mother and her son. The little boy was very afraid to go to the village school all by himself because the way to the school was through a forest. To assuage the boy's fears, his mother said that an older son of hers lived in the same forest. 'When you pass through, call out "Kaalachand Dada!" and he will surely attend to you.' The innocent child, while returning home every evening, would call out from the edge of the forest, 'Kaalachand Dada, I am going home.' And from the forest, someone would respond, 'Alright brother, go home. Don't be afraid!' The boy never actually met his Kaalachand Dada but they would converse along the way.

It should be noted here that until a few decades ago, many village schools had a solitary teacher. In the late 1800s, the situation was no different. It so happened that the teacher at the boy's school lost his father. So according to the practice of those times, he directed the students, 'Bring whatever you can, to serve at the funeral ceremony, the day after tomorrow.'

Being acutely aware of his mother's poverty and her practical inability to meet the teacher's demands, the child, on his way back, shared his woes with Kaalachand Dada, who, in turn, promised that he would cook whatever was necessary for the funeral ceremony and keep it under a particular tamarind tree.

On the appointed day, the child went to the tree and found a small pot of curd, which he carried to the school. On seeing such a small pot the teacher was incensed and rebuked the boy, saying, 'There is no need to keep this! Just serve it to that Brahmin boy.' The child obediently served the curd, but something strange happened. The pot—automatically and mysteriously—filled up again.

Now everyone was served from that same small pot, and each time it filled up again. By evening, the teacher, now amazed and somewhat contrite, enquired, 'Tell me, where did you get this strange curd?' The student replied, 'Kaalachand Dada, who lives in that forest, gave it to me.' Even more surprised, the teacher requested the boy to ask his Kaalachand Dada when the teacher could meet him. When the boy went to the forest and asked the question, Kaalachand Dada replied, while remaining unseen, 'After as many births as there are leaves on that tamarind tree. But you will meet me in this birth itself!'

Mahendranath tells us that even in London, Swamiji delighted his audiences with this story about the ever-filling pot of curd.

Here's another story of a pair of mythical birds and an ascetic. On a cold and stormy night, an ascetic sat shivering below a tree on which lived a pair of birds with their children. The ascetic had not eaten all day and had built a small fire to keep himself warm. The male bird told his wife, 'An ascetic has come to take shelter with us. It is our duty to feed him something. But we don't have anything at home—like the ascetic, we too bring our food daily and eat it. We do not store anything.' The wife said, 'I will burn myself in the fire so you can feed him my roasted meat.' The husband replied, 'If you go, who will look after the children? Let me burn myself instead.' The children heard this and said, 'Both of you stay, we will go,' and they jumped into the fire and gave up their lives. The ascetic ate their meat and felt a little better. But he still felt cold and famished. Sensing this, the wife jumped into the fire and burnt herself, and then the husband followed. Giving up their bird-bodies, all of them became one with God and went up to Heaven. Swamiji loved sharing this ascetic-meat-eating story in London.

Vivekananda's biographers have all informed us that many of his childhood stories were about fish, meat and sweets. The third story is also available to us through the kind courtesy of Mahendranath.

After practising many years of austerity, a sage was sitting under a tree, when the droppings of a heron sitting on the tree fell on him. The sage looked at the bird in anger and the bird immediately turned to ashes. Seeing his own power, the sage became vain. He went to a house and shouted for alms. The housewife respectfully asked him to wait for a while because she was busy. The sage became very angry and said, 'Do you know I can burn you to ashes right now?' The housewife did not cower down at all. She said, 'My Lord, this is not like burning down some heron in the forest. My husband is ill, and I have to look after him continuously. When I get a little time, I look after my own needs.' The sage was taken aback and was very keen to find out how the housewife managed to learn about the heron's burning. He learnt from her that by dint of serving her husband so well, the housewife had the ability to become aware of many things going on in the world. He asked her, 'Are there other people who possess similar powers like you?' The housewife answered, 'In a certain town there is a hunter who sells meat. Go and meet him.'

The sage reached the town, managed to locate the hunter and expressed a desire to speak with him. The hunter was busy selling meat and asked the sage to wait for a while until he finished his work.

After selling all his meat, the hunter went home with the sage, cleaned up the blood, fed his aged parents, fed his wife and all his children, fed the sage and then sat down to eat. The sage then asked him, 'How do you know everything?' The hunter replied, 'I treat my parents like God; I love and feed my wife and dependants as well as possible. For these good deeds, I get to know everything.' After receiving such valuable knowledge, the sage gave up all his arrogance and went back to practise further austerity in the forest.

Returning to the topic of Swamiji's legendary culinary interest, we are fortunate to have been able to learn a lot about his youth through his own family sources.

Swamiji's legendary love for cooking and feeding others has largely been established through various reminiscences, primarily from his brother Mahendranath. The rest of the elements that went into writing this book, more than a hundred years after Swamiji left his mortal remains, have emerged from the depths of oblivion, from various narrations and from recorded conversations that Swamiji had with his near and dear ones.

Mahendranath's slim book *Swami Vivekananda's Childhood* was first published in 1959. It is a collection of immensely valuable material. Here is an excerpt:

'Our Calcutta High Court's Attorney-at-law father Vishwanath Datta earned well and lived a lavish life. We had many domestic helpers; the household ate well and fed the poor and needy regularly and abundantly. He believed that for their mental abilities to develop, young children should be well fed and to enable them stay mentally fit, their diet should include spicy food. There was no need to pass on wealth to one's children, he felt. If one fed them well and provided them with a sound education, they would certainly find their own path in the world. On the other hand, if one wantonly bequeathed wealth to children, they would become foolish and recklessly wasteful . . . (Father) used to enjoy a variety of cuisines and fed everyone around him. He could also cook a range of dishes himself.'

Besides his mother tongue Bengali, Vishwanath was proficient in English, Urdu, Arabic and Persian—all pointing to his sound educational foundation. Mahendranath has also written extensively about his father's abundant love for food: 'He was particularly attentive to all matters related to food. As much as he loved to cook, he also loved to feed others. He could cook an excellent pulao and mutton curry. A cook would typically attend to the clay stove and (father) would pass on instructions from a distance. From time to time, he would bring a sample of the dish to (father), and he would patiently explain everything that had to be done to perfect it.' Mahendranath wrote that he had tasted his father's cooking many times, and even in the twilight of his life, could well remember the taste.

It is also known that Swamiji's father would invite and feed many people, often cooking for them himself. In Mahendranath's view, this is what encouraged Swamiji to become a skilful and accomplished cook.

Mahendranath's book contains innumerable old stories of the practice of cooking in families. Here are some of them.

In Bengali households of the past, once the day's cooking was done, the neighbourhood housewives and matriarchs gathered in the upper lobby of the home. They shared notes on who had cooked which dishes that day. The daughters-in-law were restrained in the presence of the matriarchs. The cooks narrated their recipes. Then questions would arise about which ingredient to put in which dish, where it was necessary to put turmeric and where a little milk could substitute it, etc. Typically, there would be various queries on specific recipes. The young learnt from the elders and this became a forum for acquiring knowledge.

Besides daily cooking, Mahendranath also shares notes on cooking during festivities at home and about the Bengali housewives' practice of sharing paan (a sweetmeat roll made of the betel leaf) and various other traditions. Women carried the paan tied to a corner of their saris as a gift for the hostess when they went visiting. In return, they also received paan from the hostess. Those days, the lime applied on the betel leaf was not the coarse lime of today. Their lime was prepared from the ash of cockleshells or natural lime. Since widows were forbidden to eat the lime prepared from an animal product, many of them used the ashes of leaves or straw in their betel leaves. They also ate candied rose petals. Both Narendranath's mother and grandmother used candied rose petals in their paan.

The housewives themselves did the cooking for all Swamiji's childhood festivities, Mahendranath tells us. Each person cooked the item they were best at, while the rest relished the dish and praised the cook. There was no practice of engaging professional cooks. We also get to know that a lot of people were invited regularly for the afternoon meals.

Mahendranath shares a lot of information about the Datta family's menus. At the time, Brahmins were forbidden (by the rigid caste system) from eating rice in other people's homes. Mahendranath tells us, 'During our early childhood days, Brahmins never had vegetable, sweets or even sugar (in our home). In Kayastha households, *luchis* (the Bengali version of the puri, an Indian wheat-flatbread deep-fried in oil) were served to Brahmin guests during festivities, while in Brahmin homes, rice was served to everyone.' *Luchis* were otherwise not often on the menu.

Calcutta then had neither cooking gas nor coal. As Mahendranath's book tells us, 'All cooking happened in clay pots on wood-stoked stoves.' We hear from the Datta family members that the dishes cooked on these stoves were very tasty.

The golden era of Bengali sweets had not yet started. As Mahendranath says, 'There were some sweets such as a basic *sandesh* and *pantua* (similar to the popular gulab jamun of North India) but *rosogolla* and various types of *sandesh* came much later. Sweets made of cottage cheese were not common and people did not like them either. Those hosts who served sweets at gatherings bought them from the Barabazar market in North Calcutta. Sweets that used sesame seeds were not common, but *Chandrapuli* (a sweetmeat made of cottage cheese and grated coconut) was available in plenty. The afternoon meal consisted largely of fish curry and vegetables.'

Before going deeper into our study of Vivekananda's love for the culinary art, let us look at some disturbing elements from Mahendranath's narration. If we do not learn about this group of antisocials named Bhojponde, then our knowledge of nineteenth-century Bengali society will be incomplete.

Bhojpondes were a group of self-appointed social guardians who got themselves invited to homes for a meal but then spread some fake news to malign the family and damage its reputation, disturbing all the arrangements. Although Bengali cuisine has been able to preserve its uniqueness through the ages, and those who had been nominated to ruin the pleasure of eating have disappeared, yet the word Bhojponde is inseparably mixed with Bengali cuisine. If these guardians did not eat the food cooked, others would not eat it either. It was only to take care of these antisocial elements that the practice of hiring Brahmin cooks first came about in Calcutta.

Mahendranath adds, 'Although these new-age cooks' culinary skills were not great, they were excellent at abusing the Bhojpondes and thwarting their efforts to create a disturbance. After being insulted at a few places, the power of the Bhojpondes diminished and they finally became extinct. The pity was that with the appointment of hired cooks, the wonderful taste of the housewives' cooking—of *sona muger* dal (the yellow mung), greens and the banana flower also disappeared.' Vivekananda's brother says, 'This is why the practice of Calcutta-housewives' cooking for feasts stopped. The ladies of East Bengal, however, continue to be excellent cooks—they do not have a practice of hiring professional cooks.'

Besides feasts, there were other culinary occasions in North Calcutta, one of which was called *phalaar*. The *purohits* (pandits or priests) were typically offered *phalaar*, particularly during post-funeral memorial services. Normally, this offering consisted of fried *chiRe* (beaten rice), ghee, sweets and sometimes popped rice and curd.

When Vivekananda was around five or six years old, the *chhakka* made with the (then foreign) red pumpkin, *patal* (pointed gourd) and peas were popular along with large *luchis*. In keeping with the rigid requirements of the caste system, salt was never added to this dish. For guests, the necessary salt was provided separately on the leaf or plate. The practice of serving salt separately was called *utsrishta* (abandoned), and perhaps, the Bengali word '*uchhchhista*' (meaning leftover scraps of food) is derived from the same word. After the *luchi-chhakka*, the next attraction was a variety of sweets such as *khaja, gaja* (both made with kneaded and rolled out refined flour and ghee, and dipped in sugar syrup), *kochuri* (a puri stuffed with savoury fillings of choice), *nimki* (a crispy savoury), *pantua, motichur* (a sweet made of roasted chickpea flour and sugar), and *kancha-golla* (a sweet cottage-cheese ball). All of these would be served in a clay bowl. Some preferred to have the sweets in a different serving leaf or plate altogether.

Vivekananda's brother tells us about two bad practices of the time. When serving, some of the servers, often sourced from neighbouring families, pilfered sweetmeats from the storeroom. When the youngsters of the house reported this to the Datta family elders, the latter ignored the delinquency and restrained the young boys to avoid embarrassing their neighbours.

Another growing menace troubled the guests at the feast. Those were the days of barefoot seating in rows on the floor, with no tables or chairs. Some miscreants took advantage of the situation and stole the shoes of the guests while they were eating. To prevent such thefts, some judicious guests would bring along a household help, whose job would be to guard their shoes while they ate in peace.

Mahendranath has lovingly chronicled many such entertaining trivia about feasts and banquets during Vivekananda's childhood. On the use of asafoetida, he says, 'People did not eat *papaR* (an extremely flat, thin and crisp dish made of lentils) because it contained asafoetida.' Normally people did not eat anything that contained asafoetida. 'Potatoes, which were quite rare, were brought in wooden ships from Bombay, which is why they were called Bombay *aloo* (potato). Slowly potato cultivation started in Bengal too. Cauliflower was also impossible to get and was never used in rituals. Subsequently, the pointed gourd and spinach began to be used for ceremonies.'

While chronicling Vivekananda's childhood, Mahendranath writes in 1929, 'Today there are innumerable types of foods, too many to even describe.' Reminiscing about Narendranath of Gourmohan Mukherjee Street, he says, 'We used to have stale *ruti* (flatbread) with the red pumpkin *chhakka*. *Chhakka* that was left overnight was really tasty. Those days, oil was pure, and cooking done on wood fires in clay pots added to the flavours. Ghee (clarified butter) was available at five poas or one and a half seers (a seer is 0.933 kg) for a rupee. So a little ghee was always added to vegetables, and housewives cooked really well.'

If *ruti* was not available, the alternative was puffed or popped rice with jaggery and water. For one paisa, one could get a lot of puffed rice. 'We ate some and fed the rest to the crows. The amount of puffed rice we got for one paisa was too much for a small boy to eat.'

'Unlike these days, there were not too many eateries at the time. There was just one in Simulia Bazaar and the next one was located in Balaram De Street.' It is learnt from reliable sources that sweetmeats with names such as *jibhe gaja, chhatur gutke gaja, kucho gaja, chouko gaja* (all sweets made of refined white flour fried and dipped in sugar syrup), *gutke kochuri* (stuffed *luchi*) and *jilipi* (the popular jalebi) were much enjoyed food items those days.

In this context, we hear the story of another sanyasi. This saffron-clad portly sadhu opened eateries in Kansari PaRa and a few other places. The shops served a variety of north Indian fare. He introduced a range of dishes in the Simulia area and had a novel way of serving his customers. While others took care of the food sale, he sat on a deer-skin mat on the road outside and sang hymns. So, the idea of presenting music to entertain guests at high-society restaurants did not originate from the productive minds of European gentlemen alone, it was also a practice for many years here in our country.

Those days, the topic of sweetmeats and savouries came up frequently in North Calcutta conversations. Narendranath, in particular, was absolutely devoted to *kochuri* and *singaRa* (both fried savouries with vegetable stuffing) at the time. Much later, he became sharply critical of the Bengalis' deep attachment to such fried savouries and declared that this affinity for unhealthy food was the main cause of the state's downfall.

Swami Brahmananda, known as Rakhal in his younger days, was Narendranath's childhood friend. In later years, he became his beloved *gurubhai*. Rakhal was celebrated the world over as Raja Maharaj and Swami Brahmananda.

In a very valuable book titled *Deliberations of Ajatshatru Swami Brahmananda Maharaj*, Mahendranath has made many observations about the savouries of those times. These reminiscences were narrated by him in November and December 1916 and written down by his disciple Sankarprasad Bandopadhyay. The book was first published after another two decades, in 1938.

Mahendranath has written about his elder brother's friend: 'In the evenings, Rakhal would come home and enjoy a generous helping of *singaRa, aloo chhenchki* and sweets. He was then a young man, and such visits came after a couple of bouts of wrestling, which is why he ate half-a-seer of food. At that time such food was priced at around six annas a seer.' The cost of savouries must have been even less at an earlier time, which is why Mahendranath further says, 'I do not remember the three-anna per seer days. Following the meal, I used to get Rakhal a glass of water and a paan and then go to study at my table. Young Rakhal, after his wrestling bout and a sumptuous meal, could not sit at the table.' He could not focus on his studies and would typically take a pillow and placing the book on it and say, 'One can study better lying down.' After a while, the book would be lying on his chest, and the Ramakrishna Mission's first president-to-be would be merrily snoring. Swamiji's father Vishwanath lovingly called the short and fat Rakhal, 'Goju' (elephant).

A lifelong aficionado of salty savouries, Swami Brahmananda (nee Rakhal) became extremely fond of sweetmeats in his last years. This alarmed many, who warned him that this kind of a sudden change in tastes heralded danger.

We have another story from Mahendranath about the singing sanyasi's eateries. Rakhal loved the food from this sanyasi's shop. 'Every time he got a little money, he would buy savouries from there. He would often tell Narendra, "Look, compared to all other shops, the food here is the best. We must get our snacks from here in the evenings."'

Many years later in Kashi (Varanasi) one morning, Rakhal Maharaj 'bought many *kochuris* and made some excellent tea and fed everyone'. Mahendranath bit into a *kochuri* and said, 'Excellent! I have never tasted such delicious *kochuris* in Calcutta.' Rakhal Maharaj replied in a serious tone, 'Have you forgotten about Simulia? Don't you remember that sanyasi's *kochuri*?'

According to Mahendranath's description, Rakhal was especially devoted to Narendranath throughout his life. Whether in wrestling bouts, while indulging in banter or even while cooking, Rakhal always followed Narendranath. Mahendranath always believed that Rakhal was of an age 'somewhere between us two brothers'. This error was discovered only in 1921, a day after Rakhal Maharaj passed away. 'On that day, I realized that Rakhal was actually a year older than Swamiji,' Mahendranath wrote.

Rakhal had scant regard for his studies, and as a result the Datta family did not have a great opinion of him. He was seen as a wastrel with no particular aim. Narendranath and his brother's only ambition on the other hand, was to 'study and become lawyers like our father and uncle'.

Rakhal, the motherless eldest son of Haranchandra Ghosh, a rich landlord of Guskora Kulin village, was married at an early age. Mahendranath believed it was in the year 1880 or 1881. The bride Bishweshwari was the daughter of the late Doctor Bhubanmohan Mitra. She and her brother Manmohan were related to Ram Dada, the Datta brothers' cousin. Bishweshwari addressed Narendranath as 'Naren Dada' and his third sister as 'Didi'. Both the Datta brothers were guests at the wedding.

Mahendranath has described the wedding feast in great detail. Fish pulao and *sandesh*, sourced from Calcutta, were served to the guests. But curiously, instead of being applauded for its novelty, the pulao managed to upset quite a few guests. Mahendranath shares an eyewitness account of the event. 'Many of the guests happened to be simple farmers, who had never had fish pulao. So, after the first mouthful itself, they were on the verge of throwing up. There was chaos and people started shouting, "Oh my God! This is smelly rice cooked with rotten turmeric and there's even fish in the rice. And, who puts oil in rice!"' And people began throwing up everywhere. To bring the situation under control, a prudent villager brought some pieces of raw onion. 'Everyone ate the raw onion and felt much better. The vomiting stopped as well. The guests were then served plain white rice and *urad* dal, which they were quite satisfied with.' It was quite apparent that the villagers were unaccustomed to pulao, and the saffron-flavoured rice offered at the banquet was found unpalatable.

Unfortunately for the hosts, their night of woes did not end with the fish pulao. The sweets also caused a problem! At the request of some discerning individuals, the *sandesh* had been deliberately made less sweet than normal. That again caused a huge upset. Guests began complaining, 'The cook has forgotten to add sugar to this sweet—it is too bland.'

'Then a lump of jaggery was served on each plate and the guests began to have that with the *sandesh*.' Mahendranath assures his readers that this was an authentic narration of the night's events at the wedding feast.

We have some more stories about Rakhal too. When his zamindar (landowner who employed labourers to work on his land) uncle's mother passed away, there was a ceremony to honour the departed soul. The uncle instructed his labourers to bring clotted milk and ghee to be served to the guests. When Rakhal saw the poor milkmen bringing pots of milk and ghee to the ceremony, he was very angry and asked his uncle, 'Uncle, is this ceremony to honour your mother's soul or is it for the milkmen to honour *their* mothers' souls?'

In Mahendranath's book on Rakhal Maharaj, there are detailed descriptions of Narendranath's favourite childhood snacks. 'In Simulia Bazaar, a man used to cook and sell delicious *dhoka* (a spicy lentil cake in gravy). In one lot he could make almost a seer of *dhoka*. I don't know how he made it, but it was impossible to replicate that taste when we tried to make it ourselves.' The Datta family's young food aficionados would regularly land up at the shop as soon as it was dusk, because if they were even slightly delayed the *dhokas* would be over and the boys would be left hungry! For one paisa they could get two *dhokas* and two spoons of gravy.

Another favourite item of Simulia was 'chaabRi'. Made with asafoetida, aniseed, ginger and *urad* dal, these cakes, now impossible to find, were similar to big *kochuris*. Culinary experts who are keen to restore the hidden gems of Bengal and win the gratitude of all Bengalis, can, with research and support from senior citizens' reminiscences, give a new lease of life to this *chaabRi*.

The memory of Simulia's *dhoka* remained fresh in the boys' minds for many years. Mahendranath has written, 'One evening in Belur *Math*, Rakhal suddenly asked me, "Brother, do you remember the *dhoka* we used to buy and eat from Simulia Bazaar as children?" Rakhal Maharaj, the then head of the Ramakrishna *Math* Missionaries, went on to say, "I have never ever tasted *dhoka* like that. The taste still lingers on my tongue."'

It was not just the shop-bought savouries however, that the young boys enjoyed. Self-reliant and keen to cook for themselves, Narendranath and his enthusiastic team carried out many wonderful experiments. But even before we evaluate the various culinary experiments and observations of Narendranath and company, it is important to have an idea of the kitchens of those days and understand the environment in which Vivekananda's love for the culinary arts took root at such a tender age.

The Bengali's history is incomplete without a detailed description of the kitchen, which is at the heart of every home. We know almost nothing about the original kitchens of Bengali homes or about the cooking implements and how they have changed over the years. We will never be able to tell in which age and in what manner, our pots, woks, ladles, spuds, plates and bowls silently entered the chaste space of the Bengali kitchen.

If our society had been enthusiastic about maintaining tradition, we would have had an impressive Social Museum next to our Industrial Museum in Calcutta. Modern citizens would have a good idea of everyday life in a bygone era. The original name of the kitchen is 'rasabati'. It is necessary to know how these rasabatis have transformed over the years in tune with the transformation in tastes.

Continuing with our perusal of Mahendranath's books, we find: 'In our childhood home, cooking was done using firewood. Mangrove wood was brought in from along the canal and three Odiya (native of Odisha, India's Eastern coastal state) woodcutters wielded their axes to cut them into blocks. These were further chopped into cubes and dried and stored away. When it was time to cook every morning, the domestic help would split those pieces of wood further and use them for lighting the fire. Those days there was no coal in Calcutta. In 1875 or 1876, coal was first used to light up Calcutta's streetlights and was distributed to all homes too, but no one knew how to use it!'

The advent of coal in the kitchen was a great event. Mahendranath writes. 'Painstakingly, the cooking stove was fashioned with iron spikes to hold the coal. Slowly coal became popular and began to cost an anna (1/16th of a rupee) a maund (approximately 37 kg)' Mahendranath later wrote about the Calcutta of 1929: '. . . But now the mangrove wood has almost completely disappeared.'

The Calcutta of Swamiji's childhood had only a few brick and cement houses. The lack of coal and gas fires meant it was a lot less warm than now, and the winters were particularly cold. A quote from an elderly neighbour Madhu Mukherjee gives us some interesting insights. 'In the Hooghly area, north of Calcutta, we had frost-drizzles in winter. Many houses in

Calcutta had thatched roofs, and a bowl of water placed in the space between the straws would turn into ice by morning. So, although we didn't have snowfall, we did experience severe cold.'

Mahendranath has provided us with some information about Calcutta's middle class of the time. Back then, the physique of the Bengali was apparently quite different. The average Bengali city dweller was of a much larger build than now. 'People were tall, broad and strong, with long arms and wide chests.' Narendranath's granduncle Gopal Datta affectionately called him 'shorty', since compared to his father, he was quite short.

There was no practice of riding a vehicle to work; everyone preferred to walk, both in the morning and evening. All Bengalis of Calcutta rubbed themselves down with copious amounts of mustard oil and bathed in a pond or at the well. Breakfast normally consisted of chickpeas and ginger, with soaked or fried *muger* dal. Fruits were favoured at lunch.

The amount of rice consumed in the morning and evening would worry today's weight-conscious young people. 'Townsfolk normally had two-and-a-half *poa* (almost 600 gm) of rice in the day and half a seer in the evening along with an equivalent amount of vegetables. People kept cows at home.' So milk was also easily available. Today's consumers will feel wistful when they hear that Calcutta's milkmen sold milk at ten to sixteen seers for a rupee. At that time, the *ruti* was still alien to the Bengali palate.

Villagers from out-of-town ate a little more: 'They would typically consume 700–900 grams of rice during the day, and a little less at night.' The children of the Datta family secretly called these guests 'demons'.

Everything was in abundance; prices of sweets were very low; making the middle class passionate about eating and feeding others. Food aficionados experienced an ever-increasing girth in the society of Narendranath's childhood.

There were manifold praises sung of Bengali food, not just at domestic festivities, but even at the *jatra* (a form of folk theatre) and theatre. Mahendranath has recorded a detailed description about this too.

'During the *jatra*, one person would stand up on the stage and rattle off funny rhymes. The speciality of his songs was that they were a recital of which fish was to be cooked with which masala and spices. His long verse spouted continuous recipes of all the fishes in the market. Sometimes, someone would recite a long poem about the various types of *phalaar* and in which months what could be added to the *phalaar*.'

Mahendranath has bemoaned the fact that no one remembers these poems, and requested that if anyone did, they should record them. 'Because these contain all the recipes of a bygone era.'

Mahendranath also writes about other rhymes from the *jatra*. All of these poems contain heart-warming descriptions of *luchi, monda, khaja, gaja* and other such sweetmeats that were available in Bengal at the time.

Curiously, those rhymes do not mention *rosogolla* or any of the present-day sweets, but pay tribute to all the sweets of yore. Mahendranath says, 'There is a need to understand all of this today—it captures the essence of Bengal's ancient history.'

Through his collection *Sangeet Kalpataru* (The Wish-fulfilment Tree of Music), Swamiji himself has assuaged a part of his brother's pain at the missing songs. Vivekananda-lovers will know that from a very young age, Swamiji was acknowledged as an authority on music. Edited jointly with

Sri Baishnab Charan Basak, this valuable collection of songs
was first published in 1887. After many years, a reprint is now
available. Dwarikanath Basak's youngest son Baishnab Charan
Basak's year of birth is not known. An affluent bookseller in
Calcutta's Bat-tala area, he was also a gymnastics teacher in a
school. He passed away in 1922.

In this collection, one particular poet, Pyaremohan
Kabiratna, a contemporary of Narendranath, has been quoted
several times. One of his songs is a eulogy to fish.

'In all the world there's nothing
as wonderful as fish.
Its fragrance helps you eat
even grubby rice with ease.
Kaliya, kofta, kabab and pulao,
the fish has much to offer.
Pure white, blood red, beautiful and shapely,
So many names—*rui*, *mirgel*, *katla*,
He who doesn't eat it,
earns the Goddess's wrath,
and burns in hell's inferno!'

In the *Sangeet Kalpataru* collection, another song by the
same poet sings praises of the black lentil.
'Of all the lentils in this world,
the black lentil takes the cake.
Ah! What delight it adds to our meals!

All the people of Bankura and Bardhaman
Are ardent devotees of the black-lentil magic.
They never know a day's illness,

and always stay healthy and fit.
If you grind it and make little fritters,
Kaliya and kababs stand no chance.
And all the Gods, leaving Heaven
will line up at your door, plate in hand!'

Some penniless fakir has also written:
'Oh goat, you are truly fortunate
Only you can create the sweetest and tastiest mutton.'
He who cooks you breaks all attachments and bonds,
He who lives with you finds a place in Vaikunth.'
(Vaikunth is the celestial abode of the Hindu God Vishnu)

Pyaremohan Kabiratna has also sung paeans of the mutton
in *Sangeet Kalpataru*:
'Mutton instantly destroys
all sin from the body.
He who eats it round the year,
has no evil in his body.'

Pyaremohan has another popular song about the potato:
'There is nothing like the potato
in this world—as you will find,
what a beautiful creation of God,
I cannot express my delight.
It has no seed, no scales, nothing to throw away,
once you skin it, it's all edible.
Winter or rain, available all year,
use it as a spicy fry or for gravy dishes,
it blends into everything.
What an amazing creator He must be
Whose hands crafted it!

He who does not love the potato,
of what use is his love?'

Sangeet Kalpataru's editor Narendranath Datta has curated
for us another poem by Pyaremohan, this time about the
eggplant.
'What can I say about the eggplant!
Everyone is enraptured by it,
the bitter gourd, ridge gourd, pointed gourd and pumpkin
just don't compare, nor the green bananas.'

Although he largely selected poems about food, Narendranath
couldn't neglect this poem about money:
'He who does not have money in this world is better dead.
Without money, there is no virtue, no importance, no
respect.'

Childhood Feasts

Swamiji's brother Mahendranath has shared with us many
aspects of the Bengali wedding feasts of their childhood.

According to Mahendranath's account, there was a time
when only '*phalahar*' (literally 'fruit-meal' but referring here, to
beaten rice, curd, fruits, etc.) was served at wedding feasts, even
at night. He infers this from the fact that 'As children, we used
to call it "an invitation for snacks".' In due course, much to the
joy of everyone in Calcutta, the *luchi* arrived on feast plates. 'In
those days, large *luchis* were served on the banana leaf, along
with a potato and pumpkin *chhakka* and a bit of salt in a corner
of the leaf. It was perfectly delicious.'

Mahendranath adds with some sorrow, 'Now we do not see
such delectable cooking anymore. Those who have tasted that

potato and pumpkin *chhakka* would know that the pumpkin *ghonto* served today is rubbish!' In the decades that followed, despite a lot of effort, the humble pumpkin has not risen in rank.

After the pumpkin, the 'banquet-*kochuri*' was served— meaning a different *kochuri* from the one normally bought in shops. Mahendranath regretfully informs us that this too has disappeared. '*Kochuri* stuffed with black lentils cooked with ginger and aniseed, *nimki*, *khaja*, square *gaja*, *motichur*, etc., were all arranged in the serving dish. *Khaja* was an important part of the feast. Since the number three was considered inauspicious, four types of *sandesh* were served at such events. And the feast did not end there—the *kheer* and curd made a royal appearance at the end of the meal, and because this *kheer* was eaten with *khaja*, it was known then as *kheer-khaja*.' Reliable sources tell us that the *rabri* had not yet reached Bengal, while Datta family sources say that it first became available in Lucknow.

Those who are keen to know about the appearance of Bengal's world-celebrated *rosogolla* will be able to find references to it in Mahendranath's writings. 'The *rosogolla* became popular in 1873 or 1874. The *tilkut* (sesame rounds in jaggery or sugar) made an appearance at around the same time.' The *aamranga* and *kaamranga sandesh* also arrived at that time, when Narendranath was around ten years old.

Mahendranath gives us elaborate information about the *sandesh*, Bengal's pride on the world stage. 'At first, there was the *atta sandesh*. *Monda* and *peneti's Gupo sandesh* were very famous. The latter was shaped like two *feni batashaas* (sugar candy shaped like half a sphere) held together.' We learn from the same source that for some unknown reason, these famed *sandeshes* later disappeared.

We also have some significant reports from the Datta family members about the evolution of wedding feasts. Mahendranath says gradually spinach appeared on the scene, followed by the fried potato and pointed gourd. 'Then, suddenly, with everyone studying English, the Bengal gram with salt was substituted by mashed potatoes with salt, while the potato and pumpkin *chhakka* died a sorrowful death. It never made a reappearance in the dishes of genteel folk. Little by little *papaR*, *singaRa* manifested themselves and the serving dish was sadly depleted to just a couple of sweets and *gujiya*.'

The Fish at Banquets

There are some enthralling stories of the serious problems that arose on the issue of fish curries being served at feasts during Narendranath's childhood days. Mahendranath, who comes across as a predecessor of Syed Mujtaba Ali, gives us some intriguing glimpses into this. (Mr Ali, celebrated for his knowledge, travelogues and humorous take on issues, was an extremely popular writer in twentieth-century Bengal.)

We have this humorous account from 3, Gourmohan Mukherjee Street's writer brother. Mahendranath writes, 'One night we went for an *Upanayana* (thread ceremony) feast to a Brahmin's house.' From his usage of 'we', readers can safely assume that Narendranath was also an invitee. At that time, the practice of salt being added to curries had commenced.

'Suddenly, with the appearance of a fish curry in the serving dish, there was complete pandemonium among some elderly vegetarian invitees, who cried out, "Oh no! What are you doing? We will lose our caste! Our dharma! We will now have to do penance!" We youngsters meanwhile eagerly eyed the fish in the hope that if by *Ma Kali's* grace that curry could meet the *luchis* on our plate, we would be in the seventh Heaven. The non-vegetarian guests however, seemed to jump up saying, "Give me! Give it to me!" until the serving dish was empty and had to be replenished. In the meanwhile, a wise guest said to us, "Well, you know, we are Kayasthas. So even if we eat the leftovers of Brahmins, our caste remains safe, and fish curry in the Brahmin's bowl is like prasad for us, so we can all eat it quite happily, day or night.'" Even at the *Upanayana* banquet, the Datta brothers had captivated the gathering. These two brothers had a talent for enthralling audiences for years, something that I have rarely seen anywhere else.

Because of the host's ignorance of the accepted customs and the consequent ruckus about the fish, 'The next morning, there was a lot of gossip about our eating it, which apparently made us great sinners. Perhaps everyone would have to do penance now!'

Fortunately, the matter was not blown out of proportion because the youngsters of the Datta family were 'unwilling to listen to the oldies'. The Kayasthas, who always loudly proclaimed themselves to be Kshatriyas (the ruling class), did, however, repeatedly praise the self-moderation of the Brahmins. 'If the Brahmins visited Kayastha families, they would only eat *luchis* with sugar, or just a sweet.' These steadfast Brahmins never even ate potato curries.

In nineteenth-century Bengal, Brahmins still played an important role in Calcutta city. They were in demand for all the big festivals such as *Dol* (A festival of colours, popularly known as Holi in North India) and Durga Puja. Devout householders often fed Brahmins to earn good karma.

Mahendranath says, during Durga Puja those days, there were at least ten guests at every meal. In Brahmin families, rice, five vegetables, curd and *payesh* (a sweet dish like porridge, made of rice and milk) were served. In the homes of Brahmins who worshipped the goddess, fish was also eaten, while in Kayastha homes such as the Dattas, having *luchi* was the practice. 'Brahmin homes cooked many tasty dishes such as the *Shaak ghonto* (a spinach dish) and the *mocha ghonto* (a banana flower dish). Everything was delicious because the ladies of the family did all the cooking. In the evenings when the maids took the children out to play, they were all given some refreshments and everyone was served with a variety of sweets.'

There were distinct rules for the occasion of *Vijaya Dashami* (Dussehra). In those days too, senior citizens received special respect. All households gave elderly Brahmins a token offering of money before touching their feet to seek their blessings.

'On *Vijaya Dashami* day, the Goddess was offered *Narikelchhaba* (a sweet made of coconut) while bidding her farewell as she returned to her heavenly abode. There was no practice yet of offering *sandesh* to visitors during the ceremonial embrace at *Vijaya Dashami*.' Mahendranath also tells us that many Brahmins received '*barshiki*' (an annual offering of money, clothes etc.) on this day from the Datta family. Interestingly, Durga Puja and *Charak* (a Hindu folk festival in honour of the God Shiva) were occasions for the return of all loans. As a practice at this time, all householders paid off debts owed to various grocery and other shops.

One hears that even larger sweet shops gave credit to customers, although no one had yet heard of credit or debit cards! To keep credit limits low, shops would hang up boards that read, 'Cash today, Credit tomorrow!'

The middle class of North Calcutta stayed poor because of their excesses of eating and feeding others. Even in the Datta household and other households of Simulia, there would be great feasting at the smallest pretext or at the slightest suggestion of an auspicious day in the calendar.

During *Dol* and Durga Puja, there was no difference in how Shaktas (worshippers of the Goddess) and Vaishnavas celebrated. Swamiji's family worshipped the Goddess Kali, while his mother's family were Vaishnavas. According to Mahendranath, 'Those days, people were invited to a big feast on *Dol* night.' Every household celebrated in accordance with their financial capacity. Guests were also given gifts. 'The main components of the gift were *chinir muRki* (popped rice tossed in sugar) and *chinir math* (hard sugar candy), *phutkaRai* (fried gram), some *abir* (the coloured powder used for Holi) and *kumkum* (vermillion). On the day of *Dol* festivities, all of us carried *phutkaRai* wrapped in sugar and roamed around with our hands and faces smeared with *abir*.' In later years, Narendranath's brother rued the fact that '*phutkaRai*, *muRki* are not so common these days and *math* has almost disappeared.'

Professional Cooks

This narrative on Bengali festivity and celebratory cuisine will be incomplete if we do not acquaint our readers with the cooks and chefs in the kitchens of those times. Mahendranath has provided us with some interesting images on the subject.

We have been audacious enough to address our epicurean and international culinary expert Swamiji in his later years as 'Chef Swamiji'. But how was the cooking done at his birthplace, 3, Gourmohan Mukherjee Street? We have not yet explored how, growing up in North Calcutta's narrow lanes, Narendranath became such an international-cuisine enthusiast.

Mahendranath tells us about '*Naphar*' Kayasthas, a particular sect among the Kayastha caste who worked in

Calcutta households. 'Within a very short period of time, having successfully handled the smaller responsibilities such as helping the cook, collecting water for the household, splitting wood for fire, etc., these people were elevated to senior roles. They served the man of the house—gave him his tobacco, oil massages and pleated and puckered his *dhuti*' (the dhoti - a garment worn by Hindu males to drape their lower limbs). Mahendranath's analysis is that from junior helps in the house they were quickly elevated to become master chefs. This practice continued even in the days of hard-core, stringent casteism.

Speaking of a lost era, Mahendranath tells us that in 1929, cooks in all Calcutta homes had to be Brahmins. But before that, during Swamiji's childhood, Kayastha households hired Kayastha cooks. The foodie Mahendranath certifies that these Kayastha cooks also prepared delicious fare. When the heads of the households travelled, the cooking was done by whoever accompanied him—not necessarily a Brahmin. There was no insistence on cooking being done only by Brahmins. Mahendranath regrets that 'such practices no longer exist in Calcutta'.

Mahendranath analyzes, 'In those days Brahmins had a level of respect, at least those in and around Calcutta did; and they believed in maintaining a certain degree of prestige. This did not allow them to accept jobs as cooks, which they believed were "menial" in nature and below their dignity to carry out.'

Those Brahmins, who took on assignments as cooks, were looked down upon by society and today's readers may enjoy a popular rhyme, which captured this feeling:

'If he's a pandit, the Brahmin's speaks into ears
if he's poor, the Brahmin speaks into the conch shell and
if he's a fool, then the Brahmin speaks into a pipe.'

Mahendranath explains, 'If he is a pandit (an erudite man), the Brahmin will teach and initiate others (into sanyas-life). If he is poor, he will work as a priest performing rituals for money, while if he is a fool, he will be a cook in other people's homes, blowing into the iron pipe to flare their wood-stoked fires.'

I have not come across any biography of a professional Calcutta cook, chronicling his joys and sorrows. The only one to our knowledge is the famous *Adarsh Hindu Hotel*, written by Bengal's pride, Bibhuti Bhushan Bandopadhyay (who also wrote the famous *Pather Panchali*—'The Song of the Road', made later into an award-winning film by Satyajit Ray).

The Advent of the Apple

The celebrities of the Datta family have written paeans about many dishes, both vegetarian and non-vegetarian. However, they have not made any enthusiastic mention of any fruits.

After a lot of research, I found the reference to a royal fruit, not easily available in those days. This was the apple, which today, even with the current levels of inflation, is almost as common as the potato! Mahendranath himself elucidates that all his siblings were fond of the apple. Mahendranath, who had a soft corner for fruits, described it thus: 'We heard about this fruit named apple, which the English ate, and which made them so clever. But we did not actually get to see an apple until much later. Subsequently we heard that it comes packed in ice and it costs a rupee for three or four of them.' To really understand the significance of the cost, we must bear in mind that later, Swami Vivekananda bought the *ilish* (Bengal's famous fish, the *hilsa*) at an East Bengal river at sixteen for a rupee and additionally received four fish as a bonus!

Mahendranath remembers, 'Once we bought four apples for a rupee and all of us brothers and sisters got to eat a small slice. It was alright but we couldn't understand what the fuss was all about!' Everyone agreed though, for the Bengalis of Calcutta, the apple was a wonder.

The Dattas had another favourite fruit. It was called the *Narkel Kul* or Bombay *Kul* (green jujube) and was sometimes available in the Dharamtala Market. However, though it is not clear exactly why, Mahendranath cautioned, it could not be used for offering to the gods.

Mahendranath was born on 1 August 1869 and graduated with FA (First Arts) from Calcutta University in 1891. His elder brother Narendranath was by then a wandering monk. Two years later in 1893, Mahendranath set sail for America in search of the unknown. That year itself, Narendranath was the cynosure of all eyes at the Chicago Parliament of Religions as he burst onto the world stage. In 1895, Swamiji travelled from America to England for the first time.

Mahendranath came to England in 1896 to study law, without his illustrious brother's permission, after taking some financial help from the Maharaja of Khetri.

Having met his brother Narendranath in London, Mahendranath declined Swamiji's advice to go to the USA to study electrical engineering. His mind was set on studying law. In anger, Narendranath said he would not pay for his voyage back to India. Mahendranath, equally adamant, decided to walk back to India! It took him five years to complete the journey, but he did it. Having spent almost two years in England, he began his incredible journey back home.

Mahendranath has spoken about another fruit, which he had while living a nomadic life in Persia. 'That was a very long and dangerous adventure,' Mahendranath tells his friend Pyaremohan. 'One day I landed up in Persia and found large red pomegranates being sold on the road. They cost only half a paisa each. Being very hungry, I bought two of them and sitting down by a well, finished them off. Almost immediately, I was hit by a severe bout of diarrhoea. I struggled the whole night and then passed out by the well. When I came to my senses, I was on a clean bed, being looked after by a wonderful couple. They fed me little cups of coffee from time to time. Finally when I was able to speak, the man asked me, "So, what did you eat?" I told him, "Two pomegranates." His response was, "Oh no! How could you! Those are poisonous!"'

Mahendranath sampled the exotic grape-jaggery in Persia. When he expressed a desire to taste it, the man of the house served him some in a little bowl. 'It was awful! Tasted like the silt from the Ganges, with just a little bit of sugar sprinkled on it. Impossible to eat!'

Mahendranath has also spoken about enjoying other fruits in the Arab world. Once as a guest at an Arab home, he was drinking coffee and waiting hungrily for some food. 'Finally, someone came with a huge serving dish. When he neared, I realized what I thought was a dish was actually a giant hand-made flatbread. The Sardar (head of the household) broke off bits of this bread and ate it. Then he handed everyone pieces of this bread along with a slice of watermelon. This bread and watermelon was our dinner that night. Do you know why he ate it first before sharing it with us? The Sardar explained, "I am your friend. To ensure there is no poison in the coffee or the bread, I first tasted and tested it myself, before giving it to you and the others."'

Another day, Mahendranath was similarly waiting for food. Everything was quiet, and there was little sign of any food arriving. 'After a while, someone entered bearing a plate with two dates, a little *ghee* and a little bit of rice powder and gave it to me. After I ate all of that and kept waiting for more, at around

2 or 3 in the afternoon, someone opened the door and, giving me a clay pot with some cloudy liquid in it, said, "Here, have a little of this. And mind you, this is not given to everyone." I asked him what this valuable drink was, and he replied gravely, "*Sharbat* (sherbet) with *tamar hind*." I tasted it and found it to be tamarind water with a pinch of salt.' Perhaps the English word 'tamarind' was derived from this term, '*tamar hind*'.

Mahendranath tells us that in the country of camels, curd and butter are made from the camel's milk, and being an adventurous traveller, he used the opportunity to taste both.

All of these were distant memories of his youth, narrated in the winter of his life. Mahendranath reached Calcutta a little after his brother's untimely death in 1902. Much later, he reminisced about his happy childhood's blissful cuisines in his home at 3, Gourmohan Mukherjee Street.

His ardent fan Pyaremohan has written about how Mahendranath once asked him, 'Have you ever eaten koi fish (carp)?'

Pyare replied, 'No Sir.'

'Mahim Babu (Mahendranath) shook his thumb at me and said, "Then, you haven't eaten anything." He continued, "As children before we went to school in the mornings, the cook would serve us hot rice on our plates even while the fish curry was boiling on the stove." We would hold our plates and holler for the fish and the cook would serve us saying, "Here it is, little Masters! Here is the koi fish!" and we would slurp up the hot rice and hot fish curry.'

The Datta Dynasty

Let us now return to the times of Vishwanath Datta, Narendranath's father, at 3, Gourmohan Mukherjee Street.

Mahendranath has described stories of Narendranath's eating and feeding others with fervour. He has reminisced, 'We really ate well in our childhood.' As mentioned earlier, Vishwanath Datta believed in feeding children well. 'Father used to say, feed the boys well and teach them well. There is no need to keep money for them.'

A Mughal housewife who was a client of Vishwanath Datta lived in Maniktala. A relative of the famed Gorgin Khan, her complexion was porcelain white. This lady sometimes sent parcels of ready-to-cook food for Vishwanath's family. Excellent pulao rice, different types of dry fruit and packets of various spices and a large quantity of excellent meat. A chef would arrive with the parcel and standing far away from the kitchen, would instruct the cook at home on how to prepare the dish. Cooking varied cuisines like this was quite a common occurrence at Naren's home. 'We ate well and also fed many people in our neighbourhood.'

Mahendranath has also described another divine dish in great detail, recorded by Pyaremohan. One day Mahendranath asked him, 'What did you normally eat in the evenings?'

'Sir, we ate *ruti* with jaggery.'

'Ah, you ill-fated one! Do you know what we ate?' The meat shops of the time did not sell goat brain. Narendra and Mahendra had arranged with all the meat sellers to save the goat brains for them. 'A walk to a couple of shops would yield us ten to twelve brains for two to four *anna*. We also bought a couple of seers of peas. This was cooked together to make a tasty curry. In the evening, Swamiji and I would return from school and have that brain curry with around sixteen *rutis* each. If you don't eat well in childhood, the brain does not develop.'

To learn more about Swamiji's food habits, let us refer to Swami Gambhirananda's famous book, *Yuganayak*

Vivekananda. In the first volume of the book, the author tells us that Narendra's father used to travel on work to many places in North and Central India. As per Mahendranath's report, Vishwanath would travel up to Mughalsarai by train and then take a horse cart to Lucknow, Delhi, etc., for his legal practice. From Delhi, he travelled to Lahore, where he earned great fame for his work.

Swami Gambhirananda adds that when Narendranath was fourteen years old (in 1877), Vishwanath went to Raipur in Madhya Pradesh. In due course, he brought his family over to live with him. In those days, the trains plied only till Nagpur, from where one would have to take a bullock cart to reach Raipur; the journey took more than a fortnight. During the trip, the family cooked their own meals and Swamiji's natural talent as a chef took further shape. Gambhirananda writes, 'Following in the footsteps of his father, Narendranath's culinary skill was well honed.'

After returning to Calcutta, Vishwanath rented a second home for Narendranath near his own, to help the latter focus on his studies. 'The rent in those days was not very much; just around seven or eight rupees a month. There was a domestic help who lived with him and looked after his needs.' Mahim Babu has given us more valuable information. It was around this time that Vivekananda decided to experiment with food on a whim and it was here that Narendranath's famous 'Greedy Club' or a club for foodies was formed. The chief function of the club was to experiment with various recipes. Swamiji's childhood friend Rakhal was a founder member of this club. Some details of this famous club are still available.

With immense pride in his brother's fame and achievements, Mahendranath informs us of a newly invented recipe. 'Well beaten and fluffed up duck eggs were mixed with rice and cooked with potatoes and peas to make a *bhuni* (fried) *khichuRi*. It was delicious.' According to Mahendranath's declarations, it was undoubtedly a far better dish than the ordinary pulao. To convince his readers, Mahendranath reiterates, 'I remember all this very well even now.'

Datta Family Adventures

On his travels back from London to India, Mahendranath had several interesting experiences. I am quoting a few here.

About the camel he says, 'The strange looks of the camel are matched by its eating habits. If he spots a neem tree (the Indian lilac, a large tropical Asian tree with bitter leaves of high medicinal value), he will refuse to budge, and if you offer him the leaves he will promptly gobble them up and chew the cud for hours.'

In Baluchistan, the people were very warm and courteous. 'One day, they brought me a few grasshoppers in a small dish and said, "Eat it up! Eat it up! We don't offer such delicacies to all and sundry."'

In Bulgaria once, when the snow was high on the roads, he fell into the clutches of a police inspector and was remanded to custody. He was locked up in a room with no food. After searching all the shelves in the room, Mahendranath found an old, hard loaf of bread and a few peppercorns. After a while, the policeman came and found the Datta offspring eating the cold, brick-hard bread.

After a few days, the inspector told Mahendranath that he could leave. The prisoner replied, 'I will not leave. It is snowing everywhere, how will I go?' Finally, a compromise was reached. The prisoner said, 'Give me a parcel with some tea to beat the cold, some peppercorns and some pipe tobacco.' When his request was acceded to, the scion of the Datta family said, 'If you give me your horse too, then I may consider leaving.' He was given a horse and an escort who would accompany him across the snow and bring the horse back. Before he left, Mahendranath used the British occupation of India as an opportunity to assert himself, saying in a loud tone, 'Who do you think you are messing with? Don't you know I am a British subject?' Hearing this, the inspector's stance softened a little.

Mahendranath observed, 'In those days, the British had tremendous power. Anyone declaring himself a British subject could proudly roam the world unharmed.'

Mahendranath also gives us a description of a startling incident in freezing Sofia, the capital city of Bulgaria. Intense cold had oppressed the town. When people stepped indoors and stood in front of the fireplace, the snow melted off their clothes and fell onto the fire. Mahendranath was almost sure he would not survive the cold. Then a very strange sight met his eyes. 'A live cow or horse—I am not sure which—was brought in and tied up. Someone pricked it with a sharp object and blood gushed out. Then the assembled people one by one, started to drink this warm blood!'

Let us now move from these cold wintry descriptions to warm Calcutta's delightful accounts. At one time Mahendranath was dictating the book *Swami Saradananda's Reflections* to Pyaremohan Mukhopadhyay. Like Vedavyas, Mahendranath dictated almost all of his books—he was unwilling to wield the pen himself. After around two to two and a half hours of continuous dictation, he said, 'Oh Pyare, today is *harimatar*,' meaning, 'We didn't get anything to eat today'. On hearing that, a devoted assistant immediately rushed off and got him some *muRi* (puffed rice) and some cold brinjal fritters. Satiated after having eaten even that cold food, Mahendranath sat back and began to pull at his hookah.

This was the nature of Swamiji and his siblings. They were as happy with food as without. They were unique in their willingness to readily give away their food to others who were more needy. Examples of this behaviour abound and have been recorded in many countries. Swami Birajananda's nephew Bimal Kumar Basu has spoken about a time when they were roaming around in a foreign country and there was a scarcity of funds. With the little money they had, Swamiji's brother bought a few pieces of bread. 'As he was about to eat it, a beggar arrived, saying he was very hungry. Mahendranath promptly gave away the bread to the man.' Bimal asked him, 'What did you eat?' Mahendranath replied, 'Do I have just one mouth? I ate with his (the beggar's) mouth.'

Mahendranath has also given us some profound wisdom about food. A devotee asked him, 'Why did the honest Bheeshma, who had conquered all the senses, side with Duryodhana in the Mahabharata war, knowing fully well that he was on the path of wrong?' Mahim Babu's unforgettable response was, 'Sinning against food is an unforgivable sin. Bheeshma was certainly nurtured on Duryodhana's food. To atone for that, even though Duryodhana was in the wrong, Bheeshma had no option but to fight on his side.'

Sinning against food is a deeply philosophical subject. In the vast Ramayana and Mahabharata, even with their great endeavours, Valmiki and Vyasa could not assess it fully. Our focus now though, is the food interest of the Datta family's elder son and his younger siblings.

Pyaremohan Mukhopadhyay has written about the Congress leader Rajarao, a South Indian Brahmin. While studying in Calcutta's City College, Rajarao spent most of his time at the Datta home. Later, as the under secretary of the National Congress Party, he visited the home whenever he was in Calcutta.

Once, on arriving, he offered salutations to Mahendra Babu and asked, 'Dada, what will we eat now?' Mahendranath responded, 'You tell me.' Raja's frank response was, '*Dahi-Mishti* (sweet curd and sweetmeats).' Mahim Babu replied, 'Listen, it is now five in the evening. No one eats curd and sweets at this time!' Rajarao said, 'We have to eat something. Please tell me what you will eat, Dada.'

Mahendranath then replied, '*Hing-kochuri*, *tarkari* (vegetable curry) and *aloor dum* (a rich potato curry) from the *Hindustani* (North-Indian) hotel.' Rajarao gave Pyaremohan one rupee and said, 'Go brother, and bring exactly what Dada says.' Mahim Babu's instructions were detailed: 'Bring one anna worth of *hing-kochuri* from the shop right next to the Thanthania KalibaRi (the famous Kali temple on College Street in Calcutta).' A large packet soon arrived, with sixteen *kochuris* and a lot of *aloor dum*. Pyare writes, 'Of that, Rajarao took one, I took two, and Mahim Babu took thirteen in a porcelain dish and sat down to eat.' Mahendranath ate an entire *kochuri* with the accompanying curry in each mouthful. Long before the others could complete their one or two *kochuris*, Mahim Babu had finished all thirteen of his share, washed up and sat down to pull at his hookah.' Clearly, the Datta family boys had a voracious appetite and bolted down their food swiftly.

Rajarao, unbeknownst to his mother, regularly smoked cigarettes. Rajarao reminisces, 'She once found some cigarettes in my pocket and asked me, "What are these, son?"' Her beloved son explained them away as candles. '"I am always travelling here and there; if I need some light, I light these." If my mother

had known that I smoked, she would never have eaten anything
I'd touched.'

Kochuri and Batabi Lebu

Kochuri and batabi lebu (grapefruit) were both favourites
of the Datta family. One evening, when Pyaremohan was
visiting Mahendra Babu, he was told, 'Sit down, some food
is arriving soon. They are buying some food—a packet of
kochuri and other eats; so eat before you leave.' Perhaps
Pyaremohan was preparing to leave after a while, because he
again said, 'The snacks have come, sit down, sit down! When
food graces us, it's best to eat it.' And in a few minutes,
some devotees did indeed arrive from Cornwallis Street with
a packet of kochuri.

Another time an admirer, who had just recovered from
malaria, arrived, weak and tired from his illness. After paying
obeisance to Mahendranath, he said, 'The fever has left but there
is no taste in the mouth—I have no appetite at all.' Mahim Babu
asked kindly, 'So, what do you really feel like eating?' The young
visitor replied, 'If I could get some grapefruit, it may help my
palate.' Mahendranath replied, 'Where will you get grapefruit
now? This is summer, not the time for grapefruits! First, the
Goddess will taste some (during Durga Puja in Autumn), then
the fruits will sweeten on the tree and only then will the rest
of us have any. But wait! Your grapefruit may be coming after
all.' Sure enough, in a few minutes, a gentleman arrived bearing
aloft a well-ripened grapefruit with its stem and leaves intact.
He explained, 'We have a dophala (a tree bearing two types of
fruits), and this is its first fruit.' Mahendra Babu was delighted
and said, 'There is your customer,' pointing to the patient. The
disappointed fruit-owner, who was keen to gift the first fruit of

his garden to the celebrated Mahendranath, gave away the fruit
to the guest instead.

Sreesha Chandra Mukhopadhyay's son Narendra Chandra
Mukhopadhyay, who was the District Judge at one time, has
written some anecdotes about young Naren's eating and feeding
stories. His uncle, Satish Chandra Mukhopadhyay had studied
with Swamiji.

'Kailash, the snacks man, used to bring an assortment of
snacks every evening, and all of us boys would enjoy them to
our heart's content. We were all small fry, but Swamiji was
the big man, in the same rank as my uncle . . . He loved *jibhe
gaja*. One evening, not being happy with his limited share of
the *gaja*, he casually picked up one, licked it, and then with a
straight face, dropped it back into the pot, laughing aloud. "Oh
no! Don't any of you eat this—it's all become *entho* (leftover –
not to be eaten by others)." He had the entire pot that day, all
by himself. He was a real entertainer.'

'Not just *jibhe gaja*, there has been a lot of fun even with the
kochuri. Once Naren was visiting the singer Pulin Mitra in a
canteen. Some delicious *kochuri* was being served, which Naren
loved. He broke off half of his *kochuri* and gave it to Pulin,
but when Pulin started to eat it, our future Swamiji changed
his mind and asked, "Give me a little of that, please! It's really
delicious, isn't it?"'

Narendranath's Food Policy

It is not clear exactly how Narendranath's father Vishwanath
Datta influenced his son's food policy. This is mainly because the
major part of Vishwanath's short life was spent outside Calcutta.
When he returned to Calcutta after acquiring considerable
wealth, he was caught up in many familial problems and then

died a sudden and untimely death. In fact, we still have not been able to get a photograph of Narendranath's father from any source. What we have is a postcard with his handwriting and signature, which is still preserved in the Calcutta High Court's archives.

In later years, his sons often reminisced about Vishwanath in various contexts. In 1940, Mahendranath, sitting at his Gourmohan Mukherjee Street residence, said, 'Father used to say that, if you complain about small things, you will become petty!' He then added, 'Don't complain when you are eating. If you eat happily, you will receive everything you desire!'

Mahendranath gives us some detailed information about the feast in Dakshineswar on Thakur Ramakrishna's first birth anniversary following his death in 1886. His disciples arranged for a festival, and both householders and sanyasis were present at the function. 'There was *khichuRi* and a few *tarkaris* (vegetable curries).' After the cooking was over, an offering was made to Thakur's idol at the *Math*'s sanctum sanctorum. Thereafter, the prasad was placed in a huge heap, on a large leaf plate, to be served to everyone.

When the prasad was being served, three emaciated sanyasis arrived at the function. With their ribs sticking out, they looked as if they had not eaten in days. They paid obeisance to Thakur's idol, and Girish Chandra Ghosh (also referred to as the father of Bengali theatre and a senior disciple of Thakur) asked them where they were coming from. They answered, 'EnReda' (a suburb of Calcutta). Girish requested them to have some prasad before leaving. They answered that being Brahmins they could not eat the *annaprasad* (rice served as prasad). Girish, however, had also offered Thakur a large plate of *sandesh* and a few large pots of sweet curd as *bhog*. So, he asked the sanyasi guests, 'Surely you can have some sweets?' They agreed and went to take a dip in the Ganges flowing outside. After a bath, they came back for their *prasad*-sweets. Girish assured them that only after they served themselves would anyone else touch the sweets or serve the others. The sanyasis went into the room to eat. A little later when Mahim entered the room, he was astonished at what he saw. The guests had each taken a large banana leaf, piled huge mounds of *sandesh* onto it and kept an entire pot of curd in front of each portion. After completing their prayers, they fell upon the *sandesh*, picking up several at a time, swallowing them swiftly and reaching for more. After the *sandesh* was done, they picked up the pot of curd and gulped it down and then licked the pots clean. They stood up and said, 'We are very happy and satisfied. Paramahansa Deb (Thakur Ramakrishna) really loved us.' Girish Babu, quite calmly and with no sign of annoyance, gave each of them a betel-leaf-wrapped paan. Mahendra Babu remembers, 'Even after their eating so much, I did not see any sign of discomfort or unease in them.'

Instead of getting all our information from Mahendranath's reminiscences alone, we should also look at what we can source from Vishwanath Datta's life stories by other authors.

In his book *Swami Vivekananda*, Pramathanath Basu has written about Vishwanath Datta: 'He was not just intelligent, educated and informed; not just vastly experienced, but he was also very keen to enjoy life. His view on life was, "If you want to live in the world, live fully, live with your whole mind and soul, fulfilling all your longings and aspirations. And, when you leave, go fully satiated in every respect. Seek, invest, enjoy, as long as you have the finances, live happily and as per your wishes, eat well, feed others too, live like a king."' According to Pramathanath, 'Vishwanath was a simple person, who enjoyed entertaining and making merry with friends and family. As we already know, he himself was skilled in the culinary arts. He was one of the rare few who could invite people with such love and care, cook such an array of tasty dishes and treat his guests to such a delightful feast.'

Pramathanath further says Vishwanath supervised the kitchen himself and regularly came up with novel recipes. 'He insisted that there should always be something new and unique to serve to the guests, and that too cooked by himself.' We also learn from Pramathanath that at Vishwanath's insistence, pulao became the daily staple food of the Datta family, perhaps because of his having stayed in Lucknow for a while.

Vishwanath concurred with his son Narendranath on many issues. Naren had an aversion to Mathematics but that did not dishearten his father. His own view on maths was: 'That is a learning necessary only for grocers.'

Pramathanath Basu informs us that while studying at the Metropolitan School, Narendranath had fallen a victim to dyspepsia and '. . . had become very weak. He would, however, give in to the temptation of his favourite fried foods and at the slightest opportunity, eating all the items that were highly dangerous for his condition.'

In his mid-teens, Narendranath lived with his father in Raipur, the present capital of Chhattisgarh, and learnt to cook various dishes from him. 'Naren was always firm in his resolve to be a better cook than anyone else.' He would often go on picnics with friends, who, based on their financial ability, contributed a few paise towards the cost of the food. Narendranath contributed the lion's share and also took on the responsibility for cooking. With the help of his friends, he cooked pulao, mutton, *khichuRi* and various other mouth-watering dishes. From several accounts, the food was very tasty, but Narendranath had a particular penchant for chillies and the food often turned out too spicy for the others.

Dr Ramachandra Datta's anecdotes tell us a little more about the Raipur stay. The author of these reminiscences is also Mahendranath Datta. 'In my childhood, under the influence of Ram Dada, I had become a complete Vaishnava. Dada (Narendranath) was fond of telling Vaishnava stories, but he never followed their practices at all. He ate fish and mutton with great joy.' Ram Dada, even with all his admonishments and teachings, could not convince Narendranath to become a vegetarian.

Mahendranath recounts the family travelling to Raipur in 1877. Vishwanath was then practising law in Bilaspur. The travel party included Narendranath, Mahendranath, their mother Bhuvaneswari Devi and sister Jogenbala. They reached a village named *GhoRatalao*, where meat was being cooked for their meal. Mahim steadfastly refused to eat the mutton curry. Then, he narrates, 'Dada (Narendranath) stuffed meat into my mouth and started thumping me on the back to swallow it.' Mahendranath admits, 'We belong to the Shakta order (a Hindu religious order that worships the Mother Goddess and is open to having non-vegetarian food unlike the Vaishnavites and Shaivites, who were strictly vegetarian). So, once the mutton touched the tongue, instinct took over.' The Datta family became very fond of mutton during their stay in Raipur.

In the family home, there was always an abundance of duck eggs, mutton and crabs. But the Vaishnavite Ram Dada, despite being extremely close to this family of meat aficionados, never touched non-vegetarian food. In later years, after he became diabetic, doctors advised a non-vegetarian fare. But although he started eating fish, he never ate mutton.

We have meticulous records on what medicines and diet were prescribed for the youngsters in the Datta family when they fell ill. Along with regular medicines, the elderly *kabiraj*

(Ayurvedic doctor) prescribed *masoor* dal (red lentil) soup and the betel fruit's *paalor ruti*. In those days, just the smell of this *ruti* apparently created a sense of illness. We also hear that unless the illness was severe, the doctor did not insist on this *ruti*.

Swamiji's father once suffered from haemorrhoids. The doctor prescribed *surua* (a soup). The recipe involved cooking oysters with shredded *kalmi shaak* (a type of spinach), onions, caraway seeds, fennel seeds and a little salt. It was cooked in a pot for a long while before it could be eaten.

Ram Dada had another concoction for any illness among the young boys of the Datta family. This was the 'quinine mixture' made with a little quinine, a little bit of yolk from a duck's egg, a little brandy and a bit of sugar. Needless to say, most medicines in Calcutta those days included a little brandy.

Ram Dada's Cooking

Ram Dada made a significant contribution to the list of the Datta boys' favourite items of food—*khaja parota* (a crisp fried flatbread with an abundance of ghee). He made this himself on his wood-stoked stove at his home in Ramtanu Basu Lane, Calcutta, where the boys visited and ate to their heart's content.

Mahendranath tells us of another favourite of Ram Dada's tempting dishes—*bhetki ghonto* (carp and mixed vegetable). Cooked carp was to be fried with a mix of potatoes, cauliflower, shredded radish, peas, ground ginger and some fried and ground spices. The *bhetki ghonto* and the *khaja parota* made a scrumptious meal.

When Ram Dada first carried apples to the Datta residence, he created quite a stir. This strange fruit was skinned using the *bnoti* (a steel knife shaped somewhat like a scythe, fixed to a wooden board and placed on the floor) and distributed. Seeing the children eat the apples with great gusto, Ram Dada asked, 'So, how is it?' The inexperienced youngsters thought it was the Bombay *kul* that was then available at four or five for a paisa. Apples were very expensive—three for a rupee. Ram Dada was rather unhappy at the valuable apple being mistaken for a green jujube!

Narendranath's maternal family used to cook yet another much-loved dish—the *kalai* dal (black lentil) with the skin left on, cooked as a thick dal, with ginger, fennel seeds and a pinch of asafoetida and without the usual turmeric.

The invention of the famous Bengali *sandesh* and *rosogolla* happened quite recently (in the 1870s). Ram Dada had received a few *talshansh sandesh* (a *sandesh* shaped like the fruit of the Palmyra tree, filled with sweet jaggery syrup) along with his fees for his treatment of an elderly lady. He carried the sweets to the Datta family home and offered one to Mahim.

The young Mahendranath was wonderstruck: 'It was amazing! I broke the *sandesh* in two and found some jaggery syrup inside!' It was a complete wonder to him how the jaggery was placed inside the sweet. The same question arose later upon seeing the *rosogolla*. Debates broke out at 3, Gourmohan Mukherjee Street on how a solid object could get sugar syrup inside it.

Mahendranath surmises that *sandesh* and *rosogolla* arrived on the scene in 1875–1876. That was the time when many new and varied types of *sandesh* and *rosogolla* appeared and with that, the *aata* and *monda sandesh* slowly disappeared from Calcutta.

Worldwide followers of Thakur Ramakrishna do not always remember that the *rosogolla* played a huge role in the first meeting of Sri Ramakrishna and Swami Vivekananda. Ram Dada had played a valuable role in this *rosogolla* project.

Mahendranath has elaborated on this meeting. From Keshub Chandra Sen's (a Hindu philosopher and social reformer of the time) discourses, everyone had heard about a kind, amicable and childlike personality, addressed as Paramahansa (the divine swan—because, like the swan that lives in water but is not touched by the water, he stayed within the confines of domestic life and yet did not allow material or carnal desires to touch him and was a highly evolved spiritual master). But people laughed at and taunted Thakur, calling him 'the great goose'. They also said he was prone to epilepsy (because of his frequent spiritual trances), but this was in fact completely denied by Thakur himself.

Sometime around 1881, Dr Ram's family was struck by cholera, and he lost his eldest daughter and two nieces to the deadly disease within a week. Unable to find any solace from his deep anguish, Ram Dada finally went to meet Sri Ramakrishna in Dakshineswar. This caused uproar in the neighbourhood. People were upset because Ram Dada had chosen to be initiated by Sri Ramakrishna over his own family guru. They were particularly offended by the fact that Sri Ramakrishna, as a Brahmin priest serving at the Dakshineswar Kali Temple, was in the payroll of 'low-caste' *Kaibarta* zamindars. Rani Rashmoni, the philanthropist heiress who established the Dakshineswar temple, belonged to the *Kaibarta* caste (a lower caste among Hindus). Undeterred by the criticism, Ram Dada continued to visit Sri Ramakrishna at Dakshineswar as often as he could, particularly on Sundays.

One day, Ram Dada asked the young Naren, who was then a college student, 'Bilay, you are always roaming around. Why don't you come with me to meet the Paramahansa?' Bilay's arrogant response was, 'He's a fool! What does he have that I should hear him? A downright fool, who worships Kali and works for the *Kaibartas* . . . do I really need to learn from him? What does he know? What does he know that he can teach me?' Finally, he impudently added, 'If he can feed me good *rosogollas*, only then am I willing to visit him! But if he does not, I will twist his ears and straighten out the fool!'

So, it was the hope of eating some tasty *rosogollas* that finally took Vivekananda to Dakshineswar. That was when Naren first met Sri Ramakrishna in the year 1880 or 1881; he was around seventeen or eighteen years old at the time. His brother Mahendranath writes in Narendranath's biography, 'Narendranath considered Thakur a lunatic of sorts and decided to step cautiously, not getting too close to him. But Sri Ramakrishna touched Narendranath, and he immediately became almost unconscious, going into a trance and lying inert, while saying incoherently, "Where are you taking me? What are you doing to me? I have parents! I have ambitions! I want to be a lawyer, I want to enjoy my prosperity!"'

Soon Narendranath began attending the Calcutta High Court along with his father and uncle. But, as Vivekananda's followers know, while in his third and fourth year at college, he would visit Dakshineswar at every opportunity and would meditate whenever he was alone at home.

In 1884, Narendranath graduated. His father was delighted that his son 'will be an Articled Clerk in my own office and will take over all my clients'.

Whenever Paramahansa visited Ram Dada's home at Simulia Street, the food arrangements were particularly fascinating. Those days the caste-driven practice was to cook potato and vegetable curries without salt and to add salt separately on the side of the leaf while serving. However, in Thakur's devotee Dr Ramchandra Datta's home, the food was salted as necessary and people of all castes and stations in life sat down together, unhesitant, to enjoy their meals. This practice of eating together was a huge step for that time, and Sri Ramakrishna joyfully supported this social change. He said that devotees must always eat together and that devotees had no caste or creed. Even uninvited guests would happily sit down with the guests and partake of *luchi* and vegetables. This again created an upheaval in the socially rigid North Calcutta society.

One evening, Naren was to sing at the Community Brahmo Samaj (a theistic movement within Hinduism, founded in Calcutta in 1828) gathering. Thakur landed up at the function, and remarked, 'The Brahmo Samaj is like a good *khichuRi*—a good mix, where rather than the complete belief of any one faith, the best ideas of all faiths find representation.' Naren was a little uneasy that day, we hear, about whether people would show Thakur due respect, but as it turned out, there was nothing to be concerned about.

Mahendranath tells us that Thakur sometimes visited the Gourmohan Mukherjee Street home to look for Naren, but he always stood outside, on the road—he never entered the Datta home.

Mahendranath records that Naren's eagerness to eat wherever he found good food had reached Thakur's ears too. Someone asked Thakur, 'Why do you love Naren so much? You allow him to use your personal hookah, making it *entho*. He goes to all kinds of places, eats at hotels. Should you be eating his *entho*?'

Thakur, we hear, was very annoyed at this and responded, 'You rascal, what is it to you whether Naren eats in hotels or does not? You rogue, even if you were to eat only the purest of vegetarian foods and Naren was to eat only at hotels, you would still not be able to equal him!'

Thakur often told his followers, 'Don't eat the food intended for rich businessmen—your stomach will not tolerate it. Only Naren can digest such stuff.' He also said, 'Naren can eat (anything), he has a fire burning inside him. Even if I offer him a tender banana plant, it will be reduced to ashes.'

Mahendranath informs us that whenever Thakur started to eat, he first offered it to the Goddess, then took his own share and only then offered the rest to his disciples.

Thakur had once told his *saha-dharmini* (a wife/partner, who is not just equal but complementary in carrying out their role of dharma under the universal law/nature of things), Ma Sharadamoni and nephew Hridu (abbreviated form of Hriday) Mukherjee, that 'When you see me offering the *aag bhaag* (first part) of my food to someone else, before eating the rest myself, know then that I will not stay in this body much longer.'

One evening, when Naren visited him in Dakshineswar, Thakur was served some *sandesh* for his evening snack. He first asked Naren to take a few, before eating the rest himself. Hridu says, 'My heart froze as I realized that he will not keep this body for very long now.' A short while after that, Thakur passed away. Mahendranath has written, 'It is important to note that the Paramahansa did not ever eat the leftovers of anyone else (other than of Naren).'

Thakur was always very eager to feed Naren, a fact also noticed by Girish Chandra Ghosh. One day, Sri Ramakrishna was sitting with a bowl of mutton curry prasad to feed Naren, whenever he arrived. Everyone present began asking to eat the mutton in jest, saying Naren was not going to turn up. But Thakur paid no heed to any of them and sat waiting. Soon Naren did appear, and Thakur was content only after feeding him the mutton.

Ramakrishna's disciples held many opinions on eating fish and mutton. Naren's *gurubhai* Swami Akhandanand used to quote from Ayurveda that expectant mothers must be fed mutton. If the child were to be musically gifted, the expectant mother would have to eat fish. If the child needed to have qualities of wisdom, virtuosity, courage and good oration or the qualities of a warrior, etc., then Ayurveda identifies specific types of meat to be offered to the expectant mother.

Ram Dada, however, used to advise the self-renounced disciples of Thakur, 'You should not eat fish and meat. It will look bad and people will criticise you.' Rakhal Maharaj responded, 'Where do we eat fish or meat? Only when we go to other people's homes and they serve us, we quietly eat it without refusing.'

One day, Thakur landed up unexpectedly at Girish Chandra Ghosh's home. An ecstatic Girish asked his helper boy to buy some *luchi* and *aloor dum* from the market. When it came, Thakur lovingly began to eat it. Girish then asked the boy to check if there was any leftover *pui shak* (the climbing spinach) and prawn curry from the morning. Accordingly, the boy brought the morning's leftovers and served it to Thakur. Thakur, who never ate leftovers, now sat happily enjoying his *luchi* with the *pui shak* and prawns. His disciple Jogen Maharaj watched him, stunned.

We must remember though, that our discussions are not about Thakur Sri Ramakrishna, but about Narendranath. Swami Gambhiranand, in the first volume of his famous book, '*Yuganayak Vivekananda*, has written that Surendranath Mitra, a devotee of Thakur, travelled frequently to Dakshineswar those days. In November 1881, when Naren was busy preparing for his FA examinations (equal to class XII in the contemporary education system), Surendranath organized a small function at his home in Simulia, with Thakur. Naren was invited to sing at the function. This was when Thakur first met Naren and was immediately drawn towards him. He requested Dr Ramchandra Datta to bring Naren to Dakshineswar some day.

When the exam results were announced, Naren had managed to only secure a second division. Despite this, he was considered an eligible bachelor and a marriage proposal arrived for him with a dowry offer of 10,000 rupees. His father Vishwanath was happy with the offer but Naren refused to get married.

Around that time, Naren visited Dakshineswar along with two friends in Surendranath's car. There, at Thakur's request, he sang a song. Narendranath himself has described to Swami Saradananda what happened after that.

After listening to the song, Thakur took young Naren aside and did something absolutely unimaginable. 'He stood in front of me with folded hands and treating me like a God, said, "I know, my Lord, you are that same ancient rishi, Narayan (the God Vishnu) in human form. You have come down to alleviate the sorrows of all human beings."'

Naren kept quiet and Thakur entered an inner room and came out with some 'butter, sugar candy and some *sandesh* and started feeding me with his own hands. No matter how much I protested, saying "Please give me the food, let me go and share it with my friends," he would not listen, and said, "They will eat later; you eat now."' At this meeting Thakur pleaded, 'Promise me, you will come back soon, alone, to see me?' Unable to refuse, Narendranath perforce agreed to be back soon.

Narendranath's own words about his eating and feeding others have been recorded in various places. 'Sometimes we would have picnics at Dakshineswar. On the first day of the picnic, seeing me cook the food, Thakur partook of all the dishes. Knowing that he would not normally have food cooked by a non-Brahmin, I had organized some prasad from the temple for Thakur. However, he stopped me from doing that, saying, "I will not incur any sin by having food cooked by a pure and meritorious soul like you." Although I requested him many times, yet he would not listen and insisted on having the food I cooked that day.'

There is a reference to some contradictory information in the biography *Yuganayak Vivekananda*. Swami Gambhirananda has written, 'In the early days of youth, when he was deeply inspired by spirituality, Narendranath had given up non-vegetarian food and would sleep on the floor on a mat or a blanket.'

But there is also another anecdote which contradicts this. 'Narendranath had eaten some non-vegetarian food at a restaurant on his way to meet Thakur at Dakshineswar. When he came into Thakur's presence, Narendranath promptly disclosed the information, saying to Thakur, "Sir, I have today eaten at a hotel, that food which the normal (Hindu) man considers unfit for human consumption." Thakur understood that Naren was not boasting about his non-conformity to social norms but said it to caution Thakur so that if there were any vessels etc. that he would not like Narendra to touch, Thakur should say so. Thakur responded by assuring Naren, "There is no sin in your eating in hotels. Even while eating pork or beef, if someone remembers God, it is equivalent to eating pure vegetarian food; while on the other hand, even if someone eats pure vegetarian food but stays immersed in material desires, then it is the same as their eating pork or beef. I don't mind you eating unwholesome food. Although if any of these people (meaning the other devotees assembled around him) had said this, I would not have been able to even touch them!"'

Either tobacco or sweets have played a role in each meeting of Thakur with Naren. A few days before Naren's graduation examinations, agonized at not having met him for many days, Thakur landed up unexpectedly at Naren's home in Calcutta.

Naren came rushing down to greet and welcome him, worried at Thakur's coming all the way himself. Teary-eyed, Thakur asked him, 'Why didn't you come all these days?' And then, untying a knot at the end of his *gamchha* (a thin cotton towel that is sometimes worn over the shoulder), and taking out some *sandesh* he began feeding Naren, saying repeatedly, 'Eat, eat.'

Whenever he visited Naren, Thakur always carried some food with him. We learn from reliable sources, however, that his beloved Naren could never eat alone—he would always share it with his friends.

After extensive research, Vishwanath Datta's biographer Swami Gambhirananda informs us that at some point in his life, a friend had misappropriated a lot of his funds and 'although Vishwanath's family continued to maintain an external appearance of financial well-being, in reality, they were in dire financial straits.'

Alongside the various troubles of a joint family, the unspoken disputes reached such a head, that 'Narendranath's father left his ancestral home and moved to a rented home in 7, Bhairab Biswas Lane'. That was probably around 1883. Narendranath was very busy at the time, attending the court with his father and uncle, visiting Dakshineswar whenever he could and enjoying himself with his friends.

Narendranath passed his FA examination in January 1884, and his father Vishwanath Datta passed away the following month. On Monday, 23 February, Narendranath was busy with a musical programme at a friend's home in Barahanagar. At almost 2 a.m., another friend brought news of his father's passing away.

While living away from Calcutta, Vishwanath was stricken with diabetes, a condition that later also afflicted Narendranath.

Swami Gambhirananda informs us that a month before his demise, Vishwanath developed some complications of the heart and was almost bedridden. But some important work took him to Alipore, from where he had to rush back home because of a chest pain. At 8 p.m., that evening, he started to vomit and by 10 p.m., his heart had stopped beating.

After Vishwanath's death, the Datta family underwent untold miseries. Naren's mother Bhuvaneswari Devi became the mainstay of the family. She, who was once used to running her household on a monthly budget of 1,000 rupees, could not even manage to raise thirty rupees after her husband's death. Despite all his efforts, her eldest son Narendranath could not find a job. Yet, she rarely expressed her helplessness.

As per the custom of the time, Bhuvaneswari Devi always signed documents as *Daasi* (the servant of God—a signature Vaishnava ladies used).

Narendranath himself writes about those difficult days: 'I had to start looking for a job even before the end of the *ashauch* period (literal meaning: 'impure'. Refers to the period of twelve to sixteen days after someone passes away, which is treated as a time of mourning, when no worldly work is done and the bereaved persons stay indoors. It ends with the *shraddh* ceremony).'

This was the first time the word 'starvation' made an ominous appearance in the life of the food and culinary enthusiast Narendranath. 'I would roam endlessly from office to office in the hot afternoon sun—starving, hungry, barefoot, with torn clothes and a job application letter in hand, looking for a job.' But Narendranath, who was to soon conquer the world with his words, found it impossible to get a job.

Even in those days of sorrow, however, a few loyal friends supported Narendranath. One of his friends, attempting to console Narendranath when he was exhausted and extremely despondent, sat down at the Ochterlony Monument (now called the *Shahid Minar*) and started to sing, 'The breath of the universe, filled with compassion, blows gently in the breeze . . .' Narendranath reminisces, 'When the thoughts of my helpless mother and siblings came to my mind, I shouted at him in anger, helplessness and hurt pride, "Ok, stop now! Keep quiet! Those whose relatives are not plagued by hunger, who have never had to endure a lack of subsistence, who lie relaxed, below the breeze of a hand-pulled fan, they may enjoy this sweet vision. I too enjoyed it one day, but today, in the face of harsh reality it seems to me like terrible mockery."'

Starvation and Fasting

This was a new experience in the life of the brave heart Vivekananda we are familiar with. Swamiji has shared with us the picture of the harsh penury of the average middle-class family in the Calcutta of those days. 'I would wake up in the morning and surreptitiously check whether there was enough to eat at home. The days on which I realized the food would not suffice for all of us, I would tell mother, "I have an invitation" and leave home. On some days I would eat what little I could manage, while on other days, manage with no food at all. My pride did not allow me to even acknowledge this to anyone at home or outside.'

To describe those days of cruel poverty, Swami Gambhirananda took the help of an excerpt from *Sri Ramakrishna Kathamrita*, (literal meaning, 'the nectar of his words') where Swami Vivekananda tells Ma Sharadamoni, Thakur's wife and consort, 'I have reached this stage after a lot of sorrow and difficulty. Mastermoshai (as Thakur's senior disciple Mahendranath Gupta was addressed), you have not had any sorrows in your life; I believe unless one goes through struggles, one cannot surrender completely to the Almighty.'

Yet, in spite of having just lost his father and having no income at all, Narendranath had immense faith in God. He always chanted God's name while getting out of bed every morning. One day finally his mother lost her patience with this. Overhearing his morning prayers from the next room, she shouted out, 'Shut up boy! From your childhood, you have kept chanting "God, God! Isn't it God himself who has caused all our problems?"

Vivekananda, influenced by her words, later described this trying situation in his life. 'It is not my nature to do anything in secrecy. So it should not surprise anyone that I then went around telling people openly and trying to prove to them that there was no God, or if there was one, it was futile or useless to pray to Him. As a result, a rumour spread very quickly that I had become an atheist and was associating with people of bad character and resorting to drinking and that I would have no hesitation to even visit brothels!'

All these rumours about Naren's supposed downfall were distorted in various ways and in due course reached Dakshineswar too. Thakur heard some of it from his disciple Bhavanath, who said that he could never have imagined in his dreams that Naren would change so much. Becoming very angry, Thakur retorted, 'Shut up you scoundrels! Ma (Goddess Kali) has said he will never go astray. Never tell me such things again, or I will not see your faces.'

During this period, Narendranath made an explosive disclosure: 'I gradually became immune to the world's applause and criticism. I realized that unlike ordinary folk, I was not born to fulfil the mundane tasks of eking out a livelihood and looking after my relatives in an indolent life until my death. This became a strong conviction and, like my grandfather, I too decided to leave my family. I began to secretly plan my departure.' The date of leaving was also finalized when Sri Ramakrishna met Naren and prevailed upon him to come to Dakshineswar.

Mahendranath has written in his brother's biography that, at the end of 1885 or the beginning of 1886, there was a complex legal issue surrounding their home and a court case had been filed. Naren went to Dakshineswar and, after listening attentively to everything he had to say, Thakur advised him, 'You go to Ma Bhabatarini (Goddess Kali) and whatever you will ask for, she will grant you.'

The Days of Kashipur

Thakur's illness was diagnosed in 1886, and at first a house was rented in Shyampukur (in the outskirts of Calcutta at the time) for his treatment. However, since there was no improvement in his condition, Thakur was then shifted to a home in Kashipur's Motijhil. Many anecdotes have been recorded during this stay, which are now available to us.

An insane woman once walked into the home. Everyone tried to shoo her away, and one of Naren's *gurubhais* actually put on a turban to imitate a police inspector and started to speak in Hindi in an effort to scare her off. The woman was anxious and began to leave when Narendranath, his head bowed and eyes filled with tears, told his *gurubhai* Gangadhar (later Swami Akhandananda), 'She has turned mad for want of food. See if there is anything here under the mat that we can give her.' Gangadhar found six anna under the mat and tied it in a corner of the woman's sari. Narendranath said with tear-filled eyes, 'Starvation is so tough! Hunger! Really difficult!'

A few days after this experience, Narendranath heard that a certain gentleman was suffering from a duodenum ailment. He did not have the money to treat himself, nor was he able to look after his three children. Narendranath organized thirty rupees to be sent to him through Jogen Maharaj. He also requested his friend Dr Trailokyanath Bandopadhyay to treat him free of cost, which the kind-hearted doctor did.

Why did Thakur agree to leave Dakshineswar and move to Calcutta during his illness? He said, 'I have come because of two reasons—the rooms there (in Dakshineswar) are musty, and there is no convenience for going to the toilet.' However, in his last stages, the rent of eighty rupees for the Kashipur villa seemed too high, and Thakur was keen to return to Dakshineswar. The then owner of the temple, however, did not agree.

There were other rumours too about Thakur's departure from Dakshineswar. Golap Ma, Thakur's householder disciple, once remarked, 'See Jogen, Thakur probably left for Calcutta because he was annoyed with Ma.' Her self-pride injured, Ma Sharadamoni arrived at Thakur's home and cried, 'I heard that you were angry with me and that is why you came away to Calcutta?' Thakur was angry when he heard what Golap Ma had said. 'She said that and made you cry? Doesn't she know who you are?' (Sri Ramakrishna had proclaimed Sri Ma as the embodiment of the Divine Mother and performed the *ShoRoshi* Puja acknowledging the divinity of the woman with her in the seat of Goddess Kali.) Ma Sharadamoni then was pacified and returned to Dakshineswar.

There had been controversies earlier too, about Thakur accepting food at Keshub Chandra Sen's home. In his defence,

Thakur first said, 'I did not have rice, only two *jilipis* (jalebis). Later, he elaborated, 'They (the hosts) were apprehensive that I would not be allowed to enter the shrine at Dakshineswar.' (That he would be stripped of his priesthood if he were found guilty of having rice at a non-Brahmin's and a lower-caste person's home.) But Thakur later admitted, 'I did once, at their insistence, have *luchi* and *aloo* during a gathering, which was served by either a washerman or a barber (both belonging to the lower castes). Keshub was then in the inner chamber of his home, with the ladies.' Thakur in all innocence further admitted, 'While Keshub held my hand and started dancing, his mother fed me.'

Another scene from Shyamapukur: Narendranath was helping Thakur have his food. Dr Mahendralal Sarkar, Thakur's principal physician, was watching closely. After he left, Dr Ramachandra Datta (Ram Dada) asked Thakur, 'Shall I look for a villa outside Calcutta for you?' Thakur assented and remarked, 'Here, I have no appetite, nor am I able to digest anything.' At that time, Thakur's diet consisted of rice gruel during the day and a little *sujir payesh* (a sweet porridge made of milk and semolina) in the evening.

On Sunday, 6 December 1885, Dr Mahendranath Sarkar arranged for some mutton soup for Thakur, which bolstered his strength. Thakur told Naren, 'Today, I am able to get up and move around because of the mutton soup.'

Sri Ramakrishna wanted to know, could mutton be offered as bhog?

Nabagopal, an associate, responded, 'No, the sacrifice happens in front of Ma Kali . . . But let them bring some *mahaprasad* (the great offering) from Kalighat for you.'

Calcutta had many Kali temples in those days. After an initial objection, the Calcutta Corporation had relented and allowed the ritual sacrifices to be carried out in front of the Goddess. The meat was subsequently sold to the devotees.

In December 1886, the ailing Sri Ramakrishna looked at his frail body in the mirror. Naren said, 'You are definitely getting better.'

Sri Ramakrishna replied, 'Am I?'

Dr Sarkar added, 'After continuing with the rice gruel and discontinuing your bathing ritual, you are certainly doing well.'

Thakur stayed for seventy days in the rented house in Shyamapukur. Seeing the deterioration of his health, Narendra had said, 'Come, let us go back to Dakshineswar. Ma Kali is there.' Of course, due to the resistance by the then owner, Trailokyanath, (Thakur's devotee Rani Rashmoni's grandson), Sri Ramakrishna could never go back to his beloved Dakshineswar.

Thakur once told his disciple Balaram Basu, 'As long as I am outside Dakshineswar for treatment, I want you to pay for my food expenses.' After coming to Kashipur, Thakur rarely had a normal meal. His diet continued as before, with rice gruel and a little gravy in the morning and sweet semolina or vermicelli boiled in milk in the evening. There was a maid and a cook to help Ma Sharadamoni. Once when Sri Ma fell down with the bowl of milk, Thakur panicked and asked, 'What will happen now? Who will feed me?' Then Golap Ma began to make the food and Naren would feed Thakur.

The doctor gave instructions for Thakur to eat mutton daily. Thakur's directions were clear: buy the meat only from a shop where there is an image of Ma Kali. Sri Ma had said, when she used to cook for Thakur in Kashipur, 'I would put the mutton in water, with some bay leaves and very little spices. When the meat became soft like cotton, I would take it off the fire.'

Thakur's disciples would get him whatever he felt like eating. One day, Thakur had the brightly coloured *sandesh* from Barabazar. Another time he wanted to eat Dhanekhali's *khoichur* (popped rice and sugar, lightly spiced) and Krishnanagar's *sar bhaja* (a dish made by deep frying clotted cream). (Dhanekhali and Krishnanagar are far-off suburbs of Calcutta).

But Thakur's condition kept deteriorating. Later, Sri Ma has said, 'On some days, the porridge used to come out from his nose or throat. It was unbearable agony.'

Immersed in nursing and tending to Thakur, Naren often did not go back home at night. One day, Bhuvaneswari Devi reached Kashipur with her six-year-old son, Bhupendranath. Thakur, sitting propped up by a large pillow on the bed, chatted with Naren's mother. 'You were right to come. Take Narendra back with you . . . I told him, "Your widowed mother and younger brothers are at home. They need you to look after them. Is it right that you should seek to be a sanyasi?"'

Returning home with Narendra, Bhuvaneswari Devi shared the gist of her conversation with Thakur. Narendranath's famous observation was: 'He tells the thief to steal and advises the householder to manage the home.' On the way back, Narendra got off the vehicle at Baghbazar and went back to Kashipur.

By February 1886, Thakur's illness slowly became more and more serious. At the time, some people were afraid that cancer was an infectious disease. To put an end to this false belief, 'after Thakur had eaten one day, Naren took the bowl and calmly had the leftovers, which were mixed with Thakur's saliva'.

Dr Ramchandra Datta had suggested that some atonement ritual be carried out to cure the illness (a Hindu belief). Thakur suggested offering a cloth, some *sandesh* and nine rupees—he did not want any feeding of Brahmins.

Sri Ma also recollects an incident in Kashipur when Thakur said, 'This illness may cause the *khajanchis* (treasurers) to say I did not do any atonement. Listen Ramlal, you take ten rupees and go to Dakshineswar, offer it to Ma Kali and distribute it among some Brahmins.'

Another day, Thakur felt like feeding mutton to those who were serving him. He asked Mahendranath Gupta, 'Will you pay for the mutton? It will cost five or six anna.' Mastermoshai happily agreed.

Not just mutton, there was also talk of Thakur having the strictly forbidden chicken. Once Rakhal Mukherjee, an anglicized gentleman from Baghbazar, came to visit Thakur. He became very concerned after seeing Thakur's condition and enquired about Thakur's diet. After consulting with the doctor, he found that chicken soup would be very good for Thakur's condition. He immediately began pleading with Thakur to have chicken soup. To calm down the persistent Rakhal, Thakur said, 'I don't have a problem eating it, but social customs stop me. All right, we'll see tomorrow.'

12 April 1886: Here are some more anecdotes about Thakur's views on eating chicken. In the second volume of his book *Sri Ramakrishna Antaleela* (Sri Ramakrishna's Last Days), Swami Prabhananda has quoted from the *Sri Ramakrishna Kathamrita* and from Swami Abhedananda's *My Life Story*.

One day, Naren was in discussion with Sharat, Jogen, Tarak and Kaliprasad, all Thakur's disciples, about 'the various superstitions among Hindus in relation to food habits'. Naren said, 'If one realizes the universal truth, they can eat food cooked by anyone and no one will be treated as low or unworthy.' Then he announced, 'Come, let us go and break all your superstitions today.'

All the young disciples went to Peeru's restaurant on Calcutta's Biden Street and ordered chicken curry. Some ate happily, while others just touched the meat to their lips to kill the superstition. Returning to Kashipur, they met Mastermoshai. Tarak declared, 'Today, we tasted all kinds of meat.'

On the effect of having chicken, Naren said, 'The mind has sunk to low depths. Let us all meditate.'

When Kaliprasad entered Thakur's room, Thakur asked him, 'Where did you all go?'

'To Calcutta's Biden Street, Peeru's restaurant,' Kaliprasad replied.

'Who all went?' Thakur asked.

When Kaliprasad told him the names, Thakur asked, 'And what did you eat there?'

'Chicken curry.'

'How did you all like it?'

'Sharat and a few of us did not like it, so we only touched it to our lips to break the superstition.'

'Excellent!' Thakur exclaimed. 'Now all of you are free of superstition.'

On Friday, 16 April 1886, Narendranath went to Dakshineswar to meditate late at night under the *panchabati* (a cluster of these five holy trees—*bel, vat, dhatri, ashoka* and *ashwatha*). Meanwhile, Girish Chandra and Mastermoshai reached Kashipur. Thakur was very happy and arranged to get *kochuris* from the nearby shop for Girish. He offered the hot *kochuri, luchi* and various sweets as *bhog* (offering) to the Goddess and then served them to Girish. Lovingly watching him eat, Thakur said, 'Leave the *luchis,* eat the *kochuri* (i.e. eat the best).'

Girish asked, 'Tell me sir, why does the mind, which is so elevated sometimes, sink again to low depths?'

Thakur said, 'Living in the world causes that. Sometimes the mind is up, sometimes it is down. Sometimes the devotion increases, sometimes it decreases. That is because you have to live with both *kamini* and *kanchan* (with sensory desires and greed). The common housefly sometimes sits on the *sandesh* and sometimes on putrid wounds or excreta too.'

Sri Ramakrishna Antaleela tells us about two of Thakur's favourite fruits. One day in Kashipur, Thakur wanted to eat the *jamrul* (also known as bell fruit, water apple or Java apple). Laatu Maharaj tells us that, being the end of winter, the *jamrul* was not available anywhere in the markets, not even in Calcutta. But a devotee had spotted some flowers on a tree in a private garden and informed Shashi Maharaj (later Swami Ramakrishnananda), who went and procured the fruit for Thakur. Thakur was surprised, 'Where did you get the *jamrul* in this season?'

Another devotee named Nagaraj came to Kashipur and heard that Thakur was keen to eat the *amalki* (the Indian gooseberry). He went away and searched every market in Calcutta for three days, without bathing, eating or even sleeping well, until he found Thakur's favourite mouth-freshener and returned. Thakur saw the *amalki* and burst into tears. He told Sri Ma, 'Make a spicy *chorchori* (a dry mixed vegetable dish with spices) for him. He hails from East Bengal, so he's used to very spicy food.'

Two days before Thakur left his mortal body, he took Naren aside and told him, 'I am leaving everyone in your hands because you are the most intelligent and strong. Make sure that you take very good care of them. Make arrangements for all of them to stay together. Let them not go back to their domestic lives but instead live together and focus entirely on devotion and chanting.'

On the day of Thakur's departure, there were many ill omens. The *khichuRi* Sri Ma was cooking for the attendants was burnt and stuck to the bottom of the pot; a water pot fell and crashed to pieces.

At the time of his departure, Thakur was hungry and tried to eat some semolina porridge, but almost all of it fell out of his mouth. He got no relief from his hunger. Thakur said, 'I feel like eating pots of rice and dal, but *Mahamaya* (Goddess Kali) is not allowing me to eat anything at all.'

As we have seen earlier, Thakur himself predicted his premature death by saying that if he ever gave anyone the first portion from his food before eating the rest himself, it would mean he was going to leave his body soon. By doing exactly that with Narendranath, he alarmed Sri Ma. By giving up his life at the untimely age of fifty, he proved that the alarm she had felt was justified.

There are other descriptions of Thakur feeding Naren at Dakshineswar. Once Naren came to Dakshineswar and said he would be staying the night. Thakur told Ma Thakurun (Sri Ma), 'Naren will be eating today—cook well.' Ma cooked with care, *ruti*, *muger* dal (tiny yellow lentils), etc. At the end of the meal, Thakur asked Naren, 'So, how did you find the food?'

'Not bad. For an invalid's meal, not bad at all!'

Thakur told Ma Thakurun, 'When Naren eats here, make the *rutis* thicker and make thick *chholar* dal (yellow chickpeas).'

The thick chickpea dal stayed a long-time favourite of Naren. After returning from the US, he met the owner of *Dainik Basumati* (the oldest Bengali daily), his dear friend

Upen. He told Upen's wife, whom he teasingly called *shakchunni* (a female spirit, according to popular folklore in Bengal), 'Today you will do sadhu-seva (serve a saint).' While she was cooking *chorchori,* he said, 'Finally, I have come to eat the *chorchori* cooked by you! With all the food at my disposal during my foreign sojourn, I remembered your *chorchori* with *boRi* (little spiced lentil balls deep fried and crumbled over the *chorchori*).'

After bathing at the well, he sat down to eat and said, 'Come on, perform your sadhu-seva! Serve me the *chorchori*.' She had also prepared the thick chickpea dal, at which Swamiji commented, 'Great! You remember what I like!'

The pain of Thakur's illness, his inability to eat in spite of fierce hunger along with occasional ritual fasting, sometimes even starving, the Kashipur villa stay was full of such stories. Yet, Thakur himself, and many of his sanyasi-disciples, loved to both eat and feed others. Many of them had a growing weakness for tobacco and tea. Before we move on, let us look at some of these weaknesses.

Swami Saradananda (earlier Sharat Maharaj) and his close relative Swami Ramakrishnananda (earlier Shashi Maharaj)'s various admissions (to being foodies) are available in many books. Mahendranath has jocularly noted the fact that many of Sharat and Shashi Maharaj's Chakraborty family members were prone to excessive eating. In his youth, Sharat Maharaj himself apparently ate more than most people. Mahendranath writes that one of Sharat Maharaj's ancestors was returning from the market one day with a pitcher of jaggery when it fell and broke. After thinking for a while, he got some oil from the grocer's shop, rubbed himself down with it, bathed in the nearby pond and sat down next to the broken pitcher for his afternoon meal. He first offered it up to the gods, then polished off the entire pitcher of jaggery, drank a pot of water and went home.

We have another example of this foodie family when Saradananda, after becoming a sanyasi, travelled to the Himalayas with Vivekananda. At that time, whatever Gangadhar Maharaj, another of Thakur's disciples, would bring back as daily alms was to be shared by everyone. Sharat, however, would go out on his own to get more alms, all of which he consumed himself.

Saradananda's relative Swami Ramakrishnananda loved *muri* (puffed rice) and chillies very much. Once at Belur *Math* he told Mahendranath, 'Hey, get me some puffed rice!' Once he had been served, he then asked for some green chillies. Ramakrishnananda could easily eat six to eight green chillies at a go. With watering eyes, he observed, 'If your eyes don't water when you eat spicy chillies, then what is the point of eating chillies?' He could easily eat two persons' share of rice, taking in large mouthfuls, and if it were served with black lentils and chillies alongside, he would be delighted.

Having contracted tuberculosis in his last years, he was lying at the Udbodhan (the monthly periodical of Ramakrishna Mission) office in Calcutta when Mahim went to meet him. An unhappy Swami Ramakrishnananda told Mahim, 'See brother, these scoundrel devotees are starving me to death. They only give me one and a half seers of milk!'

In March 1886, a few months before Thakur's passing away, Mahim went to the Kashipur villa to search for his brother Naren. Gangadhar Maharaj took him to the pond to wash up, Gopal (another of Thakur's devotees) brought tea in a large kettle while Shashi Maharaj organized some *kochuri*, *luchi* and *aloo chorchori* from a nearby shop.

Not only Narendranath but all his *gurubhais* too were addicted to tea. On the night of Thakur's demise, everyone sat

around depressed—no one had eaten even a morsel of food.
But tea? That's another story!

Many moons later, Sharat Maharaj commented, 'Listen,
there is no sin in our having tea during the Shivaratri fast (a fast
undertaken by devotees of Shiva, once a year). Do you know
why? The day Thakur passed away, the kitchen was closed. But
we burned some straw, boiled a kettle of water and made tea
and all of us drank it. So even on such a night of mourning
when we could drink tea, why can't we drink it on a day of
simple fasting such as Shivaratri?'

At the Barahanagar *Math*

A few months after Thakur (Sri Ramakrishna Paramahansa)
left his mortal body, twelve young sanyasis, gathered at a modest
villa in Barahanagar, a suburb of Calcutta. They were all college
graduates and all Thakur's disciples. This was the first *math* of the
Ramakrishna Mission. They begged daily for a handful of rice,
which they would cook and eat, spending the rest of their time
focused entirely on meditation, devotion and chanting of hymns.

Mahendranath has shared some heart-rending descriptions
of that time in his book *Memories of Saradananda*. 'The alms
contained a variety of rice grains, which were all cooked
together. Salt and chillies were cooked in a bowl. The rice was
then spread on a piece of cloth with the bowl kept in the centre.
Everyone sat around the cloth, eating some rice, followed by a
touch of the salt and chillies to their tongue. The spice on the
tongue helped the rice go down easily. There was a common
pot of water for everyone to drink from. There were no separate
plates or bowls for anyone.'

According to Mahendranath's account, there were no beds
to sleep on at night either. 'Everyone slept using their folded

arms as pillows. If anyone needed a pillow, they would place a brick under their mat.' After being bitten mercilessly by mosquitoes for months, some mosquito nets were organized. In winter, the young sanyasis would practise a few bouts of wrestling to keep warm. 'At that time, there was no practice of wearing saffron robes. Everyone wore a white *dhuti*, and a part of it was used to cover the torso if necessary. There was no practice of wearing shirts or shoes.'

Mahendranath has given us an intimate glimpse of life at Barahanagar. After the morning's meditation and bhajan, Narendranath recited from the scriptures while the others listened attentively. Chanting with rosary beads and meditation continued for a long time. They did their own cooking. At night a few *rutis* would be made. Some of the sanyasis had even given up the night's meal, eating only once in the day.

'A few *rutis* would be made for Thakur's *bhog*, along with a little semolina porridge and some vegetable curry.' There were no mantras for puja those days. Shashi Maharaj recited a mantra, 'Jai Gurudev, Jai Gurudev (salutations to our teacher)'.

According to Mahendranath's narrative, 'For the afternoon meal, sometimes there would be *telakucho* (the ivy gourd) *chorchori* or gravy along with the rice collected as alms.' That would be a special meal.

Mahendranath once asked Sharat Maharaj, 'Why do you drink so much tea?' Maharaj instantly replied, 'Because of your brother's influence. He has brought in this habit from your home to Barahanagar and got us all addicted. You are a narcotic family.' After regularly drinking strong tea to satiate their hunger, all the sanyasis at Barahanagar started showing signs of liver trouble and other ailments.

A brother-in-law of Sharat Maharaj used to live on Gourmohan Mukherjee Street, near Naren's home. He blatantly accused Naren, saying, 'Bishu Datta's *tripanda* (wayward) boy has ruined my brother-in-law. There was some "great goose" in Dakshineswar; they went to him and messed up everything. That over-smart Naren was himself spoilt, and now he's spoiling all the other young lads too.'

Mahendranath has shown us the heart-rending picture of how, within a few months of establishing the Barahanagar *Math* itself, the fury of poverty lashed out at the young sanyasis. The sanyasis jointly decided that they would not accept any material gifts from anyone. First, they gave up wearing shoes, which caused cracked and bleeding heels. When they went to bathe in the Ganges nearby, they did not even have towels. Soon, their clothes were tattered, but their detachment from the material world was so intense that they decided to abandon clothes altogether and only wear the loincloth.

According to Mahendranath's writings, 'There were just two clothes, which were worn by anyone who went outside to collect alms or for any other reason. There came a time when even the loincloth became unusable. Many of Thakur's disciples then decided they did not need that either and chose to stay completely unclothed. Only when they went out, they used those two surviving pieces of clothing kept for the purpose, and when they returned, folded them away.'

Mahendranath adds: 'On a rainy evening, I landed up in Barahanagar, and seeing everyone naked, felt both embarrassed and revolted. Whoever I turned to speak to was in the nude. And none of them were in the least bit embarrassed themselves— each was busy with his own task. Some were counting the rosary beads, some doing other work. I entered the smaller room outside and found another sanyasi (Narendranath) lying down, unclothed too. Then Suresh Mitra arrived, and Narendranath by a sign asked me to bring a cloth from the bigger room, and without getting up, he simply covered his waist with it. But Niranjan Maharaj, Shashi Maharaj and Shibananda Swami remained in the nude.' The humorous Suresh Mitra joked, 'Oh my God! All the rascals have now become Paramahansas!' Mahendranath assures us, however, that 'in a few months everyone went back to wearing their loincloth as well as their normal clothing'.

Women were not allowed in the Barahanagar *Math*. Mahendranath explains that Narendranath had disallowed it because women, besides their devotion and singing of hymns, often ended up speaking about their domestic lives. He adds, 'If any lady approached the *math*, there was a lot of bustling around . . . If any lady entered the premises, someone would shout, "*Magees* (a Bengali slang word for women) are coming!" Later, they thought someone might understand that the word *magee* related to women approaching the *math*, and promptly changed it to "Burmese"! So, the new alert call became "The Burmese are coming!"'

In the context of whether there is a connection between devotion and hunger, Thakur's nephew Hridu Mukherjee recounts how Thakur himself once complained of hunger while practising meditation. Hridu reminisces: 'One day, Mama (Thakur was his maternal uncle) had his dinner and went to sleep. Suddenly he woke up and started complaining of hunger. He was told to go back to sleep but he began to cry.' Hridu perforce began to search in the pots and pans in the kitchen for some food and found some *panta bhat* (cold, leftover rice soaked in water), which Thakur had with some jaggery, after which he happily went back to sleep.

Another time during his prayers, Thakur's excessive hunger could not be satiated with anything. Finally, he was offered a large serving dish with all kinds of food in it, and besides that a lot of *chiRe*, *muRki* and sweets were arranged all around him, so he could eat to his heart's content and overcome his hunger.

Behind the Barahanagar *Math*, there was a garden with some drumstick trees, a wood apple tree and some coconut and mango trees. The vegetables growing there included drumsticks, pumpkins, cucumbers, bananas, etc. Sometimes, when there was a dearth of vegetables at the *math*, Swami Shibananda and Shashi Maharaj would sneak into the garden and quietly bring back some cucumbers. This would often earn the wrath of the gardener as well as some choice curses. To keep him happy, the gardener was from time to time given some prasad from the *math* along with some money and clothes collected from devotees.

Financially, the residents of the Barahanagar *Math* were in dire straits. Swami Abhedananda has written that a few of the resident sanyasis would go out to seek alms every morning. A few devotees also regularly donated small amounts of money, which allowed the sanyasis to have one meal a day. In April and May 1890, after the deaths of Balaram Babu and Surendra Babu, the financial crisis deepened. Shashi Maharaj taught for a while to earn some money. Swami Gambhirananda informs us that in those days of hardship, Girish Ghosh donated steadily to the *math*. The situation was still so bad that the rice had to be eaten with *maan kochu* (elephant ear leaves), which often caused an irritation in the throat. But treating all of this as inconsequential, 'the worship, meditation, counting of rosary beads and singing of hymns all continued unceasingly'.

In those days of paucity, one gentleman named Jogen Chatterjee often came to enquire about the well-being of the residents at the *math*. If he heard there was no food, he would buy some from the market. After Swamiji returned from the USA, he initiated this gentleman into sanyas, naming him Swami Nityananda.

Swami Birajananda informs us that many sanyasis at the *math* 'shaved their heads, beards and moustaches once a month. Whatever little clothes people had were hung onto the *aalnaa* (a horizontal clothes horse) in the room. There were no boxes, cupboards, etc.'

Often the sanyasis who went out begging for alms returned empty-handed. Once, the four sadhus who went out could not get any alms at all. Hence, there was nothing to offer for Thakur's *bhog*. That day, it was decided that everyone would fast and sing bhajans all day.

Once Hirananda, a devotee of Ramakrishna from Hyderabad in Sindh (now in Pakistan) arrived at the *math*. He asked them, 'How do you manage to survive?' Narendranath responded, 'Everyone gets a handful of alms. We somehow manage with that.'

Hirananda had some six *anna* in loose change with him. He handed over those coins and said, 'Let this money buy your food for this meal.' Narendranath said, 'There is no need for the money; we have enough rice for this meal.' Within a short time, the bhajans and kirtans (hymns in glorification of the Lord) started in the Barahanagar *Math*.

In 1887, Narendranath left the *math* for a while, to travel to western India. 'Someone had bought a ticket for the journey but had not made any arrangements for food.' On this journey, Swamiji met his first disciple, the railway employee Sharat Chandra Gupta. Later that year, Sharat Chandra joined the *math* as Swami Sadananda. The Barahanagar *Math*, by then, was quite settled. Narendranath still never sought anything from anyone.

Mahim Babu writes, 'During this time, the consumption of tea and tobacco was very high at the *math*. They were young, hungry boys—they would simply add a little tea dust to hot water and glug it down without any milk or sugar.'

A lot of rumours were floating around about Narendranath. A friend remarked, 'Oh yes! Narendra has become insane. He trained his voice in music for so many years, but it has all gone to waste.' Those days, 'he was covered in dust and mud, his nails were long and overgrown, his hair dry, parched and bushy, body frail and his eyes sunken'.

Although he was able to detach himself from his familial ties, Swamiji could never detach himself from his addiction to tea. One day, Shibananda Swami joked, 'We have offered everything to the Lord, let us now offer tea!' He began jokingly reciting the mantra for an offering of tea to the Lord, '*Anen chaya*'. Once Narendranath joined in, they sobered down and the conversation shifted to the shastras.

In Barahanagar, Narendranath was often quite unwell. Besides the stomach ailments in May and June of 1887, he was racked by typhoid. Mahendranath has written that around this time, there was also a conspiracy to have Swamiji beaten up by thugs. Thankfully, Niranjan Maharaj's courage as well as his expertise in *lathi khela* (a form of martial art, where a long stick is used as a weapon to attack or defend) saved the day!

In due course, a cook named Ramachandra was hired at the *math*. However, his attendance was probably irregular, which is why Mahendranath wrote, 'At night, the clay stove was lighted and someone kneaded the dough, someone else rolled out the *rutis*, while a third sat on a kerosene tin and roasted the *rutis*. Like the rest of the sanyasis, Narendranath also participated in the cooking process.'

Once, sometime in 1887, the residents of the *math* debated about sacrificing a goat during Durga Puja at Barahanagar. Rakhal Maharaj was not in favour of the sacrifice. Narendranath allowed it, and as far as it is known, the sacrifice did happen. Narendranath, however, subsequently vowed, 'This is the last time that a sacrifice will be conducted in the name of devotion.'

Mahendranath informs us that the high levels of positive energy generated at the Barahanagar *Math* later helped both Swami Vivekananda and Swami Abhedananda achieve success in their missions amidst worldwide acclaim. During this time, our Swamiji had read many books on various subjects. On Christmas Eve, he lighted lamps and organized to have readings from the Bible all night. Swami Saradananda offered *bhog*, and, placing it in front of the photo of Jesus Christ, prayed with full devotion.

There was an interesting incident involving a seeker, Naag Mahashay. He used to live in a small hut on the banks of the Ganges. Because he was always engaged with the rosary or in meditation, he had no time to cook and would simply put a pot of rice to boil with some water. Once when the rice boiled, however, he felt it may be best to give up food altogether. 'If I have not found God after praying all day, should I put food in my mouth?'

Naag Mahashay then picked up a piece of firewood and broke the pot, deciding to give up eating forever.

Hearing the news, Narendranath anxiously rushed to visit him. Although he had already eaten, Swamiji requested to be fed. After eating some of what Naag Mahashay had cooked and served him, he insisted that his disciple eat the rest. When Naag Mahashay expressed an unwillingness to eat anything, Swamiji commanded, 'Eating a sadhu's prasad brings blessings. Eat it!'

Finally, ensuring that his disciple had eaten, Narendranath returned to Barahanagar at ease.

Now let us explore how Narendranath's mother Bhuvaneswari Devi lived her life, after allowing her beloved son to become a sanyasi. We have some anecdotes from Baburam Maharaj, a disciple of Thakur.

On one morning in 1887, Baburam Maharaj reached Bhuvaneswari Devi's paternal residence on 7, Ramtanu Basu Lane. Mahendranath gives us an account of the visit: 'Bhuvaneswari Devi was cooking on the terrace in a makeshift shed with a bamboo fencing. She called out to Baburam, "Please come son, sit down—I am just cooking something. After all we do have to eat something to sustain ourselves." Baburam replied, "I am also going to eat a little with you today." Bhuvaneswari Devi said, "Rice, dal and *chorchori*—what else shall I cook?" Baburam himself sat down to chop up the vegetables and grind the spices. Bhuvaneswari at one point said, "Your mother is such a wonderful person; she cooks so many different items of food. Instead of eating that, why are you here having our coarse rice and meagre vegetable?" Baburam had replied, "Your cooking is very pure; that is why I come here."'

Baburam Maharaj was the scion of the celebrated Ghosh family of Aatpur. His grandmother, even in her advanced years, used to enjoy cooking vegetarian food and serving guests all day. Baburam's mother had inherited the same virtue from her, and Baburam too received this quality from his mother.

Now that we are back on the subject of food, let us look at Mahendranath's accounts of how Thakur's birth anniversaries were celebrated in Dakshineswar. He informs us, 'For the first few years, the number of guests were anywhere between 100 and 500. The food for the feast was cooked under a mango tree to the west of the main room. *Muger daaler bhuni khichuRi, aloo kopir dum* (potato-cauliflower curry), curd, *bonde* (a sweet made of little balls of chickpea flour in sugar syrup), and a chutney—this was the normal fare. A few times, there were also brinjal fritters.

'Visitors who came in the morning were served *luchi* and *halua* (a thick, sweet semolina pudding). Many visitors brought vegetables, fruits and sweets as offerings to Thakur, which were also distributed among the guests.'

Baikunthanath Sanyal Mahashay and another two other persons supervised the cooking.

Mahendranath describes the meals: 'Devotees sat down in rows with *sal*-leaf (large leaves of the teak tree) woven plates in front of them and joyfully accepted the prasad. Sometimes a few devotees sat in a circle, with the prasad-laden leaf plates placed in the centre, and everyone ate off the same mound of prasad. When they finished, they would get up and another group would come and sit down. Eating leftovers of prasad is a perfectly accepted practice. There are no upper and lower castes among devotees—all castes are the same. These ideas flourished and grew at the time.'

Sometimes, Thakur's disciples had differences of opinion on what could and could not be offered to Thakur. In 1887, when a second *math* was established at the Calcutta suburb Knakurgachhi, Narendranath bought some carp fish from Maniktala and offered it to Thakur as *bhog*.

However, being a Vaishnava, Ramachandra Datta was annoyed because he believed it was improper to serve non-vegetarian food to God or to even bring it into the temple at all. Narendranath's response was, 'Does Ramachandra Datta own Sri Ramakrishna? Or was Sri Ramakrishna a Vaishnava? Thakur will be served only what he liked to eat when he was alive, and there will be no deviation from this practice.'

Mahendranath added: 'In a few days, Ramachandra Datta himself had a dream where he saw Thakur telling him to serve *bhog* with fish. After that, once a year, Ramachandra himself served fish as *bhog* to Thakur.'

There are many more interesting anecdotes about eating. A stout devotee named Kalipada Mukhopadhyay loved to eat. He could eat large quantities of *chholar* dal or *bnuter* dal (chick peas). So everyone addressed him as Bnute Kali.

In the summer of 1887, Narendranath suffered from a severe bout of diarrhoea. There was a view that this ailment happened because Swamiji, who once regularly ate meat in his domestic life, had given up everything at the Barahanagar *Math*. Swamiji would only eat whatever he and his fellow-disciples could obtain as alms and that too at most irregular times.

Alarmed at Swamiji's failing health, Balaram Basu, one of Thakur's senior disciples, brought Naren to his own home to feed him sago, barley, etc. After a few days, Narendranath was shifted to his family residence at Ramtanu Basu Lane, where fish curry and rice were arranged for him. Subsequently, Balaram Basu tried to put in place a special diet for our Swamiji at the same Ramtanu Basu Lane house. We know now that Narendranath did not like this new diet at all. Disobeying the directives about having a light fare, Swamiji once took the help of a widowed lady, Bhabini, who lived in Balaram Babu's home. Swamiji told her he was very keen to eat have some *ruti* and *kumRo chhakka*. Bhabini, who did not know about Naren's illness, cooked him some *ruti* and *chhakka* with great care and devotion, and a hungry Naren joyfully polished it off!

When Balaram Basu heard this he was very worried, but fortunately after eating Bhabini's food, Narendranath recovered quickly from his illness.

There are so many stories about Barahanagar—about the journey of the young people, willing to sacrifice everything to follow the arduous path of devotion and worship. With continuous chanting and meditation, often without any food, the young sanyasis had, at times, fallen into deep depression. Once Shashi Maharaj said, 'Naren, this is now getting impossible to bear! What have you done to all of us?' Naren replied, 'Shashi, hand me a Bible.' He opened the Bible and read: 'Jesus replied, "No one, who puts a hand to the plow and looks back, is fit for service in the kingdom of God" Luke 9:62.'

He also remembered a favourite saying of Thakur: 'When the farmer finds no rain in one season, does he close shop? Or does he sow again?' Narendranath consoled Shashi, saying 'We have lived so many lives, died so many deaths, why not this time knowingly destroy this life, why not waste it? Let us dive and see how deep the water really is!'

Naren hummed a *baul* (a group of mystic minstrels from Bengal) song:

'Dive, dive into the *rup sagar* my mind,
If you plumb the depths, you will find the precious gem
of love.'

During his stay in Barahanagar as a sanyasi in the summer of 1890, Narendranath went for a pilgrimage with Gangadhar Maharaj. He spent a few days at Deoghar, where he met the famous Rajnarayan Basu, the grandfather of the world-feted Sri Aurobindo.

Narendranath asked Rajnarayan, 'How did your health break down so badly?' His memorable reply is important to understand Bengal's culinary history. 'With every bottle of liquor, a new way of life—the English way—entered Bengal.

With that came the view that unless we drank, we would not be educated, and there would be no welfare work possible for the country. So all of us took to drinking regularly. But our Bengali constitutions could not tolerate the liquor. That is why the body broke down.'

At the end of the pilgrimage, Narendranath met an old friend, now a sanyasi—Amulya. They were both invited to dinner at another dear friend, Dr Govind's home. At this dinner, there was a competition between Naren and Amulya to see who could eat more chillies. This was where Narendranath proved his ability to become a world champion at eating spicy chillies, one after the other.

In November–December of 1891, the young ascetic disciples of Thakur moved out of the Barahanagar *Math* to a home in Alambazar.

Swami Prabhananda went on to evaluate the spiritual quotient of the Barahanagar *Math*, generated over years of meditation by the resident sanyasis. He has written that Narendranath, during his stay in the *math*, wrote that exceptionally beautiful composition, '*Nahi surya, nahi jyoti, nahi shashanka sundara*' (famous later as 'The Hymn of Samadhi') and also set it to melody. It was also here that Narendranath translated the first six chapters of *The Imitation of Christ* (Thomas à Kempis's famous Christian devotional book) into Bengali. Thakur's disciples, who had taken an early initiation into *sanyas* at the Barahanagar *Math*, numbered twelve—Narendra, Rakhal, Baburam, Shashi, Sharat, Jogen, Tarak, Kali, Niranjan, Latu, Hari and Sharada.

Many years later, when speaking with the then Viceroy and Governor General of India Lord Minto's wife, Swami Shibananda had explained, 'This *sangha* (order) was not created by us. Thakur himself had created it during his illness. That was the foundation.'

In Alambazar

The young disciples of Thakur moved out of the Barahanagar *Math* to a home in Alambazar in late 1891. There are many anecdotes of feasting and fasting during their stay at the Alambazar *Math*.

We learn that besides exploring the depths of Vedanta, Kashi Maharaj (later Swami Abhedananda) also loved preparing *borfi* (barfi, a popular Indian sweet made of milk and sugar, and sometimes, flour). He would try hard and pour the semi-solid *borfi* mix onto a plate for it to solidify and then cut it in small diamond-shaped pieces.

But as it turned out, the Vedanta guru's *borfi* could not be as good as the ones bought from the shop. However, Kashi Maharaj was unwilling to give up and kept at it until he succeeded and became a consummate *borfi* maker. Among the culinary experiments of the young sanyasi were the ash gourd-*borfi* and the gooseberry *murabba* (a spicy sweet, chutney-like dish).

Among the sanyasi brothers, tastes varied greatly. We know that Shashi Maharaj and Sharat Maharaj loved the *kaRai er* dal (another name for *kalai* dal, black lentils) but Swami Abhedananda got hay fever just by hearing the name.

Once, Baburam Maharaj's mother had expressed her keenness to invite three of Thakur's young disciples at her home for a night's meal. So she cooked *ruti* and *kumRo chhakka* for three persons. As it happened, only Sharada Maharaj (later Swami Trigunatitananda) could make it to her home that evening. So he alone finished the meal cooked for three persons!

After seeing his voracious appetite, Baburam Maharaj's mother stayed up all night, worried that he would fall terribly ill. The next morning, however, she was relieved to see him hale and hearty and affectionately remarked, 'How much does Sharada eat! He has travelled far and wide and learnt many mantras, which is why he is able to eat so much and not allow the food to touch him! Else, how is it possible for a human being to eat so much?'

A dear friend of the sanyasis, Dr Govind, once asked Narendra, 'Should human beings follow a non-vegetarian diet?' Being a vegetarian himself, Dr Govind believed that having non-vegetarian food was against the path of dharma. Narendranath replied, 'Look Govind, the tiger and lion eat meat, while the sparrow lives on grains of rice and grit. But while tigers and lions have babies only once a year, the sparrow is always keen to reproduce.' (Many Hindu religious books ordain that ascetics should practise total celibacy, while those householders on a spiritual path should engage in intercourse only for the purpose of bearing children.) Swamiji's intent was to show that eating non-vegetarian food does not necessarily go against dharma.

Now let us turn our attention to the nomadic ways of Thakur's disciples. It is quite evident from the lives of these sanyasis that a desire to travel is innate to such ascetics' lives. Swami Gambhirananda used to say lightly, '*Ramta sadhu, behta pani*'—a Hindi expression which means 'If the sadhu, like the flowing river, moves continuously from place to place, then, just like the river stays clean, so will the sadhu stay pure'.

During their stay at Barahanagar, the young sanyasis looked for opportunities to step out of the *Math* and explore the world outside. Some went for short visits, while others went for long pilgrimages and *tapasya* (practice of austerities). Swamiji himself sometimes discussed this wanderlust with his *gurubhais*. Once, to discourage his dear friend Rakhal, he said, 'Of course you should go! If you loaf around like a vagabond, God is sure to meet you in person!' But when Swamiji himself heard the call of the road, he became restless to travel too.

The Six-year Journey

Swamiji's biographers say that in the initial years of his sanyasi life, he did not travel much. However, after suffering from typhoid in 1887, he made a few visits to Baidyanath (the famous Jyotirlinga or Shiva temple in Deogarh, then in Bihar) and Simultala (a health resort in Bihar). In August of the following year, Swamiji visited Ayodhya and then Brindavan. Each time he would say, 'This is the end, I will not return to the *math*!' But each time, he perforce had to return for one reason or another. But the journey he undertook in 1891 lasted six years. Swami Gambhirananda admits that from 1886 to 1891, the details of Swamiji's travels are not known to any of his disciples.

Once Saradananda Maharaj, whom Swamiji addressed as '*Hnotka*' (fatso), was his travel companion. Because it would have been difficult to smoke on the journey, Swamiji had thrown away his pipe and tobacco. But at night, the urge to smoke was so great that he found a broken pipe and, using Sharat Maharaj's medicinal tobacco leaf, managed to have his fill.

Swamiji's brother Mahendranath has written in his reminiscences about his brother's childhood fondness for tobacco: 'My elder brother was so fond of tobacco that he used to rub the lime and *dokta* (tobacco leaf) in his palm and stuff it below his lower lip like *khaini* (chaw or quid). He was very fond of snuff too and used to ingest it often, stuffing it into his nose with a wooden pencil.'

The world-renounced Swamiji had another weakness—fish. Once, in Almora Mahendranath reports, Swamiji and

his travelling companions found a very large fish, possibly a
mahseer. The fish had lots of roe, which thrilled the Bengali
fish-lovers no end. The eggs were duly cooked and eaten but,
very soon, the sanyasis suffered a severe attack of diarrhoea. The
hill-folk were alarmed and told them that eating the eggs of the
hill-fish was strictly forbidden. The sanyasis could recover only
after the eggs were out of their systems!

Once, after practising severe austerities in Hrishikesh (now
in Uttarakhand), Narendranath fell severely ill. After a few
days, when the fever abated a little, he expressed a desire to
have *khichuRi*. Accordingly, all the required ingredients were
procured and the *khichuRi* was prepared. As soon as he put the
first morsels into his mouth, however, he made a face. He then
pulled out a long string from the *khichuRi* and asked, 'What
is this string doing in the *khicuRi*, and why is the *khichuRi* so
sweet?' They answered, 'Rakhal Maharaj has put a lump of
sugar in it.' Very annoyed, Swamiji rebuked, 'You fools, who
puts sugar in the *khichuRi*? Don't you have any sense at all?'
In later years at the Belur *Math*, even if there was the slightest
amount of sugar in the *khichuRi*, everyone would dub it the
Hrishikesh *khichuRi*.

Mahim Babu has given us several intimate details of
Swamiji's travels. At one time, Narendranath was very unwell,
too ill to even get up from the bed. Sharat Maharaj wanted to
wash Swamiji's clothes, but Swamiji objected. 'How can that
be? You are a sadhu! How can you wash my clothes?' But Sharat
Maharaj did not listen and ultimately prevailed over Swamiji.

Since their health did not improve in Hrishikesh, the
sanyasis finally landed up in Meerut. There, although the
gurubhais stayed together, they normally had their meals at
different places, probably on account of not wanting to put
additional pressure on one host. We understand that during

this period, Swamiji became very weak and emaciated. His *gurubhai* Swami Akhandananda later reminisced, 'I had never seen Swamiji so weak and frail; he had become a shadow of his normal self.' Swami Gambhirananda's assessment was, 'Living here and there and eating indifferently cooked food, acquired from various sources, just to fill the stomach, had caused the body to completely break down.'

Vivekananda had this particular weakness for smoking, even while on his travels. His biographers have recorded several incidents about this habit. One such incident occurred on the way to Brindavan. Swamiji spotted a man sitting on the roadside, smoking a hookah. As per the practice of those days, Swamiji unhesitantly asked the stranger for a few puffs on his chillum. Taken aback, the man replied, 'Maharaj, you are a sadhu, and I am a sweeper (belonging to a lower caste, often an untouchable).'

Swamiji had moved on without tasting the chillum, but a thought immediately occurred to him, 'Being a sanyasi, I have given up all ideas of caste and creed, so how can I let that come in the way?' So, he went back to the man and said, 'Please let me have a few puffs on your chillum, baba.' (Baba is used here as a way of addressing someone loved or intimate.) After sharing the chillum with the sweeper for a while, Swamiji was satiated. Later, hearing this story, Girish Ghosh commented, 'You are an addict, you must have done that while you were high.' Swamiji immediately clarified, 'No GC (Girish Chandra), I had really wanted to test myself then.'

After spending a week at Brindavan, Swamiji proceeded to Mount Govardhan for a darshan (to get a view of something or someone holy or revered). While circumambulating the hillock, he brought trouble on himself by an unusual intent. Who knows better than a travelling sanyasi that wilful fasting is not the same thing as starvation? Swamiji suddenly decided that he would not ask anyone for food and would only satiate his hunger if someone offered him alms without his asking for it.

Swami Gambhirananda's narrates the events: 'By the first afternoon, the hunger was unbearable, and then it started to rain, testing the limits of his endurance further. Tired and hungry, he (Swamiji) somehow managed to stay on the path.' At that time, the by-now ravenous sanyasi heard someone calling out to him, saying that they had brought him food. Confused, Swamiji at first tried to run, but the man ran behind him, finally caught up and requested him to have the food. 'Finding proof of God's immense grace in that lonely place, Swamiji was in tears.'

A similar incident recurred in Swami Vivekananda's life at the Hathras railway station, when he was travelling from Brindavan to Haridwar. A young railway employee found a sanyasi sitting on the railway platform. The Bengali youth, after the initial salutation, asked him, 'Swamiji, are you hungry?' The sadhu replied, 'Yes.' The railway worker responded, 'Then please come to my home.' Childlike, Swamiji asked, 'But what will you feed me?' In the style of a Persian poet the young boy responded, 'My dearest, you have come to my home; I will serve you my heart, cooked with the choicest of spices.'

The same executive, Sharat Chandra, later got initiated at the Ramakrishna Mission as Swami Sadananda. He later recalled that it was Swamiji's eyes that had drawn him. Sadananda was Swamiji's companion on some of his most treacherous travels. Reminiscing about those travels, Sadananda writes, 'When weak and tired from hunger and thirst I had fallen unconscious, it was Swamiji's tender care that brought me back to life!'

Once when Sadananda was cooking *khichuRi* for his guru and himself on one of their trips, Swamiji arrived with his stick and *kamandal* (stoup) in hand and announced, 'Now, I have to travel on my own. I cannot stay here anymore.' Sadananda sat, perplexed at the sudden turn of events. After three or four hours, Swamiji came back and said he was hungry. Later, he told Sadananda that the latter had become a shackle and that it was quite impossible for Swamiji to leave him behind and go.

After extensive travels, Swamiji returned to the Barahanagar *Math* in 1888, but despite not being physically fit, he soon became anxious to leave for a long pilgrimage again. In February the following year, while travelling to Thakur's birthplace in Kamarpukur, Swamiji had to discontinue the journey and return to Barahanagar because of fever and diarrhoea. In the same year in June, he travelled out of Calcutta in search of a place that would improve his health but was again plagued by dyspepsia.

Swamiji was very keen to meet with Pavhari Baba, an ascetic who lived in Ghaziabad. The baba did not eat anything except a few leaves of *neem* or a few green chillies. Even the *bhog* that he offered to his God was distributed among his devotees—he did not have any of it himself. Swamiji went to Ghaziabad and lived there for a while to meet and speak with the baba. But in spite of Swamiji's keenness, he could not meet Pavhari Baba regularly. At that time, Swamiji was himself unwell, suffering from backache and frequent stomach ailments. There were many lemon trees where he lived, and his diet consisted mainly of these lemons.

We do have some anecdotes from Swamiji's letters around that time. Alarmed at Swamiji's failing health, Swami Premananda arrived from Calcutta and tried in vain to take him back to Barahanagar. To escape him, Swamiji angrily left Ghaziabad and went into hiding. On 15 March 1890, Swamiji wrote to Balaram Babu from Ghaziabad, 'Please don't write to this address again since I am leaving this place.'

On the same day, Swamiji had also written to Girish Chandra's brother Atul Chandra, 'I am leaving this place tomorrow. Let me see where fate takes me next.'

In another letter to Swami Akhandananda in the same month, Swamiji writes, 'If I could manage the rent for this place, I would pay it. Therefore, please raise some money towards the rent and come.' About his benefactor who had given him shelter, Swamiji wrote, 'What can I write about such a kind and generous host? As soon as he heard about Kali's fever in Hrishikesh, he immediately sent him the travel money to come here. And he has also spent a lot of money on me. In this condition, it will be against my dharma as a sanyasi to burden him for the travel expenses to Kashmir, so I am refraining from doing so.'

In a letter written at the end of March to Pramada Babu, another of Thakur's devotees, Swamiji says: 'I am very weak, overwhelmed by maya (illusion). Please bless me that I may become strong . . . There is a continuous burning of hell fire in my mind. Nothing is working out. I think this life is being wasted in futile chaos and noise. I cannot decide what to do . . . My *gurubhais* must think me cruel and selfish. But what can I do? Who can look into my mind and fathom what torment I am suffering from?'

Many of us believe that through the length and breadth of this sacred land of India, world-renounced sanyasis are always treated with respect. However, reading the accounts of Swamiji's travels, we realize that this may not always be true.

Once Swamiji was travelling by train and alighted at TaRiaghat near Ghazipur. He was not carrying any money and hence could not get any drinking water on the train or at the platform. A North-Indian trader, who happened to be a co-passenger, taunted him severely. Despite knowing that the

sanyasi was thirsty, the man drank water without offering him
any, saying, 'See, this is cold water. You are a sanyasi who has
given up everything, so you don't have even a little money to
buy yourself some water. If you had instead tried to earn a living
like me, you would not have been in such dire straits.'

Even after they got off at the station, the man did not stop
his jibes. 'See, the power of money! You won't have anything to
do with money. See the result of that! And see the result of my
work.' He opened his food packets and mocking Swamiji, he
said, 'See, this—*puri*, *kachori*, *peda*, sweets. Do they come free?'

Swamiji tolerated all this silently.

Suddenly, a man arrived bearing a bundle in his right hand
and a pitcher of water and a mat in his left. He asked Swamiji,
'Baba Ji, why are you sitting in the sun? Come to the shade. I
have brought some food for you, kindly accept it.' This *sevak*
was a sweet-seller. He told Swamiji that during his mid-day
nap, he had dreamt that his Ram Ji (Lord Rama) was telling
him, 'My sadhu is lying hungry in the station. He hasn't eaten
since yesterday. Rush there and serve him.'

So the stranger served Swamiji with great care, and after the
meal, poured water for him to wash his hands. He also served
him tobacco. Swamiji's co-passenger, the trader, watching all
this, was ashamed of his behaviour and sought forgiveness.

Whatever his troubles, Swamiji always remained cheerful.
He often teased Hari Maharaj (later Swami Turiyananda) and
the other sadhus travelling with him. Mahim Babu writes,
'Once in Meerut, Narendranath had cooked some mutton.
Now, Hari Maharaj did not normally eat mutton, but seeing
that Swamiji himself had cooked it and was serving it too, he
decided to try some.'

Mahim Babu continues: 'There are many stories about
Meerut which are now part of folklore. Hearing Swamiji speak

about the Mohammedan religion, an overwhelmed Amir Saheb sent him a parcel of ready-to-cook food worthy of a king. The contents of the package inspired the culinary expert Narendranath to prepare some pulao. Swamiji was very familiar with the process of cooking such exotic fare, since pulao and mutton were cooked daily at his home when his father was alive, and many people were fed.' Hari Maharaj was also present on that day.

Mahendranath has also heard from Swami Sadananda and faithfully recorded the story of Ramsanaya, Rajputana's *ramta* (wandering) Vaishnava monk whom Swamiji met in Alwar. Whenever he was happy, Ramsanaya would sing bhajans using his old patched-up water pot as a percussion instrument by striking it with a pebble. 'Ramsanaya used to obtain a little wheat flour through begging, and kneading it with salt and chillies, would roast a *tikkar* (Rajasthani flatbread) on the fire.' He would then share that meagre food with Swamiji. Ramsanaya would obtain some bits of tobacco as well; the two Sanyasis would then enjoy the smoke to the accompaniment of his happy pot-and-pebble songs.

Swamiji received love and care from another old lady in Alwar. She ground wheat flour in five houses and received some flour in exchange. With that, she would make some rotis for her '*lala*' (son) Narendranath and feed him lovingly.

After returning from the USA, the world-renowned Vivekananda searched for this kind-hearted lady and managed to locate her. That reunion was a very happy one. 'You are my *lala*, and you are also poor, just like me,' she said. She then took out two *tikkars* from the fire, brushed off the ashes and handed them to Swamiji. Before returning to Calcutta, Swamiji obtained another five-grain wheat flour *tikkar* from this lady. After reaching Calcutta, Swamiji instructed that this *tikkar* be kept carefully in his room at Belur *Math* because it was made by a clean and pure-hearted person.

Starvation and Scarcity

Although there are quite a few scattered references about Swamiji's food habits, there is no detailed or chronological analysis of his starving or fasting or those occasions when he ate far less than necessary. From all memoirs written about Swamiji, particularly during his travels, we have managed to collect some information.

Nagendranath, the famous editor of *The Lahore Tribunal* and Swamiji's college-mate, has written about Swamiji, who was a guest at his house in 1897.

Nagendranath informs us that Swamiji would often decide to walk continuously, without looking back and without asking anyone for food. If someone came forward and offered him food, only then would he stop and accept it. As a result, it sometimes happened that Swamiji had no food for twenty-four or even forty-eight hours at a stretch.

Once, weak with hunger for two days, he met a syce. The syce asked the sanyasi, 'Baba, have you not eaten anything at all today?' When he heard that Swamiji had not eaten all day, the syce took him inside the stables and gave him his own night's meal—some chapattis and spicy chutney. As soon as Swamiji ate it, however, his stomach began to burn severely. The pain was so severe that Swamiji thought he was about to pass out. Just then, another man arrived with a basket full of tamarind. Swamiji exclaimed in relief, 'Ah! Just what I wanted!' He mixed some tamarind in water and promptly drank up the mix, saving himself.

Haripada Mitra once wanted to know from Swamiji (quoted from the original), '*Why do the sanyasis idle away their*

time in this way? Why do they depend on the charity of others?
Why don't they undertake some work beneficial to society?' Swamiji
commented, *'Now, look here. You are earning this money with such*
struggle, of which only a little portion you spend on yourself, and
some of it you spend for others who, you think, are your own. But
they neither acknowledge any gratefulness for what you do for them.
Nor are they satisfied with what they get. The balance you save
like the mythological yaksha *who never enjoys it. When you die,*
somebody else will enjoy it all; and perchance, he will abuse you for
not having accumulated more. This is your condition. On the other
hand, I do nothing. When I feel hungry, I let others know by gestures
that I want food; and I eat whatever I get. Neither do I struggle nor
do I save. Now, tell me who among us is the wiser—you or I?'

Haripada Mitra was amazed at his favourite sanyasi's
remarkable ability to remember things and once asked him,
'How is it that you are able to remember so much, and why
can't we remember like you?'

Swamiji explained, *'One has to read with full attention, and*
one must not fritter away the energy one draws from food.'

Replying to another of his questions, Swamiji told Haripada
Mitra, *'A religion that cannot bring peace to men must be shunned*
as a disease brought on by dyspepsia.'

About stomach ailments, Swamiji humorously said,
'Vedanta is just like tough meat to an ailing stomach—very
difficult to digest.'

Swamiji met K. Sundaram Iyer in Trivandrum in 1892, on
his way to America from Bombay via Japan. Sundaram Iyer
writes (quoted from the original), *'The Swami had taken almost*
nothing except a little milk during the two previous days . . . All
this conversation had occupied us while the Swami's food was being
prepared and . . . he was breaking his nearly two days' fast by a
hearty dinner.'

Sundaram Iyer also informs us that 'Swamiji was perhaps never greedy, at least my experience says so. Even when he lived with me in Trivandrum, I have seen he used to eat a little once during the day, and only a little milk at night. That was really all he ate.'

Swamiji's views about butter and ghee were clear when he was ill in Deogarh in 1898. When the local schoolboys came to visit him, he said, 'There is some difficulty in breathing, but I think my heart is fine. Whatever problem exists, I think is only in the lungs.'

A student later writes that Swamiji used to ask about food at the students' hostel. 'When he heard that we had a little ghee daily he said, too much ghee is not good—it is difficult to digest. Instead, a little butter may be better.' Perhaps because of his travel to the West, Swamiji was more confident about butter than ghee.

While speaking with the boys who had come to Deogarh from East Bengal, he commented, 'People in East Bengal eat a lot of fish. That is very good!'

Sundaram Iyer has described their conversations about having fish and meat when Swamiji was in Trivandrum. At the time, Swamiji's friend from his student days Manmathanath Bhattacharya was in Trivandrum on official government work. Swamiji started spending a lot of time with him, including having his lunch there. His Tamilian devotee complained and Swamiji told him frankly, '*We, Bengalis, are a clannish people*' (quoted from the original—Sundaram Iyer's reminiscences).

Sundaram Iyer adds, '*The Swami also told me that he had long taken no fish-food, as the South Indian Brahmins whose guest he had been throughout his South Indian tour were forbidden both fish and flesh, and would fain avail himself of this opportunity to have his accustomed fare. I at once expressed my loathing for the taking of fish or flesh as food. The Swami said in reply that the ancient Brahmins of India were accustomed to take meat and even beef and were called upon to kill cows and other animals in yajnas or for giving madhuparka to guests. He also held that the introduction and spread of Buddhism led to the gradual discontinuance of flesh as food, though the Hindu shastras had always expressed a theoretical preference for those who avoided the use of flesh-foods . . .'*

In his reminiscences of Swamiji, Sundaram Iyer writes, *'The Swami's opinion, at least as expressed in conversation with me, was that the Hindus must freely take to the use of animal food if India was to at all cope with the rest of the world in the present race for power and predominance among the world's communities . . .'*

Sundaram Iyer has further elaborated his own views on the matter of vegetarianism: *'The ennobling gospel of universal mercy which had been the unique possession of the Hindus, especially of the Brahmins of South India, should never be abandoned as mistaken, out of date, or uncivilized, and . . . the world can and ought to make a great ethical advance by adopting a humane diet. My belief is that vegetarianism itself can support human beings achieve great heights in their spiritual search . . . Knowing, as I fully did, the Swami's views on this question, I was not surprised to learn that while in America, he had been in the habit of taking animal food, and I think he treated with silent contempt the denunciations and calumnies directed against him on this account.'* (End of quote).

We know from many sources and through people he met on his travels, of Swamiji's opinions on eating vegetarian or non-vegetarian food. Besides this, there are also several accounts of his culinary zeal, which sometimes made his devotees both joyous and afraid. Needless to say, the cause of the discomfort was spicy food. Swamiji's cooking was undoubtedly very tasty, but his propensity to use excessive oil, spices and chillies did not go down well with his American devotees.

A pot of *rosogolla* and a bouquet of flowers.

Every devotee knows that both Thakur Sri Ramakrishna and Narendranath loved *rosogollas*. However, what many do not know is that Ram Dada (Dr Ramchandra Datta) was able to get Naren to Dakshineswar only by telling him that Thakur feeds rosogollas to his favourite visitors. So the *rosogolla* played a huge role in establishing the relationship between Thakur and Narendranath.

A plate of *kochuri, ghugni* and *chholar daal.*

Why is there a photo of *kochuris* in Swami Vivekananda's book? This question will never arise for those who have the slightest understanding of the very valuable role of *singaRa* and *kochuri* in Bengali life. At one time, Swamiji and his friends were great votaries of these snacks, but in later years he became a severe and outspoken critic of all fried foods.

A few *lichus*

Swamiji has studied and examined fruits in various countries. That *lichus* were one of his favourite fruits is clear from his asking several disciples to offer him this fruit as guru *dakshina* after initiating them.

Some *aams* (mangoes)

Mangoes were another of Swamiji's favourite fruits. He taught his foreign devotees in London how to enjoy the mango after chilling it on ice.

A few *peyaras* (guavas)

But the guava topped Swamiji's list of disliked fruits. Even today his devotees avoid offering this fruit in their worship of Swamiji.

Sri Ramakrishna Paramahansa

Of all the photos taken in Calcutta, this is the most well known and curiously discussed. Narendranath himself had helped a trainee of the famous Bourne and Shepherd Company to take the photo. It was taken on a Sunday in October 1883. The young photographer Avinash Chandra Daan became so nervous that he dropped the glass negative, shattering it. But fortunately, no harm came to the photo itself except the line over the head, giving the photo a new dimension. Thakur's response was, 'Don't you all worry! After this, they will worship me in every home.'

No photo of Sri Sri Ma was taken during Thakur's lifetime. After many years she
visited a studio sometime in 1905 for this photo to be taken.

Swamiji's original homestead in Simuliapara
The Simulia house of the Dattas was entangled in various lawsuits by various
ownership claims, keeping Swamiji distressed even up to his death. Over the next
few decades after his death, in spite of deep anxiety and worry over its ruin by
Swamiji's loved ones, nothing much could be achieved. Mona Choudhury, the staff
photographer for the *Times of India*, took this photo in 1964. We understand that
this photo had disturbed Mrs Indira Gandhi too.

Photo of the main door of 3, Gourmohan Street. The plaque above tells us that at one time the house was named Bhuvaneswari Bhavan.

Photo of the repaired and transformed main door of the homestead. With everyone's good wishes and the Ramakrishna Mission's strong intent, the old homestead has recovered its lost glory. After a complete transformation, this is the new look of the main door.

Vivekananda Kendra on Bidhan Sarani

The entrance to the new Vivekananda Kendra on Bidhan Sarani (earlier Cornwallis Street). Also, at 25 Cornwallis Street was the office of the publisher B. Banerjee, who published the novel *Sulochana* written anonymously by Swamiji's father Vishwanath Datta. In fact, the printer's office at 69 Varanasi Ghosh Street is not too far away. The printing press has a beautiful name—Hitaishi Press, meaning 'The Benevolent Press'. The printer was Sri Brajnath Bandopadhyay.

A letter written by Vishwanath Datta to his cousin

In nineteenth-century Calcutta, there was a facility of taking photographs, and the practice of family portraits was also spreading. Despite this, no photograph of Narendranath's father Vishwanath Datta has yet been discovered. What we have are a few signatures and this letter written from Lucknow to his cousin Taraknath Datta. The manuscript of Vishwanath Datta's anonymously written novel *Sulochana* is not available, but the book has been reprinted in recent times.

of the said Bissonath Dutt dec ased
intended to have jurisdiction throughout the whole of British India
be granted to your petitioner
limited during the minority of
the infant sons of the said
deceased on your petition furnishing
such security for the due adminis
tration thereof as to this Honour-
able Court will seem proper.
And your Petitioner shall
ever pray &c

ভুবন শ্রীদাসী

Explained by me

Obenash Chunder Bhad. — Interpreter

Petitioner's Attorney
Narendra Nath Das

I the petitioner in the above petition named do
declare that what is stated therein is true to the best of
my knowledge information and belief

ভুবন শ্রীদাসী

Explained by me

Obenash Chunder Bhad. — Interpreter
11-8-86

I Norendro Nath Dutt the eldest son of Bissonath
Dutt deceased named in the foregoing petition do hereby
consent to my mother the said Sreemutty Bhubannessury
Dassee obtaining Letters of Administration to the Estate
and Effects of the deceased abovenamed should it please
your Lordships to grant to her the same

Narendra Nath Dutt

Signatures of Bhuvaneswari Devi and Narendranath Datta
This is the last page of a critical document signed by Narendranath and his mother.
If you study it carefully, you will learn a lot about the Datta family. The document is
dated 11 August 1886, four days before the demise of Thakur Sri Ramakrishna.

Swamiji's grandmother
Swamiji's maternal grandmother Raghumani Basu. This exceptional lady was a
constant companion in all the joys and sorrows of her only child Bhuvaneswari Devi,
who was widowed at an early age. Raghumani Devi's husband was Nandalal Basu.

Swamiji's mother, Srimati Bhuvaneswari Dasi
We have no photos of the early life of Narendranath's mother. Bhuvaneswari Devi was born in 1841 and died on 25 July 1911. Swamiji's enthusiastic foreign devotees took this photo in Calcutta.

Swamiji's sister

Swamiji's elder sister Swarnamoyee was Bhuvaneswari Devi's fourth child. She lived at the homestead on Gourmohan Mukherjee Street and died at the age of seventy-two. The sister born immediately after her died at the age of six; we do not know her name.

Swamiji's brother Mahendranath

We have no record of the conversation the twenty-three-year-old Narendranath
had with this brother before leaving home in response to his calling. But they
met again in London in 1896 in a memorable meeting. Many years later, it led to
Mahendranath's sitting in his homestead and creating a three-volume book titled
Vivekananda in London. Six years younger than his illustrious brother, Mahendranath
was born on 1 August 1869. Belying all fears of a premature death like some of his
siblings, Mahendranath died in 1956, at the age of 88. Towards the end of his life,
legendary physicians came to see him at the Gourmohan Mukherjee Street, along
with the then Chief Minister of Bengal, Dr Bidhan Chandra Roy.

Swamiji's brother Bhupendranath
Swamiji's youngest brother Dr Bhupendranath was involved in the freedom struggle
of the country and imprisoned at a young age. It is learnt that when Thakur
Sri Ramakrishna came looking for Narendranath at Simulia, he lifted the baby
Bhupendranath in his arms. Later, Bhupendranath lived abroad for the larger part
of his life, returning in 1925 to India. He lived in the Gourmohan Mukherjee Street
home for the rest of his life. He passed away in 1961, at the age of 81. This photo
was taken in Athens.

Ram Dada
This is Narendranath's Ram Dada, or Dr Ramachandra Datta, a senior disciple of
Thakur, who had proposed to Naren that he should visit Dakshineswar and taste the
rosogollas.

Swamiji

We have not yet been able to find any photo of Swamiji's childhood, youth or student
life. The earliest two photos, which everyone has in their collection, were taken at
Kashipur in 1886, around the time of Sri Sri Ramakrishna Parahamsa's *mahasamadhi*.
It is not known who took the above photo or when it was taken. After searching all
over the world, till date, 105 photos of Swami Vivekananda have been found.

Swamiji's childhood friend Raja
Swamiji's childhood friend, Raja (1863–1922), later the first head of Ramakrishna Mission as Swami Brahmananda. He saw the Ramakrishna Sangha through a difficult time. As a wrestler when he was young, he enjoyed a large meal of *kochuri* and accompanying vegetables daily.

Having grown up under the guidance of Swami Vivekananda, this is the timeless author of *Sri Sri Ramakrishna Leela Prasang*, Swami Saradananda or Sharat Maharaj. He was born on 23 December 1865 and passed away on 19 August 1927. He was the first *gurubhai* that Swamiji took with him on his travels abroad. The book *Vivekananda in London* tells us a lot about him. He led the Ramakrishna Sangha when it was going through a period of difficulty.

Swami Abhedananda
Sri Ramakrishna's sacrificing son Swami Abhedananda was known among close circles as 'Kali Vedanti' for his deep knowledge of the shastras. Born on 20 October 1866, he too went to the US at Vivekananda's call and won the hearts of many, living there for more than three decades. He returned to Calcutta on 10 November 1921 and passed away on 8 September 1939.

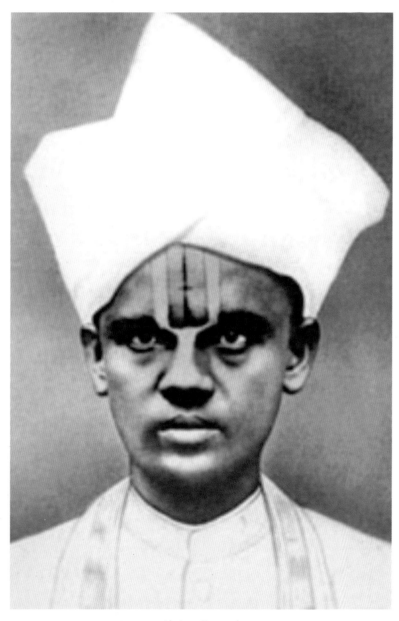

Alasinga Perumal
Vivekananda's South Indian devotee, Alasinga Perumal (1865–1909). He played a
unique role in sending Swamiji to the Chicago Religious Conference. This young
Brahmin boy's full name was Srimandam Chakravarthy Alasinga Perumal. A
significant portion of Swamiji's letters now available to us, were written to Alasinga
Perumal.

Sharat Chandra Gupta
A railway employee, Sharat Chandra Gupta (1865–1911), seeing a famished
Vivekananda at the Hathras Railway Station, brought him to his rail quarters to feed
him. Later, Swamiji brought him to the Barahanagar *Math* as his first sanyasi disciple,
whom he named Sadananda. Famous as Gupta Maharaj, this sanyasi was responsible
for the practice of addressing the sadhus of the *math* as 'Maharaj'.

Maharaja Ajit Singh

The large-hearted maharaja of the tiny province of Khetri, it was Ajit Singh who requested Swamiji to take the name 'Vivekananda' before setting out for the Chicago Conference. Bearing in mind his guru's stomach ailment, he arranged for a first class ticket on the ship for Swamiji. For many years, Maharaja Ajit Singh quietly supported Swamiji's mother and brothers with financial help and stayed in close contact with them through letters. On 18 January 1901, while visiting Akbar's tomb, he fell (some say jumped) off the eighty-six-foot high minar and that ended his life.

John Henry Burroughs
Reverend John Henry Burroughs, the world-renowned manager of the Chicago
Parliament of Religions. It was he who permitted and made arrangements for an
unknown Vivekananda to participate in the conference. After Swamiji's speech,
Burroughs took Swamiji to the basement restaurant and later sparked a controversy
in India about what it was that Swamiji had ordered.

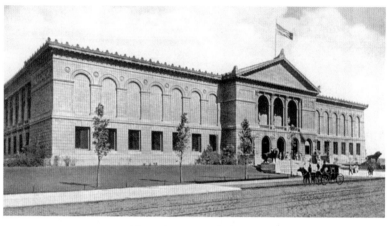

The Art Institute of Chicago
The Art Institute of Chicago, where in 1893 the Parliament of World Religions was held. After delivering an enchanting speech, what a tired Swamiji ordered at the basement restaurant with Dr John Burroughs is till today a matter of great debate.

Swami Vivekananda

Could this be the first photo of Swamiji taken after reaching Chicago? There is a large teacup on the table. The young boy standing behind him is named Narasinghacharya. Swamiji declared in a letter, 'Whether he wanders about, or whatever else he does, I love him.'

A picnic scene

Not just meditation, renunciation or praying with the rosary beads, sometimes there was also the fun of a picnic in America. There aren't too many photos of Swamiji cooking or eating.

J.J. Goodwin

Josiah John Goodwin (1870–1898) recorded many of Swamiji's valuable speeches in shorthand. Swamiji initiated him into Brahmacharya. Mahendranath has recorded some of his humorous comments at the dinner table in London with Swamiji and himself present.

Sarala Ghoshal Devi Choudhurani
Swamiji's close friend and a relative of Rabindranath Tagore, Sarala Ghoshal Devi
Choudhurani was a leading author and publisher. Swamiji has expressed important
views on the food habits of Bengal in her magazine. The daughter of Janakinath
Ghoshal and Swarnakumari Devi, Sarla lived from 1872 to 1945.

Sister Nivedita

The incomparable Sister Nivedita, whom Rabindranath had given the title of
'Lokmata' (mother of the people). Swamiji had himself cooked and fed her at
Belur *Math*, and at the table was also the poet laureate's sister, Sarala Ghoshal Devi
Choudhurani. Sister Nivedita was born in Ireland on 28 August 1867. She saw
Swamiji for the first time on 10 November 1895 and stepped into India on 28
January 1898. She passed away in Darjeeling on 13 October 1911.

Swamiji
There are no photos of our world famous Swamiji in his last months. Two
photographs were taken when he was returning from Shillong in 1901. He was very
ill at the time. Could this photo taken in Shillong be Swamiji's last photo?

The original Bengali letter in Swamiji's handwriting
Swamiji's Bengali letter written from Chicago to his beloved Shashi Maharaj.
Many of his famous letters have been written to Swami Ramakrishnananda.
Recently, a beautiful album of Swamiji's handwritten letters has been published.
This letter appears on the first page.

Sri Baishnab Charan Basak

Teacher, publisher and music lover Sri Baishnab Charan Basak, with whom Narendranath Datta compiled the *Sangeet Kalpataru* before he renounced domestic life. Consisting of 647 songs, this valuable compilation has many ballads about eating and drinking. First published in the Bengali year 1294 (equivalent to 14 April 1887 to 13 April 1888 of Gregorian calendar).

সঙ্গীতকল্পতরু

শ্রীনরেন্দ্রনাথ দত্ত (স্বামী বিবেকানন্দ)
ও
শ্রীবৈষ্ণবচরণ বসাক

The cover of *Sangeet Kalpataru*
The cover of *Sangeet Kalpataru*. With the Ramakrishna Mission's endeavours it is
once again available in print.

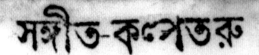

সঙ্গীত-কল্পতরু

অর্থাৎ

বিবিধ ব্যাদ্যাদি শিক্ষা, স্বরলিপি ও সঙ্গীত সম্বন্ধে
বিশুদ্ধ শিক্ষাপ্রদ বিষয় সহ জাতীয়, ধর্ম্ম-
বিষয়ক, পৌরাণিক, ঐতিহাসিক,
সামাজিক, প্রণয়, বিবিধ
এবং নানাবিষয়ক
গীত সংগ্রহ।

✦━━━◆━━━✦

শ্রীনরেন্দ্রনাথ দত্ত বি.,এ,
ও
শ্রীবৈষ্ণবচরণ বসাক

কর্ত্তৃক সংগৃহীত।

━━━━━

১১৮ নং অপার চিৎপুর রোড, কলিকাতা,
"বাণীপুস্তকালয়" হইতে
শ্রীচণ্ডীচরণ বসাক কর্ত্তৃক
প্রকাশিত।

The title page of *Sangeet Kalpataru*
The title page of the first edition of *Sangeet Kalpataru*.

Bhupendranath Datta
Swamiji's younger brother, the revolutionary Dr Bhupendranath Datta (1883–1961).
Indicted for sedition, he spent time in prison and then travelled first to America and
later to Europe, receiving his D. Phil from Hamburg University in 1923. Returning
to India in 1925, he immediately became deeply involved with the labour movement.

Mahendranath and Bhupendranath Datta
The two brothers have authored many books. After returning from abroad, both
of them settled down in their ancestral homestead and lived there in two adjoining
rooms until their death.

Kate Sanborn
Swamiji met the warm-hearted Kate Sanborn on his first journey from Vancouver to Winnipeg. The popular author commented about Swamiji, 'His English is better than mine'. Swamiji was a welcome guest at Kate's home, Breezy Meadows, and lived there for seven days.

The Hale sisters
In a far-off strange country, the love and friendship of the Hale sisters created an unforgettable chapter in Sanyasi Vivekananda's life. His letters to them mesmerize devotees even today.

Mrs Hale
Mrs George W. (Bell) Hale. This loving American lady saved Swamiji's life in Chicago and gave him shelter.

Once in New York, Swamiji told his devotees, 'Ok, ok, today I will myself cook and feed all of you.' Hearing this, his disciple Landsberg (later Swami Kripananda), went aside and began to lament, saying 'Oh God! Save me!' When asked about the reason for his prayer, he explained, 'When Swamiji lived in New York, each time he cooked, I used to tear my hair out because after the cooking was over, the mountain of used vessels had to be washed clean by me alone.'

Not just about spices and chillies, we also have accounts from Swamiji's American devotee Miss Ida Ansell about his love for pickles (quoted from the original): '*Once they bought some pickles in a little wooden dish. Some of the pickle juice ran out on Swami's hand. He immediately put his fingers to his mouth and began to lick off the liquid. This seemed undignified, and someone said. "Oh Swami!" in a shocked tone. "This little outside." Swami replied. "That's the trouble with you here; you always want this outside to be so nice."*'

Another devotee, Biraja Devi, writes, 'While living in Alameda, Swamiji cooked Indian food every Sunday evening and we had the opportunity to be close to him. Later, we used to share the food cooked by him. He was closest to us when he cooked in the kitchen. Once, after being quiet for quite some time, he said, "Madam, be large-hearted. Always remember: there are two sides to everything. When I am on the rise, I say 'Soham', meaning, 'I am that'. Again, when I am crying with a stomach-ache, I ask, 'Oh Mother, please save me.' So, always look at everything from both sides."'

Biraja Devi's original name was Edith B. Allan. Her husband was a British-American who later became the chairman of the San Francisco Vedanta Samiti. He died in 1953 at the age of eighty-nine.

Swamiji's dear friend Swami Turiyananda, who accompanied him on his second trip to the USA, has written about his perfectionist attitude to cooking. His style of cutting vegetables was exceptional—it was wonderful to watch him peeling potatoes at high speed. Even in his conversations, Swamiji often used culinary idioms and metaphors. Turiyananda reminisces, 'Once after establishing the Belur *Math*, Swamiji became very angry over a conversation and walked out of the *math* saying, "You are all small thinkers. How can I stay with you? You will argue about potatoes and pointed gourd and spinach leaves."'

Swami Turiyananda tells us, 'If he got angry, Swamiji wouldn't even spare Sri Ramakrishna. "Mad Brahmin! I wasted my life running after a fool."'

Turiyananda says, 'Along with the Vedas and Upanishads, Vivekananda also taught cooking. In Meerut, he once cooked pulao and other items for us. I cannot describe how delicious that food was! But as soon as we praised it, he gave away all the food to us without keeping even a morsel for himself. He said, "I have eaten all this many times—I am very happy feeding all of you. Eat it all up!"'

Along with cooking, there were often discussions about health. Once Swami Shibananda pointed to a youth and told Swamiji that he was suffering from indigestion for many years. Swamiji replied, 'Our Bengal is very sentimental, that is why there is so much dyspepsia here.'

Goat's Milk, Fish and Curd

Shantiram Ghosh says, 'Swamiji also experimented with various types of milk. At the later stages of his life, around 1898, fresh goat's milk was also sourced for him. In fact, a goat was kept at the *math* for this. One day, Swamiji decided that he would milk the goat himself. And he did it in a manner as if he had been doing this all his life!'

Swami Premananda's younger brother Shantiram Ghosh has also referred to a favourite rhyme of Thakur's, about the relationship between Swamiji's food and curd:

'You rascal with the curd pot in your hand,
You keep serving curd on my dish,
Are those your father or uncles,
Whose Plates are all piled with fish?

Which was Swamiji's favourite fish? Many believe it is the *ilish* (the hilsa, a herring-like fish of rivers and coastal waters, highly prized in Bengal), which was procured at his behest, even on the day of Swamiji's demise. And the *ilish* made with *pui shak* stems, as it was cooked for him once in Dhaka, was an even greater favourite.

Another favourite fish of Swamiji's was *galda chingRi* (large fresh-water prawns). Balaram Babu knew about this love and once had some cooked for him. Shantiram Ghosh informs us, 'That time, the *chingRi* had a little too much gravy, but Swamiji ate it quite happily.' When Shantiram's elder brother Swami Premananda accosted Balaram Babu, he said, 'Naren is a wonderful boy. He ate it all without any complaint at all.' Then, he turned to his wife and said, 'And see how your brother is complaining.'

We have two bits of information from Calcutta's first Indian deputy commissioner, Bhupendranath Bandopadhyay, which tell us about Swamiji's love for meat. Bhupendranath's father Mahendranath was a government lawyer in Darjeeling. Bhupendranath informs us that when Swamiji returned from abroad for the first time, among his luggage was an apparatus for roasting. During a subsequent visit to Darjeeling, Swamiji cooked some exquisite pulao and mutton. He also fed a South

Indian devotee some chicken as prasad. Bhupendranath reminisces that he would occasionally take some mutton for Swamiji to Belur *Math* because of the latter's fondness for meat. Many people are aware that Bengalis do not mix milk with their mutton, but Swamiji had no such taboos.

Ashim Kumar Basu was another devotee who met Swamiji just a week before he attained Mahasamadhi. Ashim asked Swamiji, 'How are you?' Swamiji replied, 'Like how you are. Doctors say a lot of things. But I have a terminal illness, what can you do?'

Ashim persisted, 'What will you have? Will you have milk? I have a cow at home.'

Swamiji replied, 'Yes, I will. I can't have anything else.'

Priya Nath Sinha, Swamiji's friend, indicates that Swamiji used to spend a lot of time studying nutrition. Swamiji used to address this childhood friend as 'Priya*sangi* (a play on his name, which meant 'dear friend'). Priya Nath composed the *Sri Ramakrishna Charita* under the pen name 'Gurudas Burman'. While having prasad, Swamiji once told him, 'See Singhi, we should eat concentrated food. Only stuffing ourselves with a lot of rice is just being very lazy! . . . Our two large meals stuff us up to our gills. We lose all our energy trying to digest a huge quantity of rice.'

Bengali Sweets and Vegetables

We still get to hear stories about Swamiji's many favourites among Bengal's sweets. Was it just the promise of good *rosogolla* that got him to meet Sri Ramakrishna at Dakshineswar? People those days were particularly fond of *jilipi* and *jibhe gaja*. Sometimes, though, like his guru, Swamiji too became quite concerned about who had brought the sweet (to ensure the procurer was pure of heart).

Ma Saradamoni's disciple and later Swamiji's attendant, Dheerananda (1873–1936) once visited Jodhpur with Swamiji. A saffron-clad gentleman arrived from Haridwar to meet Swamiji, in the hope of getting some financial aid, with a packet of hot jalebis. Swamiji asked Captain Sevier (James Henry Sevier was a non-commissioned officer in the British army. Both he and his wife Charlotte Elizabeth Sevier were disciples of Swamiji) to give the man ten rupees, but he didn't let anyone touch the jalebis; they were given to the elephant. About his keen-sightedness, Swamiji said, 'I have two eyes at the back and two in the front.'

Once, when speaking with the manager of the king of Mahishdol (a zamindari in Midnapore, West Bengal), Swamiji, in praise of evergreen Bengal, with its vast array of crops and vegetation, said, 'No other land has such vast quantities of vegetation like Bengal. However, Rajputana also has good arrangements for food.' In response, the manager Shachindranath Basu said, 'Maharaj, what do they know about eating good food? They put tamarind in all their vegetables.' Swamiji retorted sharply, 'Now you are talking like a child! From seeing a few people, how can you judge the entire state? Civilization started in their state—where did Bengal have any civilization? Visit the rich people (of Rajputana) in their homes and you will realize your mistake . . . When did Bengal become civilized?'

Swamiji continued, '. . . And do you think your pulao is an original dish? Many years ago, in *Pak-Rajeshwar* (India's first printed cookbook), there is a description of *palanna* (the original dish from where pulao is derived). The Muslims copied our recipe; Akbar's Ain-i-Akbari has a long description of how Hindus cook *palanna*.'

Shachindranath Basu has left a memorable description of Sister Nivedita (born Margaret Noble) in his writings. Although it is a little out of context here, I cannot control my desire to quote it. Shachindranath has written, 'Miss Noble had high endurance. She did not eat fish or meat. A slice or two of bread, along with some fruits, was her daily diet.' During Nivedita's Kalighat oration, Shachindranath informs us that he was present, barefoot, at the Natya Mandir.

Although he devoted his entire life to preaching the Vedas and Vedanta, yet Swamiji could not escape being criticized by his contemporaries. In 1899, Taraknath Rai, who later became a famous district magistrate, went to meet Swamiji in Darjeeling. He writes, 'I remember the famous "Bangabasi" magazine attempted to prove that Swamiji was a non-Hindu. Denying the strictures of the shastras, he became a sanyasi although he was a shudra travelling across the seas to America, had eaten food cooked by non-Hindus. So Bangabasi declared it was unwilling to consider him a Hindu.'

Shukto and Mocha

But whatever contemporary critics may have written about him, it is quite clear from his family sources that Swamiji was a great lover of non-vegetarian food. Our chief source is Swamiji's cousin Surendranath Datta, popularly known as Tamu. Tamu Datta, a professional stage musician, had at one time, converted to Christianity with his entire family, but in his later years, he was initiated by Swami Saradananda.

Tamu Datta informs us that Swamiji's mother and maternal grandmother were not just very beautiful, but 'the mother and daughter were both excellent cooks (too) with a varied cuisine'. Even after returning from the USA, Swamiji used to sometimes visit his grandmother's home. Tamu Babu tells us that Swamiji was his grandmother's pet. He used to bring along his band of disciples to have a meal at his grandmother's place. He particularly praised her *shukto* (a bitter and pungent mix of vegetables, light on spices) and *mocha* (the banana flower). He used to joke, 'It is worth taking birth in Bengal again, just for these two dishes.'

In 1901, Swamiji took his mother on a pilgrimage of the Kamakhya temple in Guwahati, Assam and Chandranath temple (now in Bangladesh). Sometimes he would send her gifts of fruits and vegetables from Belur.

One day, Swamiji landed up at his home, keen to have a little prasad (leftover) from his mother's plate. She had just finished her lunch, and there was only a little piece of drumstick left on her plate. She was embarrassed and asked him why he had arrived so late, but he was happy to eat that bit of drumstick, saying, 'So what?'

Of the children who lived in Belur *Math* and completed their school and college studies during Swamiji's life, Naresh Chandra Ghosh was perhaps the best known. He had travelled to many places with Swamiji.

'He was always feeding something or the other to the people around him,' writes Naresh Chandra Ghosh. 'He enjoyed cooking himself and feeding people. He used to cook *jhaler jhol* (spicy vegetarian gravy) in a novel way. Making a very thin gruel of lentils, he used that liquid to make the vegetable gravy. It was very tasty!'

Naresh Babu remembers, 'Swamiji had once made something akin to *soru chakli* (a kind of crepe or dosa) using rice powder. He would hold the pan in one hand and throw the pancake up so that it rotated twice in the air before neatly falling onto the pan again. We would have it with a diluted palm candy syrup.'

Another Chapter of Nomadic Travels

Many incidents of Vivekananda's nomadic days have been lost forever. Besides a few memories of his *gurubhais* and some personal experiences and letters of those who loved him, there is really nothing much that can be revived for our new generation of readers, curious to know more about Swamiji. Even for this chapter, we are largely dependant on his brother Mahendranath's compositions. With immense devotion, he has recorded the literary treasures of Vivekananda's life until his death, fifty-four years after his elder brother passed away.

Speaking about Swamiji's Rajputana travels, Mahendranath has given us a heart-rending description of an incident. Unable to make any arrangement for food or shelter, Swamiji was sitting beside a well under a tree. Whenever someone came to draw water he would request for and get a little water to drink and continue sitting. After a few days like this, Swamiji fainted and was lying there when the local king heard the news and, out of pity, came and took him away.

Mahendranath tells us that Swamiji, who, irrespective of any negativity in the environment around him always believed in staying open-minded, once found himself engulfed in gloom and depression. 'I am just walking around on the path, I have not received anything (spiritually); so saving my body is only a mockery.'

Lord Buddha had also once faced this same depression. Coming out of Gridhakuta Hill, he apparently spoke like a madman, saying, 'The first is hunger and thirst, the second is *kaam* (desire), the third is *sangshay* (doubt) and the fourth is *ahankar* (vanity).'

On 26 May 1890, a downcast Narendra wrote a letter to Pramada Babu signing off as 'Ramakrishna's Servant'. The letter said, 'Bengal's condition is lamentable. The people of this land do not think even in their dreams of renunciation or what sacrifice really means. Pursuits of luxury and chasing sensory pleasures are eating into their souls! May God grace Bengal with *bairagya* (renunciation) and unworldliness.'

After Rajputana, the nomad Swamiji went to Kathiawad. He did not enjoy the food there at all. Mahendranath writes, 'Haridas Biharidas had given him shelter and food, but Gujarat and Sindh's food was not at all palatable for the Bengali sanyasi. The dal was boiled and mashed up and mixed with a lot of water and given to him with a little spice and ghee. There was hardly any vegetable—mainly rice and ghee.'

Swamiji spoke in London about this difficult time. He had made friends with the cook in Haridas Biharidas's home and taught him some songs. At an opportune moment, he requested the cook 'to separate the grains of the lentils and serve them to me so that along with the rice, they can make up at least one mouthful of edible food'.

A rich man once asked Swamiji, 'Why do you eat so many chillies?' Swamiji responded gravely, 'My entire life I have roamed around and eaten (rice with) whatever I could manage. The chilli was then my only support. The chilli is my old friend. Nowadays, I am getting a few things to eat but for the large part of my life I have been forced to fast.'

Although he managed with a paucity of rice, Swamiji could not give up his addiction to smoking. Before going to the USA, Swamiji once met the Theosophical Society's Col. Olcott in the hope that he would get a few introductory notes from him. Olcott not only did not give him any, but also apparently secretly sent some derogatory notes about him. Swamiji and Col. Olcott debated on many subjects. Before leaving, Swamiji said, 'You have made me talk a lot, now please give me some cheroots to smoke.' Then, picking up five or six cheroots, he said goodbye and walked out smiling.

There are thousands of stories of how Sanyasi Vivekananda managed to find food during his travels. It is not always clear when and where those incidents occurred, but his biographers have patiently collected detailed information and recorded many of the stories.

Once a mounted policeman threatened to lock him up. 'For how many days?' asked the famished sanyasi. When he heard that the lock-up could be from two weeks to one month, Swamiji requested to be locked up for six months. The policeman asked him, 'Why do you want to be in lock-up for more than a month?' Swamiji's response was, 'The hard work in the jail will be easy when compared to walking all day continuously. I don't get anything to eat and have to often stay hungry. At least in the jail I will receive two meals a day to fill my stomach.' The policeman then lost his patience and said, '*Bhago!*' (Run!)

In 1891, in a village in Rajasthan, Swamiji was asked 'Why do you wear saffron?' Swamiji's immediate response was, 'If I wear white, the poor ask me for alms. I am a beggar myself, but if someone asks me for alms and I cannot give I feel anguished.'

Swamiji met Dewan Marfat Alwar Maharaj, who asked him impudently, 'I have heard you are an exceptional pandit and can easily earn all the money you want. Why then do you roam around begging?'

Without any embarrassment, Swamiji replied, 'Why do you neglect all your kingly duties and spend all day hunting and feasting with the British?'

Maharaj replied, 'I enjoy that.'

Swamiji smiled and said, 'So do I enjoy being a fakir and roaming around.'

Once in Alwar, a devotee asked him, 'Swamiji, is there any benefit of rubbing oneself with oil?' Swamiji replied, 'If you rub one *chhatak* (approximately 60 grams) of oil on your body, it is equivalent to eating one *poa* (25 grams) of ghee.'

On 14 April 1891, Swamiji was in Mount Abu. He had taken shelter from the pouring rain in an empty cave. He asked a follower, 'Can you make a set of doors for me (perhaps to block out the rain)?' The man replied, 'Please come and stay in my home. I am a Muslim, but I will cook food separately for you.'

Through this introduction, he then met the maharaja of Khetri. The maharaja's private secretary Munshi Jagmohan asked him, 'Being a Hindu sadhu, how are you staying in the home of a Muslim?' Swamiji replied, 'I am not doing anything against the shastras; this is permitted in our scriptures.'

Meeting with the maharaja of Khetri was a big event in Swamiji's life. The maharaja asked Swamiji, 'What is the meaning of life?' Swamiji famously replied, 'To attempt to express oneself and allow oneself to bloom and grow continuously, in the midst of an incessantly antagonistic environment, is life.'

Because of the maharaja's repeated requests, Swamiji visited Khetri thrice in quick succession. The last time was from Bombay, just before he boarded the ship to America. The maharaja instructed his private secretary Munshi Jagmohan to escort Swamiji to the dock to board his ship.

Sometime before this, Swamiji had to spend three days at a railway station in Rajasthan. Many people came to discuss religion and spirituality with him. On the third night, a *chamar* (a cobbler, supposedly of a low caste) came timidly. Swamiji asked him, 'Will you give me something to eat?' The man respectfully said, 'I am a low-caste person. Let me bring some lentils and wheat flour and you can cook your own dal and roti.'

At the time Swamiji had taken a vow to not touch fire. The sanyasi said, 'I will have the roti cooked by you.'

Watching the scene, some people at the station criticized him. 'You ate a low caste's food—is this correct?' Swamiji ignored them.

In Junagadh, Swamiji showed his culinary skills by making and treating everyone to *rosogollas*. We have still not been able to fathom when and how he learnt this difficult recipe.

In Kutch's terrible heat, he almost lost his life in the mirage of the desert. Swamiji was also in serious trouble in Central India's Khandwa, where people were largely antagonistic towards guests and would not even donate a handful of rice.

Later, the dangerously under-nourished Swamiji wrote to a *gurubhai*, 'I am roaming around shamelessly and eating in other people's homes, and my conscience does not even prick me. Just like a crow. I will not beg any more. Of what use is it to a poor man to feed me?'

It is only later, in a historic speech given in California, that Swamiji corroborates the fact that fasting is not a luxury for a sanyasi. Swamiji said, 'So many times I have faced death, hunger, with tattered feet and exhausted body. So many times, day after day, not being able to receive a handful of rice, it would become impossible to carry on walking. Then the inert body would fall in the shade of a tree and it would seem that the life breath was going out. I couldn't speak or even think. And in that state a thought would arise, "I have no fear, no death. I was never born and will never die. I have neither hunger nor thirst. Soham, Soham. The entire universe does not hold the ability to grind me down. Nature is my handmaid. Oh God of Gods, oh Almighty, show your majesty, establish your autonomy. Awake and arise! Don't hold back!' Swamiji says, 'Then I could regain my complete strength and stand up. That is why I am still alive and present here today.'

There have been many more distressing experiences in the life of the homeless wanderer, all of which can be quite easily found in Swamiji's letters and major speeches.

Travelling in Kanyakumari in South India, Swami Vivekananda won the hearts of both royalty and the common man. At the same time, preparations were on for his incredible journey, to another country.

We hear that, finding it difficult to raise the funds for his travel, Swamiji decided to travel on foot to the USA, via Afghanistan. It was this news that prompted the maharaja of Khetri to immediately arrange the funds for his dear guru's voyage by ship, and finally Swamiji travelled first class to the USA.

Even when Swamiji reached Bombay to take the ship to the USA, his eagerness to cook and feed people was very high. Mahendranath gives us an account of the time. 'One day, Swamiji wanted to cook pulao and feed everyone. The mutton, rice, *khoya* (thickened milk), etc., were all arranged. Meanwhile, the mutton stock with all the spices was getting cooked. Swamiji tasted a little mutton from the stock. The pulao was ready. Swamiji ate a bit of the mutton and then went into another room and began his meditation, forgetting everything about the food. When it was time to eat, everyone began requesting him to eat too but he said, 'I have no desire to eat. I had wanted to cook and feed you all, which is why I spent fourteen rupees and cooked a bit of pulao. Now all of you go and finish it.' And he continued his meditation.

Before leaving for the USA, while in Bombay, Swamiji one day suddenly wanted to eat some carp. The markets of Bombay did not have carp but his devotee Kalipada Ghosh sent his people to procure some from out of town. The carp fiesta gave everyone a lot of joy.

Swami Gambhirananda has written that the food on the ship was strange at first. But our Swamiji adapted himself very well to the unaccustomed food, disparate people and strange environment. 'The pure breeze of the ocean brought a joy to his mind and body.'

The Sanyasi Overseas

Swamiji set sail for distant Yokohama on the *S.S. Peninsular*. Mahendranath writes, 'Being a first-class passenger, he could get tea, coffee, etc., as soon as he desired them. He could not travel by the lower class because of his stomach ailment. The grateful Swami had written to his benefactor Raja Ajit Singh that earlier he had to visit the toilet around twenty-five times a day, but by the time he boarded the ship his stomach was fine.'

It is important to know that this maharaja himself had suggested that Swamiji change the earlier name 'Vividishananda' to 'Vivekananda'. And earlier, when Swamiji went to meet the Theosophical Society's Col. Olcott, his name was Sachchidananda.

The ship on which Swamiji sailed from Yokohama to Vancouver on 14 July 1893 was called *Empress of India*. From Vancouver, he went on to Chicago and Boston (where Swamiji taught Vedanta philosophy even before he became a renowned religious figure at the World Parliament of Religions). It became difficult to survive at times, and he sent an SOS to his South Indian devotees: 'If you cannot send me money to live here, please send money to allow me to return.'

In distant America, Mrs Katherine Abbott Sanborn, a co-traveller on a train, offered Swamiji her warm hospitality. All his devotees know the stories of Swamiji's life struggles. We also know that the Chicago Parliament of Religions began on 11 September 1893.

Just before this, on 20 August 1893, Swamiji wrote from his place of stay, Breezy Meadows, to Alasinga Perumal (a Vaishnavite propagator of Vedanta and an ardent follower of Swami Vivekananda) (quoted from the original): *'The expense I am bound to run into here is awful. You remember, you gave me £170 in notes and £9 in cash. It has come down to £130 in all!! On an average it costs me £1 every day; a cigar costs eight anna of our money.'*

In helplessness he adds, *'I have for twelve years gone from door to door of the so-called rich and great but they have only thought me a cheat. . . . When my own countrymen consider me a cheat, then what must the Americans think of this strange beggar who comes seeking alms from them!'*

In December 1893, Swamiji wrote to Haripada Mitra, 'As long as I am here, the ladies here are giving me shelter and food, organizing the lectures, taking me to the market and doing everything for me. Even if I take thousands of births to serve them, I will not be able to repay the debt I owe them. . . . There is almost no poverty in this country. But the expenses are high. Even a cheap cheroot costs four *anna*, and for a strong pair of shoes I need to pay twenty-four rupees. As they earn, so they spend.'

In his letters, Swamiji is clear about his objective. 'I have not come here to see the country, or to watch the sights or spectacle, or to count my rosary beads and chant. I have come here to find a solution to poverty.'

Swamiji has written about his encounter with racism in America: 'Whatever desire I had to become a "saheb" was crushed by the Gods of America. I wanted to shave off my beard, but as soon as I entered a barber's shop I was told "that look is not allowed here". I thought it was to do with my turban and strange saffron robe and thought I should buy myself a set of Western coat and hat. Fortunately, I met a friendly American, who explained that in fact I would be better off wearing my Indian clothes, in which I might be left alone, because if I changed to Western garb they would chase me.' Swamiji realized that the problem was not the colour of his clothes, but that of his skin. He decided to simply shave himself. He experienced discrimination not just at the hair cutting saloon, but even at restaurants.

Letter to Shashi Maharaj–Swami Ramakrishnananda

541 Dearborn Avenue
Chicago
1894

With Blessings for your well-being,

I am very happy having received all your letters. Very sorry, however, to hear of Majumdar's doings. That is what happens when one tries to push oneself forward at all cost. It is not my fault. Majumdar had come here ten years ago—and received a lot of respect and honour; now it is my turn to receive it. Everything is the will of the Guru—what can I do? It is childish on Majumdar's part to be annoyed about this. Anyway, never mind.

उपेक्षितव्यं तद्वचनं भवस्तद्दशानां महात्मनाम् । अपि कीटदंशनभीरुका वयं
रामकृष्ण - तनयास्तद्दृदयरुधिरपोषिता: । "अलोकसामान्यमचिन्त्यहेतुकं
निन्दन्ति मन्दाश्चरितं महात्मनाम्" इत्यादीनि संस्मृत्य क्षन्तव्योऽयं
जाल्म: ।

Enlightened beings like you should not be concerned by his
words. Should we, children of Sri Ramakrishna, who have been
nourished by the blood of his heart, be worried about bites
from a tiny worm? 'It is astonishing that the wicked, whose
motives are difficult to fathom, criticize the conduct of the
high-minded' (quoted from Kalidasa's *Kumarasambhavam*).
Remember all this and forgive Majumdar's foolishness. It
is God's wish that the people of this country develop their
spiritual powers—so can any Majumdar block the progress of
His desire? My name is not necessary—I want to be a voice
without a form. There is no need for Haramohan or anyone
else to endorse me.

कोऽहं तत्प्रादप्रसरं प्रतिरोद्धुं समर्थयितुं वा, के वान्ये? तथापि मम
इदयकृतज्ञता तान्प्रति

Who am I to check or to help the course of His march? And
who is Haramohan either? However, I offer my heartfelt
gratitude to them.

'Being, thus, established, one is not shaken even in the midst
of the greatest calamity' (Bhagwad Gita, Chapter 6 Verse 22)—
is a state he has not yet reached. Consider this and look upon
him with pity. With the Lord's blessings the desire for name
and fame has not yet entered my heart, and probably will never
enter. I am but the instrument; he is the craftsman. Through
this instrument, he is kindling the desire for dharma in the

hearts of thousands in this far away land. Thousands of men and women in this country offer me great love and devotion and hundreds of priests and orthodox Christians consider me the devil's brother.

मूकं करोति वाचालं पङ्गुं लङ्घयते गिरिम्

He makes the dumb eloquent and makes the lame scale mountains. I am amazed at His grace. Whichever town I visit, it is in tumult. They have named me the Cyclonic Hindu. Remember His wish—I am a voice without a form.

Swamiji wrote this open-hearted letter to Swami Ramakrishnananda (Shashi Maharaj) from Chicago. His signature appears on the next page.

'Desperate with hunger, I entered a restaurant and asked,
"Give me that thing."
"It's not here."
"But there it is."
"In simple words, you can't sit here, man."
"Why not, man?"
"If anyone eats with you, they will 'lose their caste'."
Then I began to like America a little more, like my own country.'

On 3 March 1894, Swamiji wrote from Chicago to his dear friend 'Kidi' (A. Singaravelu Mudaliar, an Indian encyclopaedist and academic): 'Whether Kshatriyas eat non-vegetarian food or not, they are really the people who have created everything that is glorious and beautiful within Hindu Dharma. Who wrote the Upanishads? What (caste) was Ram?

What was Krishna? What was Buddha? What were the Jain Tirthankaras?'

From his letter written to Shashi Maharaj on 19 March 1894, it is clear that after reaching the USA, he had not written any letters to his *gurubhais*.

Swamiji complained sharply against the bitter cold: 'Before my breath can come out, it freezes in my beard. But you know what's funny? Inside the house, no one drinks water without adding a cube of ice to it. Because it is warm inside the homes . . . These people are unparalleled in art and artifice, unparalleled in enjoying luxury, unparalleled in earning money and unparalleled in spending it . . . And I do not have a cheroot. It is now 12.15 a.m. here. These people love me, they come in thousands to hear me.'

Swamiji met the Brahmo Samaj member, Pratap Chandra Majumdar, in the USA. 'At first he was all love . . . later Majumdar became jealous. I was stunned. "Tell me baba, am I depriving you of your food?"' Majumdar then tried hard to discredit Swamiji in the eyes of the local priests saying, 'He is a nobody, a con man who comes to your country and says, "I am a fakir,"' etc. 'He said all this and got them quite angry with me. In fact, President Barrows (Rev. Dr John Henry Barrows, an American clergyman of the First Presbyterian Church and Chairman of the 1893 General Committee on the Congress of Religions, later to be known as the World's Parliament of Religions) was so angry that he does not speak well with me . . . But thanks to the blessings of my guru, what could Majumdar do? All of the American nation loves me, worships me and gives me money, treats me like a guru—what can Majumdar do?'

In his letter dated 19 November to his dear friend Alasinga, Swamiji expresses his worry about food. 'Food! Food! When

God cannot give me food, I cannot believe he will keep me happy in Heaven.'

Swamiji's letters to Shashi Maharaj are full of life and vitality. In an undated letter from Chicago in 1894, he writes, 'These people call me the "Cyclonic Hindu". Remember His wish—*I am a voice without a form*. . . . God alone knows whether I will go to England or *Yam*land (Yama is the Hindu God of death). He will organize everything. In this country, a good cheroot costs one rupee, a horse cart costs three rupees, a shirt is 300 rupees, and nine rupees daily at the hotel—God has been organizing everything.'

Did he put on weight at this time? Swamiji writes, 'My stomach has grown so much that I think we will have to break down the doors for me to pass through.'

We heard earlier how Mahendranath, without informing Swamiji and with some financial help from the maharaja of Khetri, had landed up in London, keen to study law. We know that Swamiji wanted him to go to the USA and study electrical engineering instead, which he would arrange for, but Mahendranath was adamant. He had no money to go back to India, and Swamiji angrily refused to buy the ticket. Upset and too proud to ask his brother again, he set off, penniless and on foot, to return to India via Europe, taking five years and arriving after Swamiji's death in 1902. During this time, Mahendranath did not contact his mother either.

That Swamiji was very hurt at his brother's behaviour is clear from his anguished letter to John P. Fox, written from Paris on 14 August 1900, after trying in vain to contact Mahim.

Swamiji writes, 'Kindly let Mahim know that whatever he chooses to do, my blessings are always with him. Whatever he is doing right now, I have no doubt, is far better than studying law, etc.' He further writes (quoted from the original): '*I like boldness and adventure and my race stands in need of that spirit very much . . . my health is failing and I do not expect to live long. So he must be ready to take care of our mother and the rest of the family. I may depart from this world at any moment.*'

In the summer of 1894, Swamiji wrote another undated letter in Bengali to Shashi Maharaj. 'Mr Hale's home in Chicago is my centre; I address his wife as "Ma" and his daughters address me as "Elder Brother". I have never met such a pure and kind family.'

And now some news about food, from Swamiji's own pen: 'By the way, there is an abundance of *ilish* here these days. You can eat your fill; it will all be digested. There are many fruits—banana, limes, guavas, apples, almonds, raisins and grapes—all in abundance. Many other fruits come from California—heaps of pineapples, but no mangoes or *lichu* (the litchi or lichee).

'There is a kind of *shak* which they call spinach, quite like our *nate shak*. And what they call asparagus is exactly like tender drumstick stem. Of course, I cannot get Gopal Ma's *chorchori* here. And they do not know of any dal at all. They have rice, bread and all kinds of meat and fish. Their food is like the Persians. A lot of milk, sometimes curd, but buttermilk in abundance. And cream is used in everything—in tea, coffee, in everything. This is not our cream that settles on milk, but a thick cream. And of course there is butter and iced water—summer or winter, day or night, whether they have a cold or fever, they use iced water. These are scientific people; when I tell them the cold will get worse with iced water, they laugh and say, "Drink, drink, it is very good." And they have many different kinds of kulfi.'

Swamiji's letters have innumerable references to eating, fasting and cooking. Along with that, there is some news of his health and finances. He writes to 'Sister' Isabelle (Lady Isabel Margesson) from Annisquam on 20 August 1894, (quoted from the original): *I have kept pretty good health all the time and hope to do in the future. I had no occasion yet to draw on my reserve, yet I am rolling on pretty fair. And I have given up all money-making schemes and will be quite satisfied with a bite and a shed and work on.*

Exactly eleven days later, on 31 August, he writes from some part of the USA to Alasinga Perumal (quoted from the original): *I have now Rs. 9,000 with me, part of which I will send over to you for the organisation . . .' Continuing, he says, 'You know the greatest difficulty with me is to keep or even to touch money . . . It is disgusting and debasing. So you must organise a Society to take charge of the practical and pecuniary part of it.*

In another letter to Alasinga dated 27 September 1894, Swamiji describes his frame of mind in response to others' criticism (quoted from the original): *. . . Tell my friends that a uniform silence is all my answer to my detractors. If I give them tit for tat, it would bring us down to a level with them.*

In self-criticism, he once said, 'We have a big fault—the glory of sanyasis. That was necessary in the beginning, but now we have matured; we don't need it any more. Do you understand? The true sanyasi is he who does not see himself as any different from a householder.'

On the secret of connecting with people, Swamiji wrote in March or April 1891 to his *gurubhai* Akhandananda, 'Go to all the villages of Rajputana and visit every poor home. If people are annoyed with your eating fish and meat, give it up. To sacrifice food for the benefit of others is good. These saffron robes are not for enjoyment, but a symbol of great responsibility.'

In a letter to the maharaja of Khetri, he praises the American people: 'So many thousands of beautiful family lives I have seen, so many thousands of mothers, whose pure character, selfless and childlike love, I cannot find words to describe.'

In answer to a question on why he was delaying his return to India, he writes in an undated letter to his dear *gurubhai* Mahapurush Maharaj, 'I would have left for India a long time ago but there is no money in India. Thousands of people respect and follow Ramakrishna Paramahansa but none of them will pay a single paisa. That is India!'

The immigrant sanyasi was always preoccupied with the idea of the *math* and Thakur's *janmotsav* (birth anniversary celebrations). He wrote another undated letter to Rakhal Maharaj: 'If you can build a *Math*, I will praise you for your achievement; else you are useless . . . This time the *janmotsav* should be grander than it has ever been. The food and feeding however, should be as simple as possible—just some snacks to be given as *bhog*, in little earthen plates.'

Swamiji quoted from Manu in a letter to Mrs Bull (Sara Chapman Thorp Bull was an American writer and philanthropist and an ardent devotee of Swamiji): 'In the view of Manu, sanyasis should never collect money, even for a good deed. The ancient rishis said, "All expectation leads to sorrow and denouncing expectations gives great joy."'

Swamiji describes his stay in New York with Mr Landsberg: 'Both of us together would cook some rice and dal or barley, eat quietly and then maybe we would read or write something.'

Then he quoted from Vairagya-shatakam (The Hundred Verses on Renunciation): 'From wealth comes the fear of poverty, from knowledge, the fear of ignorance, from beauty, the fear of old age, from fame, the fear of condemnation, from advancement in life, the fear of jealousy; in fact, even in life there is the fear of death . . . Only he is fearless, who has renounced everything.'

When Shashi Maharaj fell ill, Swamiji on 11 April 1895 advised him: 'Pay attention to your health . . . Let Rakhal take charge of all financial matters. No one else should interfere in that.'

Two months later, on 22 June 1895, we hear: 'Landsberg has gone somewhere. I am alone these days. I live on milk, fruits and almonds, etc. I am liking it and keeping well too. This summer I hope to lose thirty to forty pounds of weight.'

The next month he wrote from Thousand Island Park to Mrs William Sturges, 'It is as if all the sleep in the world has descended on me. I sleep for at least two hours during the day and at night I am dead to the world. I think this is the result of the sleeplessness in New York . . . The food is strictly vegetarian and I am fasting a lot . . . before I leave this place my body should lose quite a few pounds.'

On 9 August 1895, he wrote a letter to Sturdy (Edward Toronto Sturdy, a Sanskrit scholar, student of Hinduism and Buddhism, and a member of the Theosophical Society): 'I am relating some of my own experiences. When my *gurudev* passed away we were twelve ignorant, nameless, penniless youth and many powerful associations were bent on pushing us down. But with Sri Ramakrishna's grace, we have become claimants to a unique glory . . . Today all of India knows him and bows down respectfully at his feet. . . . Ten years ago, I couldn't get fifty people to attend his birth anniversary celebrations; last year 50,000 people collected to attend them.'

The various things that Swamiji has said in hurt and anger against Bengalis will fill a book. In a letter to Shashi Maharaj written from Reading in England, Swamiji's natural restraint seems to have failed him. With hurt pride and anger he asks him to tell Rakhal, 'Let people say what they will. People are idiots! Stay faithful to the path and don't go anywhere near Jesuitism (rather than being the beliefs of the Society of Jesus as a religious order, Jesuitism is a casuistic approach to moral questions and problems, so called because it was promoted by some Jesuits of the seventeenth century and popularly regarded as an attempt to achieve holy ends by unholy means).

'When was I ever an orthodox Hindu? Or even a conventional one? I do not pose as one. Does it look like the Bengalis themselves made me a human, sent me here with their money and now are looking after me? Huh! So we will now only have to follow what they like? Why should we even care what the Bengalis say or do not say? Their daughters become mothers at the age of twelve. They are not willing to give even a single paisa towards him, whose birth consecrated their land, but they want to talk! Do you think I will ever go back to Bengal? They have ruined the name of India . . . We should build the *math* in Rajputana, Punjab or even in Bombay. But Bengalis! Ram! Ram! They eat snails and drink from ponds stinking of urine, eat from torn banana leaves and sleep on wet floors mixed with their sons' defecations. They live with witches and wear "half-naked" clothes, and yet they speak with such arrogance. How does it matter what they think? You all keep doing your work your way. Why do you watch men's faces? Watch God's face.

'Don't trust those *&%#'s with any money. We will not lose any funds over them. Take care of all finances yourself. Madho—just do as I say, don't try to act smart with me. Now ask your Bengalis to send me a *Vachaspatya* (Sanskrit Dictionary)— let me see how good your great orators are!'

Later, from E.T. Sturdy's home in Reading, Swamiji directed his attack on Swami Brahmananda. 'There are two problems with all letters, particularly yours. First, you don't reply to any of my questions, and second, your letters come very late. You are after all sitting at home, while I am struggling day and night here and spinning like a top . . . I can quite well understand now that I will have to do everything myself . . .

'Business is business, which means that work must happen swiftly; there is no time for laziness. I will be going to America at the end of next week, so there is no hope of meeting whoever is coming.'

He has written in the same tone to Swami Akhandananda on 13 November 1895: 'You are young, you do not understand the spell of gold. When the opportunity arises, even the most principled person will turn swindler. That is life. So, don't share any information about money with X.'

In some letters, the normally nonchalant Vivekananda's voice sounds immensely despondent. In 1895, he writes to Alasinga from the USA, 'When I chose to become a sanyasi I was well aware that I will have to starve often. So what? I am a beggar, my friends are all poor, I love the poor and I gladly welcome poverty. I am happy that I sometimes have to spend the day fasting. I do not need anyone's help. Where is the necessity for that?'

It is clear that what we consider a huge success overseas also had some invisible fissures. Else, why would he mention starving?

Alongside this, he also sometimes felt disgusted at the world. Why else did the ever-optimistic sanyasi write so clearly to his countryman Alasinga, 'This is the world; those you love the most and help the most are the ones who want to cheat you. Disgusting world!'

Chef Swamiji

And now, it is time to look once more into our 'culinarian' Vivekananda's work. On 24 January 1895, he writes from New York to Swami Yogananda, who in his pre-sanyas days was Yogeendranath Rai Chaudhury. He was born into Dakshineswar's famous Sabarna Choudhury family in 1861 and was the Ramakrishna Mission's first vice president in 1897. (The Sabarna Ray Chaudhury family were the zamindars of the Kolkata area, prior to the arrival of the British. On 10 November 1698, they transferred, by lease, their rights over the three villages—Sutanuti, Gobindapur and Kalikata—to the East India Company.) The subject of Swamiji's letter was the ingredients of Bengali cooking, received as per 'Maharaj' Vivekananda's order placed on him.

Brother Yogen,

The *arhar* dal, *muger* dal, *aam sattva* (clotted mango juice), *amsi* (dry mango pulp), *aam tel* (mango pickle), *aamer murabba*, *baRi* and masalas have all arrived. There was a mistake in the signature in the bill of lading and there was no invoice, so there was a little delay. However, in the end, everything reached the destination well. Many thanks. Now, if you can please send the same dals and a little pickle to Sturdy's address in England—High View, Caversham,

Reading, then I will receive it as soon as I reach. Don't send any fried *muger* dal. I don't think that lasts very long. Send some chickpeas. England has no duty, so there will be no problem sending the goods. If you write to Sturdy, he will receive the material.

Yours,
Vivekananda

On 14 April 1896, Swamiji wrote from New York to the Hale Sisters that he would board the *S.S. Germanic* at midday the next day.

Swamiji was very keen to go to England, but found time in the interim to express his annoyance at his dear *gurubhai*: 'What do you mean by "*muger* dal is not yet ready"? I have already told you not to send the fried *muger* dal; I asked for the chickpeas and the raw *muger* dal. The fried *muger* dal loses its taste by the time it reaches this far and also becomes difficult to cook. If you send it again, it will all go into the Thames, and your labour will be wasted. Why do you work without reading my letter? . . . And why do you lose my letter? Why is it not filed?'

We have some more interesting news about his cooking. On 18 March 1896, Swamiji expressed his desire to cook some Indian food for his devotee, with whom he was staying in Detroit. During this time, his room had the Upanishads in one corner and all his spices in another. Maharaj Vivekananda was ready to show his magic at his devotee's home. This word 'maharaj' is truly wonderful. On the one hand, it means the king who sits on a throne, while on the other it denotes a sanyasi. There are just a few saffron-clad sanyasis in the entire world who can be addressed as 'Maharaj'. And the third meaning is that of a culinary expert, or a chef.

The magician Maharaj Vivekananda took out several dozen packets of spices, pickles and chutneys from his pockets, all of which had arrived from India along with books on the Vedas and Vedanta and the dictionary he had asked for.

It is no secret that wherever Swamiji went, he always carried a variety of spices with him, and his most valuable possession was a bottle of chutney, which was sent to him as per his wish from Madras. As all his followers know, his cooking was extremely spicy, and his Indian cooking was done slowly and painstakingly. Many were worried that this food may be harmful for the liver, but our sanyasi was not afraid of death.

Having won over the USA with his Vedanta's *pashupat astra* (an irresistible and most destructive personal weapon of Shiva and Kali), it is not clear how much time Swamiji could devote to cooking. But one of my school friends has done some research, and the curious reader can look for more answers in Swamiji's various letters.

Swamiji has written from New York, to Mrs Ole Bull, whom he addressed as 'Ma', letting her know he is happy and is the proud possessor of a gas stove that Miss Hamlin has very kindly sent him. He will have to cook in his bedroom itself. However, he is happy to let her know that below his rented home there is a very good public kitchen too.

It is important to know that Swamiji was never hesitant to cook himself, but he rarely did it to feed his own hunger. It was in fact a weakness for this Simulia Datta family to feed everyone around them at the slightest opportunity.

We also hear that Swamiji participated in cookery contests and dinners in various star-studded restaurants! The world-renowned Waldorf Astoria cordially invited Swamiji for a dinner. My school friend tells us that Swamiji, who had sometimes spent up to three days without food now went to a glittering dinner party, which started in the evening and carried on till 2 a.m. in the morning. But we know he did not enjoy this, because in tiredness, he wrote in March 1895, 'I am going to a dinner tonight. This is the last.'

Swamiji also thought about marketing and selling Indian food to the Americans, as conveyed in a long letter from New York to his favourite Trigunatitananda. He said he received the Sanskrit version of the Bhagwad and was happy with it. He also offered some business-related advice to one Ramdayal Babu. (quoted from the original): '*Tell Ramdayal Babu that a flourishing trade can be set on foot with England and America in Mung Dâl, Arhar Dâl, etc. Dâl soup will have a go if properly introduced. There will be a good demand for these things if they be sent from house to house, in small packets, with directions for cooking on them and a depot started for storing a quantity of them. Similarly Badis (Pellets made of Dal, pounded and beaten.) too will have a good market. We want an enterprising spirit. Nothing is done by leading idle lives. If anyone forms a company and exports Indian goods here and into England, it will be a good trade. But they are a lazy set, enamoured of child marriage and nothing else.*'

A quote from another book:

Shishya (disciple): 'What business will I do? And where will I get the money?'

Swamiji: 'Why are you blabbering like a lunatic? You have indomitable strength inside you. Just by saying "I am nothing", you are becoming powerless. Not just you, all of Bengal has become like this. Step out of Bengal once and see how the rest of India is moving ahead swiftly. And what are you all doing?

Even after studying so much you are crying at other people's doors, shouting, "Give me a job! Give me a job!" After getting kicked so much, are you all still human? Now you are not worth anything at all.

In a beautiful land like ours, which nature has blessed a million times more than any other, with clear streams and orchards, which nature has bestowed with more prosperity than any other—that is where you are born, and yet you have no food to eat and no clothes to wear! The land whose riches and prosperity are propagating civilization to the world, in that *Annapurna's* (of abundant food) land, why are you living in such misery? Your condition is worse than a detested dog's. And then you boast about your Ved-Vedanta! The people who cannot provide for their own food and clothes, who depend on others for running their lives, how can they boast? Drown your dharma and karma in the Ganges now and first focus on getting your life running. So many things originate in India. Foreigners take those raw materials and use them to grow their armies while you sit like loaded donkeys and hanker after their goods. Foreigners have taken those commodities that originate here, and using their intelligence, added value to make many new things and they have become big. And you have locked up your brains in the safe and are going around crying "Give me food! Give me food!"'

Student: 'What can I do to organize some food, Sir?'

Swamiji: 'The answers are all in your hands. You are blindfolding yourself and crying, "I am blind, and I cannot see anything." Tear away your blindfold and see—the world is aglow in the light of the afternoon sun. If you cannot get money, then join a ship as a khalasi (a manual worker, especially a docker, porter, or sailor) and go abroad. Sell Indian clothes, *gamchha*, *kulo* (a woven plate of sorts for various household purposes) or a broom on the roads of America and Europe. You will see how much people appreciate Indian things. I saw in America how some Muslim boys from Hooghly district have sold things like that and become rich. Are you less clever than they are?'

To his question about where to find the seed money, Swamiji promised, 'I will somehow get you started.'

Even after this, the student said he did not have enough courage to do what was suggested.

Swamiji: 'That's what I am saying, you people don't have devotion—you don't have self-belief either. What will become of you? Neither will you have a family life, nor will you have dharma. Either follow the business path with confidence and become successful in the world or leave everything and come to our path. Advise people here and abroad on dharma and help them. Then you will also get alms like us. Despite so many struggles in doing a job for someone else, in being a servant to someone else, you are still not waking up! That is why your sorrows are also unending!'

Swamiji's intention was that after spending five years seeking alms and another five years studying in the *math*, i.e., a total of ten years of training, students could receive initiation from the swamis in the *Math* and enter the *sanyas-ashram*. Of course, this would be subject to their wanting to become sanyasis and the *math's* administrators considering them suitable to become sanyasis.

Student: 'Sir, what will be the objective of these three branches in the *math*?'

Swamiji: 'The first is *anna daan* (giving food), the second is *vidya daan* (giving learning) and then the most important, *gyan daan* (giving knowledge). The *math* will synthesize these three ideas.

'While seeking alms, the *brahmacharis* (a student of the Vedas and a celibate) will learn to serve others and the intention to spend their lives learning *Shiv gyan* (the knowledge of Shiva) will become firm and strong in their minds. From there, their heart will become pure, and the *sattva gun* (the quality of positivity and goodness) will awaken in them.'

Student: 'Sir, if *gyan daan* is the most important, then what is the need of the *anna daan* and *vidya daan*?'

Swamiji: 'You still have not understood the issue. Listen, instead of wailing for food, if you can somehow—through begging or learning—manage to collect a handful of rice daily and feed those poorer than you, then not only will you benefit the recipients, the world and yourself, but you will also earn the sympathy of everyone for your good work.'

In the last chapter, writing about the need for perseverance in creating a successful business, Swamiji said, 'Persistence is required; idling at home gets zero results.'

At different times in the USA, Swamiji had small and big problems related to food, some of which his well-wishers have recorded in their memoirs of him.

Once in New York for example, due to a paucity of funds he had rented an apartment in a dirty area. After spending one night there, Swamiji told Sara Ellen Waldo, 'The food here is very dirty. Will you be able to cook my meals for me?' Miss Waldo, after taking the permission from the landlady to use her kitchen, arrived the next morning with all her utensils and ingredients to cook for Swamiji.

During the Chicago Parliament of World Religions in 1893, Swamiji was a guest at the home of Mr and Mrs John B. Lion at 262 Michigan Avenue. The host of the family that had welcomed Swamiji into their home during the Chicago Conference said, (quoted from the original): 'This Indian is the most brilliant and interesting man who has ever been in our home. And he shall stay as long as he wishes.'

Their granddaughter Cornelia Conger has later written (quoted from the original), *'As our American food is less highly seasoned than Indian, my grandmother was afraid he might find it flat. He told us, on arrival, that he had been told to conform to all the customs and the food of his hosts, so he ate as we did.*

My grandmother used to make a little ceremony of making salad dressing at the table, and one of the condiments she used was Tabasco Sauce, put up by some friends of hers, the Mrs Ilhennys, in Louisiana. She handed him the bottle and said, "You might like a drop or two of this on your meat, Swami." He sprinkled it on with such a lavish hand that we all gasped and said, "But you can't do that! It's terribly hot!" He laughed and ate it with such enjoyment that a special bottle of the sauce was always put at his place after that'.

Cornelia Congar has also written that Swamiji did not possess any wallet. He kept his money tied to a corner of his handkerchief! (quoted from the original): *'He had no purse. So he used to tie it up in a handkerchief and bring it back—like a proud little boy—pour it into my grandmother's lap to keep for him.'*

Swamiji's initiate Mary C. Funke informs us, '(Once) Swamiji jokingly said, "Today I will cook for all of you—ok?"' She continues to say, (quoted from the original): *'The food he prepares is delicious but for "yours truly" too hot with various spices; but I made up my mind to eat it if it strangled me, which it nearly did. If a Vivekananda can cook for me, I guess the least I can do is to eat it. Bless him!'*

We have seen how Maud Stumm described her receiving Swamiji and Swami Turiyananda when they got off the ship at New York in August 1899. She further says that Swamiji was very happy when he got something he liked. (quoted from the original): *'Ice cream, for example. How many times I have seen him rise from the table after salad, excusing himself to smoke or walk, when a very quick word from Lady Betty (Mrs Francis H. Leggett) that she believed there was to be ice cream would turn him back instantly, and he would sink into his place with a smile of expectancy and pure delight seldom seen on the face of anybody over sixteen.'*

One Sunday evening Swamiji was to speak at the 'Home of Truth'. He had invited some friends. Before the speech Mrs Steele had invited Swamiji and Ida Ansell for dinner. Everyone had expected that as per Western customs Swamiji would say grace before eating. But Swamiji surprised everyone by starting to eat without saying grace. Later, he said, 'It is better to praise the Lord after eating than before.'

For the last course of the meal, Mrs Steele had organized dates. Later when she praised Swamiji's lecture, he said, 'Madam, the credit really goes to your dates.'

Normally after a lecture, the followers took Swamiji to a café or a restaurant and depending on the weather, they decided to have coffee or ice cream. On that day, even though Swamiji was shivering in his overcoat, he ordered his favourite, ice cream!

Once Swamiji made *misri* (sugar candy) for his friends abroad and told them, 'Among sweets, this is the purest. Since it is continuously cooked, all the impurities are gone.'

Another time, after meditation, Swamiji supervised the cooking and even cooked a vegetable. He showed how spices are ground in India. He took a shallow bowl-shaped stone and squatted on the ground with it in his lap. Then he placed the spices for grinding in that bowl, and taking another smooth stone, ground the spices finely.

Ida Ansell says, 'We would normally place the spices on a plate and use a knife's flat edge to crush them, but we could never get it as fine as Swamiji did.'

Whenever he sat to eat, Swamiji used to keep some small and very spicy chillies on a side of his plate. Once he took a chilli and handing it to Ida said, 'Let me see you eat this up. It will help you.'

Writer Hiranmay Bhattacharya lived abroad for many years and was deeply respectful of Swamiji. In his book *Humourist Vivekananda*, he has meticulously presented some stories of Swamiji's food, eating and cooking. Some of his anecdotes are quoted below.

Omnivorous Sanyasi?

Swamiji was in Memphis, Tennessee's largest city, for around ten days. He was under the care and hospitality of an influential lady. The first day, at breakfast, Miss Gene said, 'Swamiji, I have got some special hickory ham for you. I hope you do not mind eating ham.'

'I am a monk, Miss Gene. Sanyasis should not have any objection to eating anything.' Swamiji was not an overly self-denying sanyasi. He believed that God's children must always be happy. He always ate whatever he received, without any concern for customary taboos. Fish, mutton, pork or anything else that was served, from the West's boiled potatoes and vegetables to Eastern Europe's fare, spiced with chilli oil.

But do we know what Swamiji's favourite food of all times was? He has admitted, 'I believe that it is definitely worth taking rebirth just to once again enjoy our rice, dal, *chorchori*, *shukto* and *mochar ghonto*.' Till his last days he would go to his grandmother's home to eat *mochar ghonto*. He had a few more such havens of culinary delight. He would say, 'Yogen Ma, after I complete all my work today, I will come to your home to eat. Please cook well.'

At 'Mayer BaRi' or Sri Ma's home in Baghbazar, Naren's love for her prawns cooked in *pui shak* was Golap Ma's weakness. In later years she would say, 'Whenever I make prawns with *pui shak* I always remember Naren. He used to love that dish. Smiling from ear to ear he would say, "Golap Ma! (This is scrumptious!) Let me touch your feet!" The joy he gave me was incomparable.'

Swamiji had a deep relationship with spicy masalas! Unless the dish was overflowing with spices, he was not satisfied. And when he cooked himself, the disciples had no choice but to eat it, even if it killed them in the process!

But the process of eating it nearly did kill them. Once Swamiji entered the kitchen, the room would be full of smoke and with eyes and noses continuously streaming, everyone would beseech God's mercy. Swamiji, of course, would be ecstatic with devotion, saying, 'Now God is awakening! All of you, particularly the ladies, can step out and save your souls if you like.'

While cooking, Swamiji would often give a little something in somebody's hand and say, 'Eat it up, it's good for you.' Even if Swamiji had given poison, his devotees would have respectfully obeyed him and eaten it! So, frequently, the one instructed to 'eat it up' would be crying after having the spicy crumbs, while the others would be rolling on the floor with laughter. Swamiji may have simply sprinkled some chilli powder on the devotee's palm! When he sat to eat, Swamiji would always keep that red poison next to him and occasionally, opening his mouth, would sprinkle it on his tongue!

The Chef's Artistry

Swamiji had a wide diversity in his culinary abilities. He was not absorbed just in Bengali food but also combined Eastern and Western tastes to create amazing international recipes. Besides, when it came to spicy masalas, he was a militant! So it would not surprise anyone if the dishes were overpowered by spices. As he himself has written, 'Last night I cooked myself. Saffron, lavender, mace, nutmeg, kebab, sugar, cinnamon, cloves, cardamom, butter, lime juice, onions, raisins, almonds, pepper and rice and dal—altogether it was such a crazy mix that I couldn't eat it myself! There was no asafoetida at home, or it would have been good to add some of that too.' You may well wonder from where he obtained all these ingredients!

Let us listen now to the descriptions of the multi-course French dinners. The dinners are divine affairs. Not just one or two courses, but course after course flows, like poetry, quite comparable to the paeans sung for the Goddess Kali, with a falchion in one hand and ambrosia flowing from the other.

But let us set aside the frills now and get to the real meat of the meal. Hiranmay gives us Swamiji's own description: 'At first, savoury fish or fish roe with some chutney or vegetable (would be served). This was an appetizer—something to stimulate hunger. Next, in the modern-styled dining hall, some fruit would arrive, followed by fish with gravy. The main course would then make an appearance—barbecued steak, served with fresh salad. Wild meats followed, venison or game. Ending on a sweet note, sweetmeats were served and finally ice cream.

'In exclusive restaurants, the plates and cutlery would be replaced with fresh ones at each change of course. With each course, the drinks would also be replaced—sherry, champagne, sometimes with frozen liqueur. After the meal, black coffee would be served, and then tiny glasses of brandy served along with cigars.

'A restaurant would only qualify as fine dining if the spread of drinks matched the spread of food. The amount of money the French spent on a single dinner would quite easily destroy even a moderately wealthy man in our country.'

Once, Swamiji was in California as the guest of a rather conservative family. One morning at the breakfast table, it was discovered that the bottle of cream that was normally left at the doorstep early each morning by the milkman was missing. Everyone wondered what could have happened because the milkman always delivered on time, and it was unimaginable of course that anyone would steal it!

Swamiji listened quietly and then concluded the conversation by admitting that it was he who had picked up the bottle early in the morning and had finished it all! The hosts did not know whether to laugh or cry!

Another time, living with a family in California, he'd had two cups of coffee in the morning. He was offered a third cup. Enticed more by the cream than the coffee itself, Swamiji asked, 'Wouldn't that be a bit too much?' In the end of course he couldn't resist the lure of the cream but said in jest (quoted from the original): '*All right. Woman's business is to tempt man.*'

Reading a news article about a man dying of hunger in Calcutta, Swamiji reportedly told Haripada Mitra, 'Now our country will be ruined!' Someone dying of hunger was unheard of, largely because of our habit of regularly giving a handful of rice to mendicants. 'Other than during famines, this is the first

time I am hearing about someone dying of hunger in Calcutta,'
he said.

In 1892, before leaving for the USA, Swamiji was asked
some questions in Belgaum about his food habits. G.S. Bhate
records that when Swamiji was asked (quoted from the original)
*'whether he was a vegetarian or a meateater, he said that as a man
belonging not (to) the ordinary order of Sannyasins but to the
order of the Paramahansas, he had no option in the matter. (The
Paramahansa, by the rules of that order, was bound to eat whatever
was offered, and in cases where nothing could be offered he had to go
without food).'*

He was also asked whether he had any hesitation in
accepting *bheeksha* (alms) from a non-Hindu. Swamiji replied
that Muslims had several times fed him when he was hungry.

Cooking and Eating in London

In the nineteenth century, most people travelled from India to
the USA via London. But our Swamiji travelled in the opposite
direction, going first to Japan and then entering the US
through Canada, to celebrate and acclaim India and Hinduism
at the Chicago Parliament of Religions. By the time Swamiji
whispered Vedanta's mantra in the ears of the world, captivated
all of America and started to think of heading for England, two
years were over.

Even before he could touch England, however, Swamiji
was in France for a dear friend's wedding. Francis Leggett was
getting married to Betty (Sturges), his friend's sister. Swamiji
was at Paris, the Mecca of all high society, as the bridegroom's
guest for the wedding held on 9 September 1895. Sanyasis do
not normally attend weddings, but this is apparently not true of
Christian priests. We understand that Swami Vivekananda also

ignored the rule and attended several weddings while abroad. He left for England on 10 September, the very next day after the wedding.

In his book *The East and The West*, Swamiji has written a humorous account of his stay at a grand hotel in Paris, often considered 'Heaven on earth!' I cannot resist quoting from it: 'A wealthy friend invited me to Paris. He put me up at a palatial hotel—with royal dining, but alas, no bathing facility! After two consecutive days of staying there I could not take it anymore. I told my friend, "Brother, you can stay here and enjoy the royal treatment, but I will have to leave." It was peak summer and with no bathing room, I was like a panting dog. My friend was both sad and angry and said, "We cannot stay here, let's go find a better hotel." We looked at twelve leading hotels in Paris; none of them had bathing rooms. There were many bathing rooms in the city where one could pay four or five rupees and take a bath whenever needed! My God!' The addresses on Swamiji's letters give away the names of two of the hotels he stayed at: Hotel Continental and Hotel Holland Rue de la Paix.

Back in London, Swamiji at first stayed at the home of Miss Henrietta Muller at Regent Street, Cambridge, and later at Caversham, Reading, at the home of his disciple Edward T. Sturdy.

It was clear from Swamiji's letters that he liked England very much. In October that year, he wrote to Mrs Leggett (quoted from the original): '*The Englishmen here are very friendly. Except a few Anglo-Indians, they do not hate black men at all. I am getting plenty of vegetables cooked, you will be surprised to hear,* à la Indienne *perfectly.*' Going one step further he wrote to Miss MacLeod on 20 October about England, '. . . *this being in a sense my native country . . .*'!

About food and eating Swamiji wrote to Alasinga Perumal from Paris in September (quoted from the original): '*I am surprised you take so seriously the missionaries' nonsense . . . If the people in India want me to keep strictly to my Hindu diet, please tell them to send me a cook and money enough to keep him. This silly bossism without a mite of real help makes me laugh. On the other hand, if the missionaries tell you that I have ever broken the two great vows of the Sannyâsin—chastity and poverty—tell them that they are big liars. Please write to the missionary Hume asking him categorically to write you what misdemeanour he saw in me, or give you the names of his informants, and whether the information was first-hand or not; that will settle the question and expose the whole thing . . .*'

The sanyasi Vivekananda's anger at this repeated attack of falsehoods has been expressed with great force in this letter to Alasinga (quoted from the original): '*I require nobody's help. I have been all my life helping others . . . They cannot raise a few rupees to help the work of the greatest man their country ever produced—Ramakrishna Paramahansa; and they talk nonsense and want to dictate to the man for whom they did nothing, (but) who did everything he could for them! Such is the ungrateful world!*'

After completing his work in England, Swamiji returned on a tedious, ten-day voyage, arriving in New York on 6 December 1895. Two days later, he wrote in a letter, 'The sea was terribly rough, and this is the first time in my life that I was so seasick.'

Swamiji was amused by many incidents about eating and drinking in the USA. Sister Nivedita quotes one such incident: a Chinese American was caught for stealing pork. The American judge believed that the Chinese did not eat pork. When asked, the defendant, speaking in broken English, told the judge, 'Oh but I am American now sir! I drink brandy, I eat pig meat, I eat everything!'

Back to Britain

Swamiji again boarded the White Star Line's *S.S. Germanic* to leave New York for England on 15 April 1896. We have a lot of information about this second trip to England, because Swami Saradananda reached England on 1 April to welcome Swamiji. Another unexpected meeting for Swamiji on this trip was with his brother Mahendranath. The third person present in England was Swamiji's stenographer J.J. Goodwin, but for whose single-minded efforts to record them, many of Swamiji's speeches would have been lost forever.

We are particularly grateful to Mahendranath, whose faithful recording (in a three-volume book) of the intimate details of Swamiji's stay has given us a complete picture of the London chapter. Mahendranath tells us that he arrived in London just a week after Swami Saradananda. In the preface to his book, Mahendranath gives us some upsetting information. Goodwin had taken many of Swamiji's lectures down in shorthand but had not been able to transcribe them all. His desire was to publish Swamiji's discourses and lectures in at least seven volumes, but his unfortunate and untimely demise caused us to lose all those invaluable resources. Goodwin died suddenly in Madras, and his elderly mother, not recognizing the worth of the shorthand notes, threw them all away!

Narendranath was born in 1863, and his brother Mahendranath in 1868. Mahendranath has gifted us almost everything that we know of Swamiji's childhood. When Swamiji gave up the material world at the age of twenty-three, Mahendranath was very young. But the mother and two brothers of the Datta family ensured that communication continued with Swamiji until he boarded the ship for America.

We came to know from the confidential sources of the maharaja of Khetri that, as per Swamiji's wish, the maharaja provided regular financial support to his mother and brothers. Although the letters indicating this were discovered rather late, it does not take away from the fact that they are invaluable.

The subject of our research, however, is not the maharaja's contribution to Swamiji's mission; it is on the other hand, to understand how a culinary chef-sanyasi managed to survive the critical test of starvation and hunger to teach the fine art of cooking biryani and pulao alongside his talks on Vedanta.

Swamiji's second visit to London is special for us, because we have been able to learn a lot about this visit from Mahendranath's book *Swamiji in London*. Swamiji's brother began writing this book in Calcutta in 1925, publishing it a few years later in 1931. Were this book not written, we would have been denied the gift of knowing about this vibrant, warm and loving Vivekananda. In the introduction to the book, Mahendranath writes, 'Swamiji travelled from America to London in 1896. Swami Saradananda had arrived in London, at Sturdy's home in Reading, a few days before that, and I reached there a week later. A young Englishman named J.J. Goodwin who was Swamiji's stenographer also lived with Swamiji.'

It will not be an exaggeration to say that although people of this country have not yet recognized the value of this book, this three-edition treasure trove has given us unparalleled access to Vivekananda's life. Even if we were to set aside Vivekananda the Vedanta teacher, nowhere else have I seen such intimate images of Vivekananda the person.

Swamiji was then thirty-three years old and Mahendranath twenty-seven. The two of them, along with Swami Saradananda, were hosted by various people, chief among them being Miss Henrietta Muller, Mr E.T. Sturdy.

Swamiji was surprised to see his brother in London—he had no idea that the maharaja of Khetri had supported his brother to travel to England. But he lovingly gifted the brother with five pounds and a golden pen and sent one Mr Krishna Menon to drop him back to his place of stay.

Mr Menon took Mahendranath to a coffee shop and with that began Vivekananda's brother's initiation into the Western way of life. In those days, all famous coffee shops in London used only silverware, and the bill for the two of them was nineteen shillings. The rupee was nineteen to the pound, Mahendranath informs us. He tells us that the British had tea at breakfast and coffee in the evenings.

He continues to say that the well-known coffee shops run by French ladies in London served coffee without milk. They added a little mastic (a resin from the mastic tree found in Greece) cognac and very little sugar instead.

We learn that on the way back, they noticed some oysters, lobsters, crabs and shrimps being sold at a roadside store near Victoria station. Mahendranath estimated that the lobsters were twice or thrice the size of Calcutta's, but the crabs were about the same size as the ones on our Puri coast.

Mahendranath informs us that the English do not eat fish heads, nor fish roe. If they accidentally eat the roe, they nearly throw up! Mahendranath, however, certifies that England's roe is tasty and in no way inferior to Calcutta's. His elder brother Vivekananda had cautioned, 'It is inappropriate to judge the food of another person or place.'

In another example of Swamiji's love and affection for his younger brother, the very next day he sent eleven pounds through Menon to buy some clothes for Mahendranath.

Did Londoners also use cow dung cakes for fuel like us in India? Swamiji himself saw cow dung cakes being used to warm the room in Miss Muller's home. It will be news to today's readers that while in Bengal, we make flat cow dung cakes and in other parts of India they are like thick hemispheres, in London they were like tubes—almost nine inches long.

In Western countries, the evening meal is always called dinner. Before we look at some of the memorable dinners at Miss Muller's as narrated by Mahendranath in the third volume of his abundantly descriptive book, it will not be out of context to listen to what our humorous Swamiji had to say about eating and drinking in the Western countries.

Swamiji says, 'They serve themselves huge portions, but eat little. They eat a few spoons and throw the rest away. They eat well, and they work as hard. But look at Indians! How do they survive on so little food? How do they live on half-empty stomachs? And they have neither courage nor perseverance. They are always sad and helpless. . . . They have forgotten that the *mahashakti* (great energy or power, also represented by the Goddess Shakti) resides within them.' Swamiji's large eyes were overflowing with tears at the thought.

Now let us turn to the dinners at the vegetarian Miss Muller's courtyard. The visitors were first served a thick, milky, salted macaroni soup. Newly arrived Saradananda Swami was unaware of how to hold the fork and knife. Unseen by the others, Swamiji nudged his foot and whispered to him in Bengali: 'Hey Sharat! Not like that. Don't hold the fork in your right hand; hold the knife in the right hand and use the fork in the left hand to put the food in your mouth. Don't take such big bites. Take small bites. And don't let your teeth or tongue be visible when you eat. Also, don't cough! Choking or coughing while eating is considered obnoxious. And never sniff while eating!'

Later, an annoyed Swami Saradananda complained, 'Who has ever heard of our Hindu boys drinking milk with salt? I was nauseous at the thought but couldn't throw up. . . . But the milk here is very thick and we get thick vermicelli too. We also get oranges. One day, I will make some sweet clotted cream and enjoy it with oranges!'

There was a tricky situation at breakfast another day. Mahendranath asked for a slice of toast in a very soft and gentle tone. Miss Muller was angry and said, 'Why are you asking like that? We are not cruel people (to deny you food).' Swamiji explained that in India when an elder brother is present, the younger one always expresses his wants softly. Still angry, Miss Muller retorted, 'This is not your India. This is England, where elder brothers and younger brothers are all equal.'

The guests at the breakfast table all had coffee, but Miss Muller poured herself some green tea in a Japanese teacup and began adding milk and sugar to it.

Another day, the breakfast table talk turned to a Jain gentleman, Birchand Gandhi, who was staying at a vegetarian hotel in America. One morning, he noticed that his coffee had some egg mixed in it! 'The attendant was called, who immediately said that egg is not considered non-vegetarian. It is vegetarian.' Swamiji humorously remarked, 'How can you be so orthodox in an alien country? You have to adapt to everything.'

In the context of vegetarianism, the Empire of India Exhibition also opened in Earl's Court during that time. (The **Empire of India Exhibition** took place at Earls Court in 1895. Indian scenery was reproduced and there were displays, which reflected the country's past and present states. The overall theme was clear: modern India was the product of British patience and genius.) Workers from India fried spicy chickpeas, popped rice, puffed rice and made *borfi*s. This group had both Hindus and Muslims. They were happy to find Bengalis in this alien land with whom they could speak their language. These people did not touch water or food touched by the foreigners; nor did they touch meat handled by them. They bought their own goats, which were slaughtered by the Muslims among them and eaten by both Hindus and Muslims.

Even today I enjoy reading Mahendranath's descriptions of the lunches and dinners at various homes in London—still captivating more than a century later. He also tells us that Swamiji often went out for his lunch. Aristocrats and other distinguished people would call on him and he would have his lunch with them, returning after evening tea at 4 p.m.

The description of tea at home is also interesting. The elderly housekeeper would bring tea in a teapot along with some raw milk in a small jug, some very thin slices of buttered bread and sugar lumps. The English, unlike us, take their tea very light. Sailors drink strong tea, which is called sailor's tea as a result. The English in those days never boiled the milk but had it raw.

Mahendra Babu has noticed that the milk is salty, because the cows are fed a lot of salt. There is no concept of what we in Bengal call the cream of the milk. Because they never boil their milk, they don't know what cream is. That is why there is no English word for the cream that settles on the top of a boiling pot of milk. The sugar is beet, i.e., derived from the beetroot plant. They are small, thin squares and placed one on top of the other, three of them form a cube. Nothing is ever touched by hand. A pair of sugar tongs made of German silver or similar material is used to lift lumps of sugar and then dropped in the teacup as required.

We also understand that both Sturdy and Miss Muller were pure vegetarians. Fish and meat were strictly forbidden in the house. The American Mr Fox, who was a non-vegetarian, occasionally went out for his meals.

Goodwin, although a devout follower of Swamiji, sometimes asked difficult questions in humour. One day, when Sturdy and Miss Mueller were out, a fish and cauliflower curry was made. Goodwin himself was a vegetarian by then. Swamiji was pacing up and down and Goodwin asked him, 'You always lecture people on giving up meat. Why then did you have the fish?' Swamiji laughed and responded, 'Oh that old lady had cooked it. If I hadn't, it would have been thrown in the drain. So I threw it in my stomach instead; what's the problem with that?' He followed it up with a Sanskrit sloka: 'I never eat; the body is the receptacle and everything is offered up inside.'

Although a devotee, Goodwin could not be deterred by a Sanskrit sloka and did not give up that easily.

'Why do you eat fish?'

To annoy him some more, Swamiji said,

'Bipadi dhairya kshama chabhadaye tatha.'

Which means, 'Stay calm in times of misfortune, be forgiving when you prosper and advance and don't harbour thoughts of revenge.'

At around 4 p.m. on another evening, Swamiji returned home and sat down to tea. Instead of having his usual tea with milk however, he sliced a lime in half and squeezed one half into his teacup, added a little sugar and savoured it slowly. He said, 'I don't enjoy tea any more and tea with milk is best avoided; it creates a lot of problems for the stomach. The Americans enjoy their tea with lime and this is good.' Then he turned towards Swami Saradananda and said, 'These Americans overdo everything. They drink their tea with lemon and a chunk of ice. They drink a lot of iced tea in the summer. They eat just a little but serve themselves a huge amount. Everything they do is strange. So during winter they use steam

pipes to warm up their homes but add a whole lot of ice to
their drinking water!'

On another day, Desai, a newly arrived young Gujarati boy,
asked Swamiji about Hatha yoga and Raja yoga. His question
was, why was Swamiji only concerned with Raja yoga? Why
didn't he ever say something about Hatha yoga? Swamiji's reply
is memorable: 'Hatha yoga requires timely food, covering oneself
with blankets . . . Those who have access to good food . . . who
can afford the time to indulge in looking after their body, only
they can practise Hatha yoga.' According to Swamiji, Hatha
yoga does not develop the mind—only the body. For the mind,
Raja yoga is the only way forward.

Swamiji was concerned about providing appropriate food
for newcomers Mahendranath and Saradananda, but staying as
guests in someone else's home, it was not always possible to
obtain what one wanted to eat. He told Mahim one day, 'You
will lose your appetite if you have the same food daily. Tell the
Aunt (cook) to sometimes make a poached egg or an omelette
for you.'

Swamiji speaks of the difference between poached eggs
and omelettes. To poach an egg, you make a small hole in the
pointed end of the egg and pour its contents in a pan of boiling
water, while fluffing up and frying the egg makes an omelette,
with some shredded watercress adding flavour.

A lot has been written about mutton recipes used abroad,
but it is not quite clear whether the writer is Swamiji or
Mahendranath. 'After removing the bones from the mutton, the
flesh is cubed and dropped in a pan of hot water. When it is
cooked well, some curry powder is sprinkled on it and a little
flour is added to thicken the soup. Salt is then added as per taste.'

Swamiji and Goodwin would joke endlessly on the matter
of food. Goodwin would tease poor Saradananda saying, 'You

cooky Swami, you don't meditate; you simply close your eyes and think about food, wondering when the food bell will ring!'

We have found a lot of information about breakfast, lunch and dinner abroad, but it is necessary to also add something about the fruits. Did Vivekananda, who loved green chillies, consider it a fruit? His particular weakness for chillies is still a matter of discussion among today's chefs. Mahendranath's book tells us that Swamiji was undeterred in his quest to find chillies in London too, but at the rate of one shilling per chilli they were expensive. Sometimes Swamiji's disciple Krishna Menon would buy him three green chillies from the shop of William Whitely, the famous fruit seller of London. We hear that the chillies were called cayenne peppers—no one knew what the word 'chilli' meant.

Mahendranath informs us that a messenger arrived daily from William Whiteley's shop with a paper bag containing a variety of fruits for Swamiji. Later, it became known that this mysterious sender was Miss Josephine MacLeod. Perhaps because she had heard of Swamiji's love for fruits, Miss MacLeod had deposited some money with William Whiteley's and asked them to send some fruits across every day for Swamiji. Mahendranath writes, 'The fresh fruits would reach around three weeks before they became available in the market.'

The pineapple was not easily available in London those days, and at almost a guinea a fruit, it was quite expensive too. Yet, Swamiji would regularly receive this fruit at home.

Mahendranath writes, 'Swamiji was very happy to see this rare pineapple at home. An excited Goodwin quickly fetched a knife and tried to peel the pineapple but didn't know where to start . . . Swamiji then took the knife from him and slowly started peeling it himself . . . They were cut into small cubes and Goodwin served everyone in little plates with a sprinkling of powdered sugar on them. He was very happy to eat the pineapple and had no idea that this fruit was available in India.'

Swamiji then told everyone that the pineapple was a Chinese fruit, brought by either the Portuguese or the Dutch from China. It was originally called 'ananas' but later the name was distorted to 'anaras' (the Bengali word for pineapple). Swamiji continued, 'India's soil is so fertile that many foreign fruits grow in profusion.'

Mahendranath has also written about the English cherry. When the cherry had just made an appearance in the London markets, two packets were bought at a penny each. Goodwin claimed, 'The English cherry is the tastiest in the world. Enjoy, enjoy!' We discovered that in some parts of the Himalayas, the cherry is called 'the hill jujube', and in Kashmir it is called 'gilaas'.

And now let us turn to the summer fruit—grapes. One afternoon at around 3.30 p.m., Swamiji told his brother, 'There are some grapes in the glass bowl—new grapes of the season. Go and eat some. Grapes help clear your blood.' And he himself got up to get the grapes for his younger brother. Mahendranath surmises Swamiji 'was in a happy mood that day'.

At the end of our discussion on fruits, let us look at the mango—the king of fruits. On another summer day, a box of mangoes arrived from India for Miss Muller. An enthused Swamiji told Goodwin, 'Go get some ice and soak the mangoes—the taste will improve.' The ice duly arrived from a fishmonger's and the mangoes were chilled and then sliced. The American gentleman Mr Fox did not know how to eat it. Swamiji affectionately advised him, 'Scoop it up with a spoon.' The ice-cold mangoes tasted very good, writes Mahendranath. Swamiji then began narrating interesting stories about different varieties of mangoes in various parts of India.

Besides *Vivekananda in London,* Mahendranath's other books also contain descriptions of fruit shops abroad. 'In London, there once was a fruit seller named McDonald. He kept his shop open for just long enough to get sufficient money to run his life. Then he closed shop and studied.' He was dressed in a vest, always barefoot. Once the police took him away saying he was 'half-naked'. McDonald asked the magistrate, 'What is the need for a hat? For shoes?' The magistrate ordered his release. Mahendranath had become very friendly with this fruit seller. He once asked McDonald, 'What do you eat?' McDonald replied, 'Almonds, walnuts, dates and water.' Built like an ox, McDonald had a large collection of books at his home. He would often attend the classes conducted by the Ramakrishna Mission sanyasis.

We have spoken about the lunches and dinners of the English. Now let us look at how Swamiji tried to popularize Indian cuisine abroad. Mahendranath gives us some gems here too. It is important to quote some excerpts so that the story of Swamiji's London trip is complete.

Mahendranath writes in his inimitable style about how, for a change of taste from the monotonous food, Swamiji once told him, 'Come let's go to the kitchen and cook ourselves something—a spicy *aloo chorchori* or *aloo dum.*' But when Mahendranath wanted to join him he said, 'No, you stay here. People here do not approve of others entering their kitchen.'

'Then,' says Mahendranath, 'he went ahead and cooked a delicious potato *chorchori* with butter and pepper and came back. Tasting just a little of that *chorchori* made me come alive again. We realized then, how much we love and cherish the food of our own country.'

There have also been various conversations around the chapatti of India and the bread of England. Indophile Sturdy once told everyone after breakfast, 'When I was in India, I used to eat chapattis. It is made with fresh flour and not fermented. At first I found it difficult to digest but in a day or two I was fine. I realized that unlike the loaf, the chapatti is very nutritious . . . If it is introduced in England, it will improve the health of many.'

On another day, some white peas were cooked in a Dutch oven 'with a little curry powder and salt, garnished with butter' and served with rice. Goodwin loved the peas, and said, 'I can live on something like this all my life.'

At the London dining table, the conversation sometimes veered to the history of various foods at various times in the world. One day Swamiji spoke of the Roman Emperor Vitellius (15–69 AD). Referring to the historian Edward Gibbon's work, he said that throughout his reign, all the emperor did was to eat. Many birds and animals were sent to Rome from various parts of the world. The starling was sent from far away Assam and peacocks from other parts of India. The Emperor apparently boiled the starling's head with milk and clarified butter and ate it! Stunning his listeners, Swamiji also said that the Siberian white fox was also imported to Rome because the emperor loved to eat its liver.

While staying in London, Swamiji did not hesitate to sometimes speak about his personal struggle too. One day after breakfast, he said to Swami Saradananda, 'I have tried all paths. Tried teaching, tried law, but I found all routes blocked. Finally, I found this path—it opened up for me and I found success here.'

Once Swamiji jokingly said about his teachings, 'I am pushing Vedanta into the very bones of the sahebs' ('Saheb' is the term used in India for an Anglo-Saxon gentleman). One afternoon, Swamiji told his dear disciple John Fox, 'Oh! We can't have the same old monotonous food every day. Come, let us go to a hotel and eat.' The two of them left the house thereafter.

Sitting in far away London, Swamiji worried about the lifespan of his beloved countrymen. One day at breakfast he asked Saradananda, 'Why do our people die so young? Whoever I enquire about I hear has passed away. Are we going to become extinct?' In America and England people have long lives. 'But in India they die too soon. Their food is wretched; it is necessary to change their eating habits . . . The people of India are sluggish—as if they are sitting all day. I walked around all the villages of India, preaching Vedanta in case they absorbed it, but instead of doing that they actually began to ridicule me! I was very upset.'

There were sometimes wide-ranging discussions about food. Once Swamiji said that cooking onions with mutton is a very old tradition. Onion was called 'palandu' because it was cooked with mutton, which was called 'pal'. Fried onions are difficult to digest and may cause stomach disorders, but cooked onions are very useful and serve as an antidote to the constipating nature of mutton by clearing the bowels. That is why onions have always been used in cooking meats in all countries.

One evening Swamiji asked his younger brother, 'Where did you go this evening?'

'I went to have dinner at Mrs Turner's home. She can really cook well.'

This lady had mastered a few Indian dishes, which is why several Indians visited her from time to time. It was like a homely Indian hotel.

'What did she cook?'

'Ruti, a mutton curry, a few other vegetables, a mint chutney and rice payesh.'

Swamiji laughed and said, 'Why doesn't she come here and cook one day? I will get to eat something good and refresh my palate.'

'She is a householder; not a paid cook. Why would she come and cook here in someone else's home?'

Swamiji smiled and said, 'Ok, then maybe I will go and eat at her home one day.' But sadly, says Mahendranath, 'No one actually remembered to visit Mrs Turner's home for a meal again.'

We know that the famous people of London often called on Swamiji and took him to their palatial homes for lunch. ICS Behari Lal Gupta (1849–1919) went abroad for higher studies in 1868. He visited with his wife and listened to Swamiji's lecture. Swamiji later spoke personally with them and was all praise for Mrs Gupta. This lady's special talent was that she would curdle the milk and make *pantua* and other Bengali sweets from scratch by herself and feed all her visitors. Later, Mahendranath was also very happy to meet her at her home.

In order to meet special people, there had to be some preparation too. Mahim Babu tells us that Swamiji 'would shave himself daily, and whenever he was visiting someone's home in the evening, he would shave again and wash up, comb his hair, change his collar shirt and only then leave. He would also pay attention to whether his shoes were polished or not'. We also learn that the cost of polishing one's shoes on the road was two pennies at the time.

Not content with just being a guest for meals at others' homes, Swamiji also lost no opportunity to cook Indian food himself. He arranged to get various condiments from home like pickles, *aam tel*, dal, *boRi*, etc. Swamiji always kept his favourite ingredients with him. Whenever he felt like cooking, he used these to cook some vegetables and serve Goodwin too.

Goodwin could not bear the smell of asafoetida. He pronounced the Bengali names of spices with an English accent, and when he tasted the mango pickle, he made a terrible face and said, '*What nasty stuff!*'

We are still enthralled by our chef Swamiji's various endeavours in London. Mahim Babu described these events thirty years after they happened, in 1925, naming the chapter '*Aloo kochuri and Jhal Chorchori*'.

The picture he draws of our connoisseur Swamiji is unforgettable! 'Once Swamiji went to the basement kitchen, and melting butter to get some ghee, made some excellent *kochuri* and a very nice and spicy *aloo chorchori*. He brought it up to the dining room and the three of us began to eat. There was no one else in the house at the time. While eating, Swami Saradananda suddenly said, "Oh! Keep some of this for Miss Cameron, otherwise she will scold us when she comes back in the evening."'

The maid in the house was called the 'housekeeper'. English housekeepers worked very hard; they could work equal to almost three or four maids of India.

'Miss Cameron was around forty-five years old and a friend of Mrs Sturdy. She was absent from home that day but returned at around four the next evening. As soon as she entered the house, she asked us, "Tell me, what have you cooked? You are always cooking nice things for yourself and not keeping anything for me." She teased Swami Saradananda, shaking her head and saying, "You cooky Swami, you keep eating and putting on weight and never save anything for me," and so on.'

Swami Saradananda turned to Mahendranath and said, 'Go, bring the *kochuri* from the upstairs room!' Mahendranath swiftly brought the two *kochuris* and *aloor chorchori* kept for her in a saucer. Miss Cameron asked, 'What should we eat this with, sugar or salt?' Starting to eat it with sugar, she did not find it palatable.

'Swami Saradananda said, "Why don't you try it with salt?" Then, putting a spoonful of the *aloo chorchori* to her mouth, Miss Cameron screamed out, "Oh what a lethal dish! They have cooked black pepper with cayenne pepper!" With that she began slapping her face with both hands and started to curse Swami Saradananda, "Oh! This is poison!"'

Once Goodwin and Miss Cameron were discussing heaven. Goodwin asked her, 'What would you consider heaven to be?' Miss Cameron's response was, 'A lot of eating and drinking and no hard work at all.'

'What will you drink in heaven?'

'Of course, champagne!'

Swamiji was an expert at blending conversations of history and economics along with food and drink, as we see from Mahendranath's beautifully written memoirs. Swamiji has narrated the story of our own home-grown British soldiers' high-mindedness. When the British were once under siege in Madras, rations were declining, and capture—possibly death— was imminent. The dutiful soldiers began to give their own share of rice to the British, keeping only the drained-out starch for themselves. The fort, along with the lives of the British, was ultimately saved. But in spite of this, they expressed no gratitude! Swamiji's observation was, 'Your country has no gratitude. You are a selfish and ungrateful lot. That is why no one in the world trusts you.'

Besides history, Swamiji has, during various speeches, given useful information about food too. Mahim Babu his given us some examples.

Swamiji said, 'During meditation, you should not eat anything which excites the body and mind. Rice, chapatti, milk, bananas, etc., are best. It is best not to eat fish or meat, though fasting is not necessary. Milk, chapatti, fruits, butter, etc., can be had three, four or even five times. It is good to eat light and not overfill oneself. Be careful to ensure that there is no flatulence and there is no indolence in the body.'

Continuing to speak about eating meat, Swamiji has said that the lion eats meat and is always restless; his strength is overpowering. The elephant on the other hand, eats vegetables and 'is always calm and stationary. It is best to not eat meat while meditating because the mind is restless and it becomes difficult to focus'.

Knowing that the Western world gave a lot of importance to etiquette and conduct in the home, Swamiji at various times advised his brother Mahendranath on this matter.

One morning in the month of April or May, it was still a little chilly. Unused to the cold, Mahim sat on a chair with his hands in his pockets to keep them warm. The elderly Miss Muller entered the room then and greeted him. Swamiji later explained to Mahim, 'When you sit in a room, particularly where there are ladies present, never keep your hands inside your trouser pockets—that is considered bad manners. Place your hands on your knees or elsewhere; don't cross your arms either. Miss Muller is particular, so when she comes into the room, always stand up, wish her and ask her a few things like how she is, etc., so that she is not offended.'

Swamiji was also experienced in table manners and often showed his brother and *gurubhai* Saradananda how to handle themselves. 'Hold the knife in your right hand and use the fork in your left hand to pierce the food and place it in your mouth. But if you are using a spoon, then that is to be held in the right hand. It is discourteous to ask for a second helping. It is to be indicated by the way the fork and knife are placed on the plate.

If the points of the knife and fork meet each other (i.e., if the knife and fork are placed parallel to the edge of the table in the centre of the plate), then it is understood that more food is needed to be served, while if the knife and fork are placed parallel to each other in the centre of the plate, then you know that the eating is done and nothing more is required.' Since they do not know these norms, our youngsters who go there face a lot of problems initially.

Swamiji has described the custom of English tea—with toast and butter—to perfection. 'There is a special skill in slicing the bread at teatime in England. First the two ends of the bread are sliced off and thrown away. Then, using a sharp knife, the rest of the bread is sliced very thin, with such precision that it is a joy to watch. The cut slices look like pieces of pasteboard. After all the slices are cut, they are gathered together and placed like the original, uncut loaf. The English ladies are experts at slicing the bread like this.'

One morning after breakfast, the tea-lover Swamiji sat chatting with everyone about various incidents from his life, in the context of tea. He spoke about the tea, which Sri Ramakrishna's disciples had made with burnt straw after Thakur's demise at the Kashipur bungalow.

When we speak of Swamiji's eating and drinking, the topic of his health also comes up. We have heard about Swamiji's first heart attack in London through Mahendranath's writing. While travelling in Cairo, Josephine MacLeod has written that Swamiji had another heart attack. This is why Swamiji was anxious to return to India immediately and surprised everyone with his unexpected arrival at Belur *Math*. From Josephine's use of the word 'another', we know that Swamiji must have already had a first heart attack, and Mahendranath's book confirms it.

Besides Mahendranath, Swamiji's disciple, the Harvard graduate John Fox was also in London at the time. He met Swamiji in Harvard and New York and then met him again in London in June–July 1896. He was in London to study architecture. One day after lunch, Swamiji was sitting and meditating in his armchair, while Fox and Mahendranath were also sitting in front of him. 'Suddenly Swamiji's face was twisted with pain. After a while he took a deep breath and said (quoted from original), '*See Fox, my heart almost failed. My father died of this ailment. The pain in my heart was unbearable. It's a family disease.*' Mahendranath was very disturbed by all this, but he did not say anything. We do know, however, that later in Belur Swamiji had the same attack again.

Beyond the Ocean

There are many scattered descriptions of Swamiji's travels in America, of which the most reliable is Sister Gargi's. (A leading literary figure of the Ramakrishna–Vivekananda movement. Born Marie Louise Burke, she is known for her widely read and discussed six-volume work, *Swami Vivekananda in the West: New Discoveries*.)

This American writer's guru Swami Ashokananda also conducted detailed research and discovered new information on Swamiji in later years. Of this, the most delightful experience was his meeting and conversation with Mrs Alice Hansbrough. The famous writer Swami Chetanananda has blessed us by translating this into Bengali too. I am very happy to be able to present some passages from this memoir, *Bahurupe Swami Vivekananda* (*Swami Vivekananda in Many Forms*). Interested readers can enjoy this entire book in Bengali. With deep

respects to Swami Chetanananda, I am presenting just a few
excerpts from his book.

*One bright Sunday morning in March 1941, Swami
Ashokananda invited Mrs Alice M. Hansbrough to drive home
with him from his lecture at the Century Club in San Francisco.
On the way, driving by a roundabout route over San Francisco's
many hills to enjoy a sun made welcome by weeks of rain, the
swami asked Mrs Hansbrough if she could not give an account
of her contacts with Swami Vivekananda during his visit to
California in the winter of 1899 and 1900. Mrs Hansbrough
had met Swamiji in Los Angeles a few days after his arrival
there, and from the day of the meeting, had become a faithful
follower.*

*Mrs Hansbrough readily agreed to give whatever recollections
Swami Ashokananda desired. The swami evidently had already
given considerable thought to the proposal, and ways and means were
discussed. It was arranged that he should go to Mrs Hansbrough's
home and that, through questions, he would suggest to her a direction
of conversation. (The conversations would be) recorded by Mr A.T.
Clifton (later Swami Chidrupananda).*

Monday Evening, 3 March 1941

*Swami Ashokananda arrived at Mrs Hansbrough's home a little
after eight o'clock in the evening. She was living with her daughter,
Mrs Paul Cohn, at 451 Avila Street, near the broad Marina
parkway on San Francisco Bay. As the swami walked to the door
of the handsome Spanish-style residence, he caught a glimpse of Mrs
Hansbrough reading beside the fire in the living room. In a moment
she had greeted the swami at the door and escorted him to a seat
before the fire.*

Mrs Hansbrough was now well on in years [seventy-five years old], but still was blessed with a keen intelligence and a ready humour, which must surely have endeared her to Swamiji. She was slight and below medium height, dignified and unvaryingly good natured in her manner, and possessed of a natural peacefulness which communicated itself to others. Her memory was clear and her conversation therefore filled with interesting details.

Swami Ashokananda: 'How did you first hear about him?'

'I first learned of Swamiji in the spring of 1897 at a lecture in San Francisco about three years before he came to California . . .'

On the way to Alaska, Mrs Hansbrough read Swamiji's book, *Raja Yoga*.

Mrs Hansbrough: 'Yes, I came through San Francisco on the way, and arrived in Los Angeles on 23 November 1899. Swamiji had been in Los Angeles only a few days, I later learned.'

Swami Ashokananda: 'How did you first happen to meet him?'

Mrs Hansbrough: 'Well, perhaps you would like to hear first what circumstances brought him to the West Coast! Swamiji at the time was in Ridgley, close to New York. The brother of Miss Josephine MacLeod at whose home Swamiji had been staying in New York, had been ill in Arizona with tuberculosis for some time. By the time November came, Mr MacLeod was not expected to live; and the wife of his business partner, a Mr Blodgett, wired Miss MacLeod to come west to see him, which she did. The brother died on 2 November 1899, however, and Miss MacLeod stayed on in Los Angeles, at Mrs Blodgett's house at 921, West 21st Street, where Swamiji later came.'

Swami Ashokananda: 'Can you get a photograph of the house?'

Mrs Hansbrough: 'I might be able to. Well, when Miss MacLeod first entered her brother's bedroom at Mrs Blodgett's house, the first thing she saw was a full-page newspaper picture of Swamiji—you know that one that you have in your office in the Berkeley Temple, where he stands partly turned to the left—which Mrs Blodgett had taken from a Chicago paper and had framed. It hung above her brother's bed.

"'Where did you get that?' Miss MacLeod exclaimed. Mrs Blodgett told her she had heard Swami Vivekananda speak in Chicago and had cut the picture out of one of the papers at the time. "Well, Swami Vivekananda is our guest now in New York!" Miss MacLeod said. (Later, Swamiji came to Los Angeles at Mrs Blodgett's invitation.)

'It was on December 8, 1899 that my sister Helen came home that evening and said: "Who do you think is going to speak in Los Angeles tonight? Swami Vivekananda!" All during the two years I had been reading his books in Alaska I had never expected to see him. Well, we rushed through dinner, made up a party, and went in.'

'How was Swamiji dressed?' Swami Ashokananda asked.

'He wore a yellow robe and turban.'

'And how did he look?'

'His voice I should say was baritone—and it was the most musical voice I have ever heard. At the end of the lecture he closed with that chant, ("Chidananda rupam Shivoham, Shivoham") "I am Existence Absolute, Knowledge Absolute, Bliss Absolute." Everyone was enchanted with his talk.

'When it was over, the rest of our party went up on the platform where a number of people had collected to speak to Swamiji. I sought out Professor Baumgardt, however, to find out when and where

Swamiji was going to lecture again. When I asked him he inquired, "Are you interested in the swami's teachings?" I told him I had been studying them for two years, and he said, "Well, I will introduce you to the swami's hostess." He introduced me to Miss MacLeod, who, when I told her I had been studying Swamiji's works for so long, asked if I wouldn't like to go to call on him. Of course I said I would be delighted, and so it was arranged . . .

'He (Swamiji) either phoned or wrote me whenever he wanted to leave any place. For instance, later in San Francisco he was the guest of some physician and had expected to stay for some time. But the very day he went to the doctor's home he either phoned or wrote me—I forget now, which he did—to come for him. When I arrived, his hostess came in, introduced herself, and then withdrew again.'

'Was Miss MacLeod present at (your) first meeting (with Swamiji)?' Swami Ashokananda inquired.

'She was there at first,' Mrs Hansbrough said, 'but she went out after a few minutes.'

'And how did you feel about Swamiji when you met him?'

'I can only describe myself as enchanted by him,' Mrs Hansbrough answered.

'And what did he talk about with you at this first meeting?'

'The conversation was only general. He was rather shy and reserved in manner, as I remember. He said that if we cared to arrange a class, he would be glad to address the group.

'Naturally, with such an offer, we eagerly went about getting a class together, and the first meeting was in the Blanchard Building, 19 December. There were three meetings over a period of a week [December 19, 21, and 22] in this first series of classes . . .'

'And when was it that you asked him to visit you?'

'I think it was at Mrs Blodgett's home, once when Helen and I were there together.' Mrs Hansbrough smiled. 'Sometime before—as a matter of fact, before we had even met Swamiji, though it was after his second lecture—I one day said to my sisters, "Do you know, I think Swami Vivekananda wants to come to visit us." My sisters thought I was crazy. However, I defended my thought by pointing out that the swami was not well and that he might find our home restful. We were then living [at 309 Monterey Road] in Lincoln Park, which is now called South Pasadena, in a rented house.'

'Of course we know that Swamiji was not well, but how did he look at that time?'

'When he declined my invitation to visit us, he was very gracious. I had explained that our home was very unpretentious, but that we would be very happy to have him with us. He smiled and said, "I do not need luxury," and explained that he was comfortably situated at Mrs Blodgett's.

'Later on [in late December] I asked him to come for Sunday dinner [probably on Christmas Eve]. He readily accepted and asked me to invite Miss MacLeod also. When I asked Miss MacLeod, she wouldn't believe Swamiji had accepted my invitation. She herself went to ask him about it, and he told her, "Yes, and you are to come too."

'It was about an hour's ride on the electric train for them to reach our house. After speaking to each of us as he came in, Swamiji turned and walked into the living room. . . .Then he turned and spoke, answering again the question I had asked him at Mrs Blodgett's: "Yes," he said, "I will come to visit you!"

'Then he wanted to come right away, and he soon did. He had but one trunk, but he had many clothes, for he was always well dressed when he went out or met strangers. At home he cared little for his dress; he was most casual about it.

. . .

'Swamiji brought the matter up again himself one morning after breakfast, when he and I were sitting alone at the table. "Well, when are you going to San Francisco?" he asked.

'Not long afterward a letter came from Dr B. Fay Mills of the Unitarian Church in Oakland, inviting Swamiji to go there. So I said to Swamiji, "Well, I needn't go now." However, Swamiji wanted to give his first lecture independently . ... (i.e. not under the aegis of the Unitarian Church or any other body).'

'Tell me now,' Swami Ashokananda began, 'how long Swamiji stayed at your home in Los Angeles.'

'It must have been all of four weeks,' Mrs Hansbrough replied. 'He came in late January 1900 and it was on 21 February when he left to come to San Francisco.'

'How long would these conversations last in the evening? About what time would Swamiji retire?'

'He would talk as long as we wanted him to,' Mrs Hansbrough said, 'though actually it was never later than around ten or eleven o'clock.'

'And did he have a room to himself in your house?'

'Oh yes.'

'Well, now, let us see how he spent his day,' the swami said. 'At what time would he come down from his room? What time would he take breakfast?'

'He usually came down about seven o'clock. There was a bathroom on the second floor where his room was, and I presume he would bathe in the morning, but he didn't comb his hair.'

'He didn't!' Swami Ashokananda exclaimed.

Mrs Hansbrough smiled. 'No,' she replied. 'Though he was very careful about his dress when he went out, he was very careless about it at home.

'. . . He would come down about seven in the morning, in his bathrobe and slippers and his long black hair not yet combed.

He would have some kind of undergarment under his robe, which showed a bit at the neck. I remember that his robe had seen many winters. It was a black and white tweed of some kind, probably with a herringbone pattern in it, and with a cord around the waist.

'When Swamiji first came to Los Angeles, his hair had grown long, and it was beautifully wavy. In fact it was so beautiful, and it set off his features so well, that we would not let him cut it again.'

'What time would you have breakfast?'

'Breakfast would be at about seven thirty, in order to accommodate Helen, who was working, and Ralph, who had to get to school. Swamiji would pass the half hour walking outside.'

'In his bathrobe?'

'Yes. You see, at that time that part of town was not very closely built up. There were no houses across the street and the neighbours on either side were separated from our house by trees and shrubs. Swamiji would walk in the garden behind the house, or along the driveway at one side, and no one could see him there.'

'And what would he usually take for breakfast?'

'He always had fruit, usually an orange or grapefruit, and he liked poached eggs. He would have toast, and coffee usually.'

'Did he like his coffee with cream?'

'Yes, he took cream and I think he took sugar also.'

'And how big a breakfast would he eat?'

'Swamiji was a moderate eater. Usually he took two eggs, two pieces of toast, and two cups of coffee. Once I offered him a third cup of coffee. At first he declined, but when I urged him he finally yielded and said: "All right. Woman's business is to tempt man."

'Breakfast would usually last about an hour, for we never hurried. Ralph had to be at school at eight-thirty, and Helen would leave for work, but the rest of us were not occupied. After breakfast Swamiji would stroll in the garden again or browse through the library.'

'What would Swamiji wear to the meetings? Would he wear his robe?'

'No, he wore the black garment we see in several pictures of him, something like a clerical frock, but looser. Sometimes if it was not too warm he would wear his overcoat over this. He would take his gerua (saffron) robe and turban in a suitcase, and put them on when he arrived at the meeting place.'

'Was he a heavy smoker?'

'No. He would smoke after breakfast, lunch and dinner, but never to excess.

'Sometime before he left for San Francisco he said one day, "I always leave something wherever I go. I am going to leave this pipe when I go to San Francisco." He left it on the mantelpiece in the living room, and we kept it there for a long time as an ornament.'

After a minute or two Swami Ashokananda returned to the routine of Swamiji's day. 'Now, what would he do after lunch? Would he go to his room for rest?' he asked.

'No, he very rarely went to his room after lunch. He would usually recline on the couch in the living room and read there, or talk, or do some such thing.'

'It was probably during an after-lunch conversation when he was walking up and down the living room that Swamiji told us: "The master said he would come again in about two hundred years—and I will come with him. When a master comes," he said, "he brings his own people."

'Was he at all susceptible to heat or cold?'

'Cold did not bother him, but he was sensitive to heat. We always had a fire in the grate after dinner in the evening, and once when it had gone out, he exclaimed, "Praise the Lord, that fire's out!"'

'Did you ever have guests for meals?'

'Yes, often there would be luncheon guests. We would go to class or lecture in the morning, and Swamiji would ask some to come for lunch afterward. Mrs Leggett and Miss MacLeod especially were frequent luncheon guests. Miss MacLeod was also a houseguest for a few days. She asked Helen one day, "Can you put me up for a few days?"'

Swami Ashokananda said. 'Tell me about the evening meal. What time would you sit down to dinner?'

'Dinner would be about six-thirty. We would usually have soup, and either fish or meat, vegetables and dessert—pie, perhaps, which Swamiji sometimes liked, or something else. Usually he did not take coffee in the evening.

'It is Lent now, and this reminds me of one evening when Swamiji was walking up and down in the dining room while the table was being set for dinner. We always had a plate of spring fruit on the table, and on this evening there were some guavas among the others. We were speaking of Lent and the custom of giving up some favourite food or pleasure during the forty days. Swamiji said that a similar custom existed in India, which was always observed by the monks. "All but the wicked fellows like me renounce something," he said. "Now I, for example, will renounce these guavas!" We took the hint and did not have guavas anymore after that!

'When the evening meal was over, instead of going into the living room we would clear the dining room table and sit there, where we could light a fire in the open grate. Some would sit at the table, others would sit in easy chairs. We had an easy chair for Swamiji, which was large enough for him to sit cross-legged in, which he used to do. He usually wore either what you would call a dinner jacket or smoking jacket or his robe.

'At another time, Swamiji had prepared some dish for Lalita to try. When he asked her whether she liked it she said that she did. After a moment's pause, Swamiji inquired, "Was it true, or just for friendship's sake?" Then Lalita confessed, "I am afraid it was for friendship's sake."'

'Tell me,' Swami Ashokananda asked, 'did Swamiji ever use slang?'

'. . . Regarding missionaries, he was once speaking of their antagonism toward him, and he told of a dinner to which he had been invited in Detroit. For some reason he suspected that his coffee had been poisoned. He was debating whether or not he should drink it, when Sri Ramakrishna (appeared at) his side, and said, "Do not drink—it is poisoned." He always spoke of his master as "Atmaram". Whenever there were difficulties he would say, "Well, if things do not go well, we will wake up Atmaram."

'Mrs Allan has told me of another occasion when Bransby had been to see Swamiji while he was in Alameda. When he returned, he said, "How do you think I found the great man? Sitting on the floor, eating peanuts!"'

'Do you think that when Swamiji came to San Francisco he felt as free as he did in your home?'

'Not while he was in the Home of Truth. This was natural, for quite a number of people were living there and he could not feel as free or at home as he had in our house. After some time there he told me one day, "I must get out of here." It was then that Mrs Aspinall and I took the apartment on Turk Street, and Swamiji came.'

There was some conversation about the attendance at the swami's lecture that morning, and this led the swami to ask if Swami Vivekananda's lectures in San Francisco were well attended.

'His Sunday morning audience usually ran from five to six hundred people,' Mrs Hansbrough said. 'At evening lectures there were not so many, but usually he did not lecture in the evening on Sunday.'

'And classes?' the swami asked.

'Class attendance averaged from one hundred fifty to two hundred—which was not bad, considering that there was a charge of fifty cents for each class. That is, the charge was a dollar and a half *for a series of three. The lectures were free. We followed the custom of the day.'*

'Did Swamiji talk in a loud tone, or quietly?'

'No, he talked in a low tone of voice,' Mrs Hansbrough said. 'Even in private conversation he was always a calm man, except when he was giving someone a dressing down. (This he never did to Helen or Carrie.) The only time I ever saw him get excited was when the missionary woman called him a liar. . . .

'Swamiji liked to prepare one meal of the day himself, at our home in Lincoln Park, and he often helped with meals. He cooked curries, and especially chapattis (flathread, same as ruti), of which Ralph and Dorothy used to be very fond. He liked the way I cooked rice—in fact, he told me I was the only woman in America who knew how to cook it! In the Turk Street flat he often cooked pulao, that rich dessert made with [rice and ghee]. Sometimes he would cook breakfast; he used to like potatoes cooked in butter with a little curry powder.

'Several of the ingredients he used had to be ground, and since he did not like to stand beside a table, he would sit cross-legged on the floor with a wooden butter bowl on the floor in front of him. One day during this ceremony we were talking about his health. Someone suggested that he had a weak heart. "There is nothing wrong with your heart," I told him. "If you mean that," he answered, "I have the heart of a lion!"'

'And how did he spend his day while he was in San Francisco? Was his routine about the same as in Los Angeles?' Swami Ashokananda asked.

'When he had no class in the morning we would often go out during the day. Swamiji liked to go to the market with me, and sometimes we would go out for lunch or go for a ride here in Golden Gate Park, which he liked.

'Sometimes when he was not lecturing in the evening we would go out to dinner too. He never ate dinner before a lecture; he said it *slowed his thinking. He was a hearty eater; in fact, Molly Rankin, one of the housekeepers at the Alameda Home of Truth, said that no person could eat as much as Swamiji did and be spiritual! Lucy Beckham and George Roorbach were quite agreeable, though. And Swamiji demanded what he felt he needed. Once, for example, he said: "See here, I must have meat. I cannot live on potatoes and asparagus with the work I am doing!" So they got meat for him, although they themselves were vegetarians.*

'. . . Incidentally he had a fascination for the Chinese. They would just flock after him, "shaking themselves by the hand" as the saying went, to express their pleasure at his presence. Mr Charles Neilson, a well-known artist who lived in Alameda and who became an admirer of Swamiji, invited us to have dinner one evening in Chinatown. We sat down and ordered, but the food had no sooner been put on the table than Swamiji said he could not eat it and rose from the table. Of course we went home. Mr Nielsen was very disappointed because he knew the Chinese person who owned the restaurant; but Swamiji later explained that it was because of the character of the cook that he was unable to eat the food. One other such occurrence took place when we had had fried shrimps somewhere. When we got home Swamiji vomited his dinner. I said fried shrimps were always hard to digest and probably these were not good, but he insisted that it was the bad character of the cook that was responsible. "I'm getting like my master," he said. "I shall have to live in a glass cage."

'He went to the theatre once in Los Angeles to a play . . . He did enjoy going out to dinner.'

'What was the usual routine of Swamiji's day at Camp Taylor?'

'We would usually have breakfast sometime between seven-thirty and eight. Then about ten or ten-thirty Swamiji would hold a meditation, which took place in Miss Bell's tent, as she had requested it.'

The Barrows Controversy

In the matter of eating non-vegetarian food, Swamiji's detractors not only criticized him, but also spread many colourful rumours about him at various times. In due course, those rumours travelled all the way to India and hurt Swamiji. These eager detractors were not just Christian missionaries, but Swamiji's own people too.

If we look back, we will realize that on the same day that the unknown young man was going to become famous at the Chicago Parliament of World Religions, the foundation of his later disrepute was also laid. At the root of both was also the very same Dr John Henry Barrows, but for whose kindness Swamiji could never have become a representative at the Chicago conference at all! Swamiji was deeply indebted to Dr Barrows, but the chief proponent of the bad name that pursued him, was also this famous Christian clergyman.

Later, Sankari Prasad Basu (a Bengali writer and critic, and researcher on Swamiji) diligently collected various pieces of information about this controversy and threw light on the entire matter.

Swamiji has in several letters expressed that the chief source of the ill reports that spread about him, immediately after his Chicago speech, was the Brahmo Samaj's Pratap Chandra Majumdar. Swamiji has written that Pratap Chandra had succeeded in spreading these false rumours to the extent that Dr Barrows did not even make a show of courtesy to Swamiji. The relationship became even more bitter and uncomfortable later. And yet, we cannot but accept that the lifting of the veil of anonymity and presenting Swami Vivekananda to the world was possible only through Dr Barrows. We Indians owe him a huge debt of gratitude.

Sometime after the Chicago conference, Dr Barrows visited India to deliver the first Haskell lecture through the Haskell Foundation. Before that, in 1894, he expressed his hope through a letter to Pratap Chandra Majumdar that 'through the Brahmo Samaj it may be possible to spread an understanding of Christian thought in a way that India may be able to receive it'.

Travelling through India, Dr Barrows began deliberately saying various things about the Indians at the Chicago meet. He was asked, 'How did the Indian representatives to the conference conduct themselves in the USA? He replied, 'The Jains ate non-vegetarian food, the Buddhists sometimes had fish and the other delegates ate everything that the Americans normally eat.'

Swamiji's leaving Madras without meeting Barrows caused some misunderstanding. But in a letter to Mary Hale written at the time, Swamiji says, 'When I returned from London to South India and was being felicitated by the people with feasts and celebrations and also being used to achieve their needs, at that time suddenly *an old hereditary disease (diabetes) made its appearance. The tendency was always there and excess of mental work made it "express" itself.* I had to immediately leave Madras and go away to North India.'

Dr Barrows himself has written an account of the meeting organized at Madras. He said that it was not just Christians who considered beef more necessary for building one's strength than the sacrificed goat offered to the Goddess Kali. '*After the first session of the Parliament of Religions I went with Vivekananda to the restaurant in the basement of the Art Institute, and I said to him, "What shall I get you to eat?" His reply was "Give me beef!"*' This story burst like an explosion in society, creating deep dismayed silence all around.

Swamiji called Barrows' remark a 'downright lie'. When *The Mirror* published Barrow's article, Swamiji was in Kashmir. On 15 November 1897, he wrote to Shuddhananda (Swamiji's disciple) that Brahmananda must refute that lie. Sankari Prasad writes that although Swamiji normally did not rebut any of the rumours about him, he thought Barrows' blatant lies deserved to be rebutted. He did not, however, see any refutation in *The Mirror*. 'Perhaps I missed seeing it or in the end Swamiji may have decided that the fitting reply to Barrows' low-down behaviour was contempt, not denial.'

Swamiji was not normally provoked by false accusations. On 6 July 1896, he wrote from London to Mr Leggett: '*You will be pleased to know that I am also learning my lessons every day in patience and, above all, in sympathy. At twenty years of age I was the most unsympathetic, uncompromising fanatic; I would not walk on the footpath on the theatre side of the streets in Calcutta. At thirty-three, I can live in the same house with prostitutes . . .*'

On 23 August 1896, Swamiji wrote a remarkable letter to Shashi Maharaj where he says, 'I received a letter from Ramdulal Babu today. He says that at the Dakshineswar *Mahotsav* (the Kalpataru festival, celebrated at the Kali temple in Dakshineswar on the first of January every year), many prostitutes visit the temple and as a result many gentlemen are unwilling to go there. If prostitutes cannot go to the great pilgrimage place that Dakshineswar is, then where will they go? The Lord manifests himself more to sinners than to the virtuous.'

In a letter written on 7 October, Swamiji apprised Miss MacLeod of his diet. '*I now live mostly on fruits and nuts. They seem to agree with me well . . . I have lost a good deal of my fat. But on days I lecture, I have to go on solid food.*'

The Son Returns Home (1)

On 20 December 1896 Swamiji wrote a letter from Florence, en route to India, to his dear friend Rakhal. Among other things, he instructed Rakhal, 'If there are oranges in Calcutta, please send a hundred to Alasinga's address in Madras so that I may get them when I reach there.'

On arriving at Darjeeling, Swamiji wrote to Mrs Ole Bull on 26 March 1897: '*The result of this steady work in the West and the tremendous work of a month in India upon the Bengalee constitution is "diabetes". It is a hereditary foe and is destined to carry me off, at best, in a few years' time. Eating only meat and drinking no water seems to be the only way to prolong life—and, above all, perfect rest for the brain.*'

In a letter written to Lala Badri Shah (his host at Almora), Swamiji gives further details of his hereditary illness: '*. . . the doctors . . . do not want me to move about, as that brings about a relapse.*'

In the last week of April, he gives his opinion on various matters in a detailed letter to the Indian publisher Sarala Ghoshal. An excerpt: 'About vegetarian diet, this is my view—firstly, my guru was a vegetarian; yet if anyone gave him the prasad meat offered to Ma Kali, he would respectfully touch it and raise his hand to his head. There is no doubt that killing a living being is a sin. But until science is able to make vegetarian food that provides everything the human body needs, there is no alternative to eating meat . . . It is true that Emperor Ashoka saved the lives of millions of animals through the use of his sword, but isn't slavery of a thousand years even more terrible? . . . Let those belonging to the upper class, who do not have to labour to receive their food and clothing, not eat meat, but to force vegetarianism upon those who have to struggle and labour hard to earn their bread is one of the causes of our country losing its freedom. Japan is an example of what a nourishing diet can accomplish!'

Four days later, in another letter from Darjeeling to Miss Mary Hale, Swamiji says Ajit Singh, the maharaja of Khetri had wanted to take him to England.

'. . . But unfortunately the doctors would not hear of my undertaking any physical or mental labour just now. So with the greatest chagrin I had to give it up . . . My hair is turning grey in bundles, and my face is getting wrinkled up all over; that losing of flesh has given me twenty years of age more. And now I am losing flesh rapidly, because I am made to live upon meat and meat alone—no bread, no rice, no potatoes, not even a lump of sugar in my coffee!! . . . I am going to train a big beard; now it is turning grey. It gives a venerable appearance . . . O thou white hair, how much thou canst conceal, all glory unto thee, Hallelujah! . . .'

Two letters written that month from Almora give us important information on Swamiji's diet. The recipients were Swamiji's intimate friend, Swami Brahmananda and Swamiji's favourite Shashi Doctor (Dr Shashi Bhushan Ghosh), written on 20 and 29 May 1897, respectively.

In his letter to Swami Brahmananda, Swamiji writes, 'My feverish feeling has gone. I find that with the slightest effort at walking or from the slightest heat, the liver begins to act up. I am trying to see if I can get to an even colder place. The air is so dry here that there is a burning sensation in my nose all the time and my tongue feels like a block of wood. You all have stopped criticizing, else I would have gone on to a colder place by now . . . Why do you listen to all those fools? Like you refused to let me eat black lentils because it had starch! As if the fried rice and *ruti* did not have starch! What amazing knowledge! The truth is, I can now clearly see that my old temperament is returning.

'Every place seems to have its own special ailment. In this country the illness reflects this local colour and in that country the illness reflects that local colour. I am thinking of switching to a very light dinner. I will eat well in the morning and afternoon and restrict my dinner to fruits, milk, etc. That is why I am lying in an orchard, expecting fruits, oh God!

'Now, don't be afraid, does the inner spirit die so quickly? The evening lamp has just been lit—we have a whole night of festivities ahead. I am not so irritable any more and I can see clearly that the feverishness is all due to the liver. I will soon control that too—why do you fear? Brace yourself well and start working hard. Let us create a mighty uproar!'

Almora, 29 May 1897
'My dear Shashi Doctor,

'I received your letter and the two bottles of medicines in time. I have started using your medicine from last evening. I hope that combining both medicines will have a better effect than having only one.

'I have started extensive exercise on horseback in the mornings and evenings and I am really feeling a lot better as a result. In fact, after the first week of gymnastics, I felt so much better that I don't think I have ever felt so well since my childhood wrestling days! Then I used to really believe that having a body was a joy. I enjoyed the experience of strength in every movement, in every turn of the muscles. That sense of exhilaration has slightly abated, but I still consider myself quite strong. I could have overcome both GC and Niranjan in a test of strength.

'In Darjeeling I always felt as if I have become another person, but here I feel as if I have no illness whatsoever. There is just one noticeable difference. All my life it would take me around two hours of tossing on the bed before I could sleep. I never managed to sleep as soon as my head hit the pillow, except from Madras to my first month in Darjeeling when I accomplished that feat. That ability to sleep instantly has gone and now I am back to tossing and turning at night and feeling exceptionally warm after dinner. I do not feel this heat after a day meal.

'Since there is an orchard here, I am consuming even more fruits than I normally do. However, the only fruit to be had here is the apricot. I am trying to organize some other fruits from Nainital. Although the days are extremely warm, I don't feel any thirst. . . . On the whole, I am finding a return of my strength and energy and feeling completely healthy. The only thing is I seem to be putting on a lot of weight, perhaps because of the high quantity of milk in my diet.

'Don't pay any attention to Yogen. He is a hypochondriac himself and wants to make everyone else one too. I ate one-sixteenth of a *borfi* in Allahabad, and in his view, that was the cause of my illness in Almora. Yogen is expected here in a few days and I am going to take him in hand. By the way, I am susceptible to malarial influences. My first week's indisposition here may have been because of the journey through the Terai region.

'Anyway, I feel really strong now. You should see me, Doctor, when I sit meditating in front of the beautiful snow-peaks and repeat from the Upanishads: "न तस्य रोगो न जरा न मृत्युः प्राप्तस्य योगाग्निमयं शरीरम् — "*He has neither disease, nor decay, nor death, for, verily, he has obtained a body full of the fire of Yoga.*" . . .

Yours in the Lord,
Vivekananda

On the day of total solar eclipse at Calcutta, the *shishya* Sharat Chandra Chakraborty cooked and fed his dear guru. Sharat Chandra has drawn for us the picture of the loving epicure Swami Vivekananda.

'Today is solar eclipse. Astronomers have travelled to various places to see this total eclipse. Men and women have travelled from far in their thirst to acquire dharma by taking a dip in the holy river and are eagerly awaiting the start of the eclipse. But Swamiji is not very interested in the eclipse. His directive is that today his disciple will cook and feed Swamiji. The disciple has already gathered all the ingredients for the meal and arrived at (then deceased) Balaram Babu's home at around eight in the morning. Swamiji, on seeing him, has said, "You have to cook like they do in your home state (East Bengal, now Bangladesh), and the meal should be over before the *grahan* (eclipse) begins."

'None of Balaram Babu's daughters are in Calcutta at this time, so the house is completely empty. The disciple has gone to the kitchen and started to cook, while Yogen Mata (Ma Saradamoni's attendant and close companion) stands nearby, advising the cook and from time to time handing him the necessary items. Sometimes Swamiji himself comes into the kitchen to see the progress and to encourage the cook and to tease him by mimicking a typical East Bengali accent and dialect, "Don't forget! Make sure the fish curry is exactly like in East Bengal!"

'The menu is rice, *muger* dal, carp fish curry, *shuktuni* (fish with vegetables) and *machher tak* (fish with sour lime). Before the cooking is completely done however, Swamiji comes out of his bath and sits down with a leaf plate in front of him. Although the disciple says the cooking is yet to be completed, Swamiji does not listen and, like a small child, says, "Quickly give me whatever you have cooked, I am dying of hunger." The disciple quickly serves him the first dish and Swamiji promptly starts to eat. After he finishes serving Swamiji with all the dishes, the disciple begins to serve Swami Yogananda, Swami Premananda and the other sanyasis. This disciple was never a great cook, but Swamiji repeatedly praises his cooking. People of Calcutta normally make fun of East Bengal's *shuktuni*, but Swamiji eats it with delight and says, "I have never had such tasty *shuktuni*." After eating the fish with sour lime he says, "This is just like they make it in Bardhhaman (a district of Bengal)." Swamiji finishes his meal with curd and *sandesh* and, after washing up, sits on the bed of the inner room. The disciple sits in the front veranda and receives his prasad. Swamiji says, as he pulls on his hookah, "He who cannot cook well, can never make a good sanyasi. Unless the mind is pure, the food can never be tasty."

'After a short while, there is the sound of blowing conch shells and ululations by the ladies. Swamiji says, "Oh! I think the *grahan* has started. Let me sleep; please massage my feet." Swamiji goes to sleep and the disciple sits in peace, pressing his guru's feet and thinking to himself, "In this auspicious moment, my *seva* (service) to my guru itself is equal to a dip in the Ganges and all the chanting." Gradually the total eclipse covers the sun and cloaks the world in darkness.

'When there are fifteen or twenty minutes left for the eclipse to end, Swamiji awakes, freshens up and begins smoking. He jokes with his disciple, saying, "People say that whatever you do during the eclipse you will receive a thousand-fold. So I thought, *Mahamaya* has not blessed me with good sleep in this body; if I sleep a little during the eclipse, then I will get good sleep later, but that was not to be. I could barely sleep for fifteen minutes."

'After that everyone comes and sits down before Swamiji and he instructs his disciple to say something about the Upanishads.'

On another day in 1898, during the construction of Belur *Math*, Swamiji and his dear disciple Sharat Chandra Chakraborty were conducting a hair-splitting analysis over food.

Disciple: 'Swamiji, is there any correlation between food and spirituality?'

Swamiji: 'Certainly, to an extent there is.'

Disciple: 'Is it proper or necessary to have fish and meat?'

Swamiji: 'Eat your fill my boy! Any sin that arises out of that is my lookout. Look at the faces of the people in your country. Sad faces, no courage or enterprise in their hearts, large stomachs but weak limbs—cowards and funks!'

Disciple: 'If eating fish and meat gives only good results, then why do Buddhism and the Vaishnava faith teach, "अहिंसा परमो धर्म:" i.e. "Ahimsa (non-violence) is the greatest dharma?"'

At this point the disciple has added a footnote in his book, which it is necessary for us to read.

'Footnote: No one should think from Swamiji's reply that he did not have an authoritative view about eating meat. In his books on yoga and other subjects, he has clearly instructed against this practice. That food which is indigestible and causes disease in the body, or even if it does not, which needlessly heats the body and excites the mind and senses, is always to be avoided. Therefore, Swamiji always advised those individuals inclined towards spiritual growth and who also had an appetite for meat to eat bearing in mind the above two norms. Or else he asked them to give up non-vegetarian food altogether. He told people to decide whether to eat meat or not based on their own physical health and mental well-being. However, Swamiji was always in favour of the poorer sections of India eating meat. He said that in order to match up to the tough competition in every walk of life provided by the meat-eating Western cultures, it was absolutely necessary for the common man to eat meat.'

Swamiji: 'Buddhism and the Vaishnava faith are not different. After the decline of Buddhism in India, Hinduism adopted a few cardinal tenets of Buddhism, and this has now become the Vaishnava faith. The teaching that "Ahimsa is the greatest dharma" is excellent, but to impose that principle on all by law without actually studying its effect on them has caused Buddhism to wreck this country. As a result, some people are feeding sugar to ants (for love of all living creatures) but plotting to ruin their brother for money! I have seen many such "hermit herons" (meaning, a pretender to religion. There is a story of a heron who apparently took to religion and decided to stop killing fish but when it stood on the shore of the river pretending to meditate it was actually searching for fish to eat). On the other hand, the Vedas as well as Manu dharma prescribe the eating of fish and meat. And yet, they also contain injunctions to follow ahimsa too. The Vedas say, 'मा हिंस्यात् सर्वभूतानि' or 'Cause no injury to any being'; Manu also says, 'निवृत्तिस्तु महाफला' i.e. "Cessation of desire brings great results". Therefore killing and non-violence have both been directed (in accordance with the law).'

Disciple: 'I have seen that at the slightest leaning towards dharma, people first give up eating fish and meat. In the eyes of many it is a greater sin to eat non-vegetarian food than to commit adultery! From where did these ideas come?'

Swamiji: 'How does it matter where they came from? You can see, can't you, that these ideas are ruining your country and your society? Just see how the people of East Bengal eat only a lot of fish, meat and turtle—which is why they are much healthier than the people of West Bengal. Even the affluent of East Bengal has not adopted the practice of eating *ruti* or *luchi* at night. That is why they do not suffer from dyspepsia like us. In fact, I have heard that the people in the villages of East Bengal do not even understand what dyspepsia means!'

Disciple: 'That is very true, Swamiji. There is nothing called dyspepsia in our land. I heard that term only after coming here. We eat rice and fish in the morning and evening.'

Swamiji is obviously in favour of fish and rice. His advice to his disciple is clear.

Swamiji: 'Yes, eat well. All these flat-stomach, grass and leaf eating "babajis" are ruining the country. That is not a sign of *sattva guna*; in fact, it is the shadow of excessive *tamo guna*—the shadow of death. The signs of *sattva guna* are brightness of the face, undaunted enthusiasm, tremendous activity; while those of *tamo guna* are indolence, lethargy, attachment to *maya* (worldly desires), sleep and other such traits.'

Perhaps the disciple was not fully satisfied with the guru's answer, so he asked again:

Disciple: 'But Swamiji, fish and meat only increase *rajo guna* (passion, activity, good or bad, self-centeredness, ego, individualism, being driven, moving, dynamic).'

Swamiji: 'That is what I want now—*rajas* is what we need. More than ninety per cent of people you think are steeped in *sattva* in this country are actually deeply into *tama* way of being. Even if you can find one-sixteenth of our people practising *sattva* that is more than enough. Now we need the awakening and inspiration of the *rajasik* energy. Can you not see the entire land covered in the darkness of *tamas*? We have to feed fish and meat to the people and make them awake and active, and we have to do it swiftly. Otherwise the entire country will become inert—like trees and rocks. That is why I tell you, eat a lot of fish and meat, son!'

The disciple wants a more detailed analysis.

Disciple: 'But Swamiji, when one has developed the qualities of *sattva*, does the desire to eat fish and meat persist in the mind?'

Swamiji: 'No it does not. When *sattva guna* is fully manifested in the soul, then there is no appetite for fish and meat. But watch for these signs that *sattva guna* is developed—willingness to stake everything for another, complete indifference to bodily pleasures and money, no vanity and a complete lack of ego. When somebody has all these traits, they will not have an appetite for non-vegetarian food anymore . . . When you yourself attain that level of *sattva*, you can also give up fish and meat.'

Disciple: 'But Swamiji, in the *Chhandogya* Upanishad it says, 'आहारशुद्धौ सत्त्वशुद्धिः' i.e. the *sattva* quality in a man becomes pure through pure food. Isn't it the intention of the verse, that in order to become *sattvik*, one should give up all food that is *tamasik* or *rajasik*?'

Swamiji: 'Sankaracharya has used the word "*ahara*" to mean everything that we absorb through our senses, while Sri

Ramanuja Swami has used it to mean just food. My view is that we should choose a meaning that merges both the points of view. Should we pass our lives constantly assessing the quality of the food we eat, or should we control our senses? Controlling our senses should be our main purpose, and in order to achieve that we need to be discerning about the food we choose to eat. Our shastras tell us that there are three ways in which our food can become impure.

(1) *Jati* dosha—the natural impurities of a class of food like onions, garlic, etc., cause disturbance in the mind and we lose our intelligence;

(2) *Nimitta* dosha—caused by external impurities like dust, dead insects, hair, etc.;

(3) *Ashraya* dosha—caused by the impurities arising from evil in the source, such as the people who have handled it. (The belief is that if we eat food cooked by an evil person, we imbibe their evilness and if we eat the food cooked by a virtuous person, we imbibe that too.)

'You should always be alert and check if the food has either *jati* dosha or *nimitta* dosha . . . But in this country, we do not pay attention to these two doshas. Instead, we keep looking for the third dosha, which in fact other than a yogi no one can discern! We fight over this third dosha and are constantly shouting, "Don't touch! Don't touch!" We create a huge ruckus with our shouting from one end of the country to the other. But those shouting do not actually discern whose hands to take food from. I have only seen Thakur catching out this *ashraya* dosha. It has happened many times that he hasn't been able to eat food touched by someone. After detailed investigation, we found that there really was some particular taint in the person concerned. Now all your dharma has ended up in the pot of rice! As if by just avoiding another caste touching your pot of rice, you will find God! You ignore the fruit of the sublime truth in the scriptures and instead just fight over their peels!'

Disciple: 'Then Swamiji, are you saying that we should eat food handled by everyone?'

Swamiji: 'Why should I say that? You are a Brahmin. Even if you don't want to eat food from another caste, what stops you from eating the food of other sub-castes within the Brahmins? Because you are RaRi class of Brahmins, why should you object to eating food from the Barendra class? And why should they not eat from you? And for that matter, why should not the Marathi, Telugu and Kanauji Brahmins not eat your food? In fact, Calcutta's class consideration is even stranger! You can see many Brahmins and Kayasthas secretly eating in public hotels and after washing up, coming out and posing as great social leaders, creating laws in support of casteism.'

The Son Returns Home (2)

In his famous and invaluable book *The East and the West*, Swamiji has written many things about food and drink in our country and other countries. Although it is a long passage, if we do not quote some of it here, Swamiji's ideas about food will remain incomplete.

In his impeccable Bengali, Swamiji has conveyed his thoughts to the people of our country. As we have seen in the previous passage, Swamiji writes, 'Ramanujacharya has asked us to avoid three types of doshas or defects, which make the food harmful for us. Of the three, it is very easy for us to avoid the *jati* dosha and the *nimitta* dosha, but almost impossible to discern the *ashraya* dosha. It is only to avoid this ashraya dosha that we have people screaming, "Don't touch! Don't touch!"

'Regarding *jati* dosha, no other country in the world provides a better place to learn this than India. No other country in the world consumes food as pure as we do as regards *jati* dosha. When it comes to *nimitta* dosha we are in a terrible state of affairs. As you can see, it has become very common for us to eat food that is dirty and rotten from the street corner shops open to dust and dirt and to eat from the bazaar, and the results are clear for everyone to see. The dyspepsia in every home is because of this impurity in the food. The diabetes that you see in every home is a result of eating this impure food from the streets. The reason why the people in the villages do not have these illnesses is because they do not get to eat these "poisonous" *luchis* and *kochuri* from the roadside.

'. . . There are several controversies about certain rules, both in the ancient times and now, in modern times too. Firstly, from the ancient times till today, a great argument is on about vegetarian and non-vegetarian food. Does eating meat help or harm the body? Besides, the question of whether it is right to take the life of a living being has also been a matter hotly debated over the years. One group says, "It is a sin to kill an animal for any reason," while the other group says, "That is rubbish! Unless there is killing how will the life cycle progress?" Even among those who follow the shastras, there is a huge commotion because the shastras themselves are contradictory. In one place it is said, do sacrifices at the yagna, while in another place it says, "never hurt living creatures". Hindus have decided that other than at yagnas, it is a sin to kill and eat animals, yet after a sacrifice, you eat the meat with impunity! . . .

'. . . The modern-day Vaishnavas find themselves in a difficult spot because, as per incidents in the Ramayana and Mahabharata, their Gods Rama or Krishna seem to be happy eating meat and drinking wine! Sita Devi had vowed to offer meat, rice and a thousand jars of wine to the Ganges!

'Western civilization is divided too. One group says eating non-vegetarian food causes all kinds of illnesses and vegetarianism is far healthier. The other group says that is all fiction; otherwise the Hindus of India would not have had any illnesses at all and the Western countries would have by now become extinct with all their illnesses. One group says that if you eat goat meat, you will have a goat's brains and if you eat pig's meat, you will have the brains of a pig and if you eat fish you will have the fish's brains! The other side says, if you have a cauliflower you will have a vegetative brain, if you eat potatoes you will have potatoes for brains and if you eat rice you will have dull rice-brains! And that it is far better to have the intelligence of a live animal than that of an inert, dead vegetable. One group says the chemical composition of rice and dal is the same as in meat. The other group mocks them, saying then the same must be there in air too—so why don't you simply have air instead of food? One group says even on a vegetarian diet people can be healthy and work hard and long. The other group says, if that were true, then the vegetarian countries would have been stronger, but that is absolutely false. All the strongest nations of the world are those eating meat. Those who are in favour of eating vegetarian food— say, look at the Indians and Chinese—they live on a meagre diet, eating only rice and vegetables, and see how miserable they are. Japan used to be like that too, but ever since they have started to eat meat, they have completely transformed themselves.'

Swamiji has arrived at his own conclusion, which he presents to us in his book:

'. . . After carefully evaluating all arguments and seeing all sides, I believe that the Hindu way is the best. By that I mean, the principle that people's station in life and the work they do determine what they eat. It is true that eating meat is barbaric and eating vegetarian food is of course purer. So those who only want to practice dharma should eat vegetarian food while those who have to do hard labour and compete with all the worldly forces to steer the boat of this life should certainly eat meat. The modern Hindu, however, will listen neither to the shastras nor to any sage.

'. . . Now the unanimously approved decision is to have food that is nutritious but is also digested quickly. The greatest nutrition that is available in the smallest volume of food is required, and the body should also quickly absorb it. Otherwise, it will have to be taken in large quantities and the entire day will go in the body trying to digest it. If all one's energy is spent in digesting food, then where will the energy be available to do the rest of the day's work?'

Although in his childhood and youth Swamiji himself was a great fan of eating fried foods bought from shops, yet, as is clear from his book, at some point in his life he completely disapproved of them. The erstwhile lover of *kochuri* writes with a sharp pen!

'Fried food is the real poison. The sweet shop is the home of Yama. In a warm country like ours, the less ghee and oil we use the better. Butter is more easily digestible than ghee. Refined flour has no nutrition—it just looks white. Whole wheat has all the nutrition. The diet that is followed in the villages of Bengal is still the best. Which ancient Bengali poet sings paeans of *luchi* or *kochuris*? These *luchis* and *kochuris* are imports from the

(North-) Western provinces, and even there they are only eaten occasionally. I have never seen anyone who lives only on fried food. The Chaube wrestlers are fond of *luchis* and laddoos, but within a few years Chaube's digestion is ruined and he has to live on *churan* (a mixture of powdered herbs and/or minerals used to aid digestion).

'There is nothing nourishing at all at the sweet seller's shop. On the other hand, there is poison, poison, poison! In the olden days, people ate those occasionally, but now people who live in towns, particularly those who have come in from villages, eat them daily. It is no wonder then that these people die untimely deaths from dyspepsia! Even if you are hungry, throw away the *kochuri* and *jilipi* in the ditch and buy muri for just one paisa. It will not only be cheap but also healthy and filling. It is sufficient to have rice, dal, whole wheat *ruti*, fish, greens and milk.'

Swamiji cautions his devotees about eating dal though!

'. . . Dal has to be had like the South Indians have it—have the soup only; give the rest to the cow! Dal is high protein, but difficult to digest. Dal soup made from tender peas is both tasty and easily digestible. This pea soup is a favourite dish in Paris. First boil the tender peas very well; then grind it well, make a paste of it, and mix it with some water. Then strain it well through a strainer like the milk strainer, so that all the skins come off. Now add turmeric, black pepper and cumin seeds, pepper, chillies or whatever else you want for taste, and cook it well. An excellent pea soup or dal is ready—tasty and easy to digest. If you want, you can add the head of a fish or goat to make it even more delicious.

'If you have the money to buy meat, have it by all means, but do not add the heat-producing spices like they do in the (North-) Western parts of India. The spices are not worth eating—they are only added out of poor habit.'

Swamiji clearly and compellingly declares to his disciples
and readers of *The East and The West* what they need to do to
remain healthy. 'There is a huge escalation of diabetes cases
in the country—and at the root of it all is indigestion. Just
putting something in your stomach does not mean the body is
assimilating it! Eat only what you can digest. Getting a paunch
is the first sign of indigestion. Losing weight and gaining
weight are both symptoms of indigestion. If there is sugar or
albumen in your urine, don't let that bother you at all. Pay full
attention to what you eat, so that you can avoid indigestion.

'As far as possible, stay in open spaces, take long walks
and work hard. Whatever be the cost, do take a vacation
from your work and travel to Badrikashram on a pilgrimage.
From Haridwar, you have to walk and climb a hundred *krosh*
(approximately 200 miles) to get to Badrikashram, and if you
undertake that journey just once, all your problems of diabetes
will simply disappear. Your legs will be strong like iron.'

Swamiji advises, 'Don't let doctors come anywhere near
you. They are normally after what you can pay them rather
than how they can cure you. As far as possible, don't take
any medicines—they are normally deadlier than the disease
itself. If you can, every year, during the Puja break, walk from
your town of work to your native village. In our country, to
be wealthy has come to mean being indolence personified. If
someone has to be helped to walk or to eat, he is a wretched
invalid. He who is eating only the crisp outer crust of the
luchi, fearful of indigestion, is already dead. And if he cannot
walk twenty miles, is he a human being or a worm? Who can
save the man who invites disease and premature death of his
own will?'

Swamiji also has no respect whatsoever for bread. He says,
'Bread is also poison! Don't ever touch it! As soon as you mix in

yeast, the flour changes to something else. Don't have anything fermented. It is very true, as our shastras say, we should never have any fermented food. Any sweet that turns sour is called *sukto* in the shastras and is absolutely forbidden. The only exception to this is curd, which is very beneficial and should be eaten. If you must eat bread, toast it very well over the fire before you do so.'

To understand Swami Vivekananda's food, fasting, his love for cooking and his food philosophy, the two books that must be read are *The East and the West* and *Paribrajak* (*The Nomad*). He has made it abundantly clear to all of us that to really cook well, it is not enough to simply put the vegetables or fish and meat in the pot and place it on the fire. It is necessary to have an excellent understanding of the history of civilization and the philosophy of food!

We know that from childhood itself, Vivekananda had a keen interest in food. We also know that one of his earliest purchases of books was one on French cuisine, purchased in easy instalments. What is remarkable, however, is that his interest went beyond Hindu and Bengali food to Muslim recipes through the interests of his father, to European food and American food too, both of which he had an opportunity to personally observe and learn during the last decade of his life, an opportunity he fully utilized. Yet, a big question persists. As a penniless sanyasi in a strange land, Swamiji received a roof over his head because of the kindness of strangers—he never stayed anywhere for more than a few days and was also quite frequently ill. Despite this, he managed to learn so much about Western culinary art! We have never had a person like Swamiji before, and I don't believe we ever will.

Swamiji's vast range of experiments with food is another wonder. As a sanyasi, he was sometimes a special guest in a palace, sometimes the chief visitor at a banquet in a palatial hotel, sometimes a first-class passenger in a luxury liner at sea and sometimes an unbidden caller at a poor hamlet. I know of no other person so varied in his culinary experiences.

Let us look at some examples of his counsel to us. The speciality of Vivekananda's writings is that each one of his instructions is crystal clear and needs no explanation—everyone can quite easily understand them.

For example, his basic tenet is this: to be able to eat and digest rich food one's body should be strong enough to bear the consequences. In comparison to the Western world, our lifespan, strength, courage, etc., is very different. We are vegetarians—all our illnesses are related to the stomach. We grow old and die of digestive ailments, while they, with their high meat diet, die mostly of heart ailments.

Now, instead of commenting on his writings, let us quote directly from what he has written. 'If the food is pure, the mind will be pure; if the mind is pure, it leads to permanent self-awareness—this statement from the shastras is accepted by all communities in our country. Although Sankaracharya refers to food as anything that enters through our senses and Ramanujacharya refers to food as actual food that we eat, the unanimous understanding is that both are correct—for unless we eat nutritious food, how will our senses work effectively? It is quite certain that poor food habits will negatively impact our sense organs' ability to absorb. This is evident to all. Everyone is aware that with a lack of food, our sight for example can be severely impaired. It is also obvious that particular foods can cause particular physical or mental issues for people. All the discriminations that we create about food in our society are also rooted in this fact, although we often forget the essentials and fight over marginal issues.

'India has one and a half lakh soldiers. See how many out of them eat meat. The best soldiers are the Gurkhas and the Sikhs, who have never been vegetarian. The argument, however, continues. One group says that eating meat causes indigestion, while the other says that is not true at all—in fact, it is the vegetarians who always suffer from stomach problems. And just because your green leaves can help bowel movements and cause purging, do you want the whole world to eat only that? The net result of the argument though is that it has always been the meat-eaters alone who have been brave warriors, rulers, thinkers, etc. The non-vegetarians have said that when yagnas used to be performed across the country (sacrificing animals and having everyone eat them as prasad), only then did great intellectuals emerge among Hindus. Now, in the age of 'babajis' there is not a single great thinker. Because of this thinking, non-vegetarians are afraid to give up on their non-vegetarianism. Even among the members of the Arya Samaj in our country, this controversy persists—one group says it is critical to eat meat, while the other says it is a great sin to eat meat. The debate continues.

'As long as the human race follows the principle of "might is right", we will have to continue to eat meat or discover a way to get the same nutrition through some other diet. Otherwise, the weak will get crushed under the feet of the strong! Just saying "X or Y is quite healthy and strong in spite of being a vegetarian," is not good enough. Compare the entire class of vegetarians and non-vegetarians.'

The Vegetarian Arguments

'Even among vegetarians, there are arguments. One group says rice, potatoes, wheat, millets, etc., are all high sugar and starchy and not food at all. They are all man-made and cause all illnesses. Starchy foods house all ailments. Even if a horse or cow are kept indoors all day and fed these foods, they will fall ill. But if you send them off to the field and let them eat grass and green leaves, they will become healthy again. Green leaves and vegetables contain very little starch. The forest-dwellers of ancient times ate nuts and leaves—they did not eat potatoes or wheat, etc. Even if they did eat starchy food, they ate it when it was raw, i.e., when the starch content had not developed! This quibbling continues.

'One side says roasted meat, fruit and milk are the only diet to ensure a long and healthy life. Particularly fruits go a long way towards maintaining the youthfulness of the person because the acid in the fruits does not allow the joints to become arthritic.

'All illnesses are caused by impure food and impure water. Purifying drinking water has become a craze in America these days. The filter has served its time and is no longer useful. Now it only strains the water without removing the germs, and over time these filters have themselves become a hotbed of germs! When the filter first made an appearance in Calcutta, it was said that there was no outbreak of cholera for five years, but after that things returned to exactly the way they were before. So the filter has now started to proliferate those germs! Of all the filters available to us, the one where three earthen pots are placed one above another on a three-legged bamboo frame is the best. However, the sand or charcoal needs to be changed or reheated every second or third day to kill germs. In the villages on the banks of the Ganges, the method of straining the water through a cloth with a piece of alum in it is the best. The alum slowly dissolves, taking all the germs and other impurities and it settles at the bottom of the jar. This is a simple system, which puts to shame the expensive filters of the West and is far better than the tap water. Of course, the safest is to boil the water.

Boil the water after sedimentation with alum, then drink that
water and throw away all the filters. In America these days the
drinking water is first vaporized, so all the impurities are gone.
Then that vapour is cooled to form pure water and alongside
that fresh air is pumped into the water again to replace the air
that was pushed out during vaporization. This distilled water is
pure and used in all homes for drinking.'

Swamiji has given us his unique comparison between
today's rice and *ruti* and the nineteenth-century staple diet of
kochuri, *monda* and sweetmeats.

'In our country, anyone who has a little money will daily
feed his children *kochuri* and sweets fried in ghee and dipped in
sugar! As if it is below his dignity to have simple rice and *ruti*.
How else can you then expect these children to turn out other
than pot-bellied, weak-structured animals?

'Even the strong Englishmen, who live in a cold climate,
who work hard and exercise hard, are scared at the thought of
eating any sweetmeats or fried food. And we, who live in a very
hot climate, who are unwilling to exercise even to the extent of
simply moving from one room to another; only eat fried food
and sweetmeats! Everything fried in ghee and oil!

'In the old days, the village zamindars would walk twenty or
thirty miles at the drop of a hat, would think nothing of eating
forty carp fishes, bones and all, and would live for a hundred
years. Their progeny come to Calcutta, wear spectacles, eat
luchis and *kochuris*, never walk at all but travel in carriages all the
time and die prematurely of diabetes. That is the sad result of
their trying to become "Calcuttans"!

'And the scoundrel doctors and vaidyas (practitioners
of Ayurvedic/indigenous medicine) have ruined it further by
pretending to know everything, by pretending that they can
resolve all issues. When someone has slight flatulence, instead

of telling them "Go and walk four miles and you will be fine!", they medicate him.

'I have travelled to many countries and seen many different types of food. But I believe it would be worthwhile taking rebirth just to again enjoy our rice, dal, *chorchori*, *shukto* and *mocha*. My great regret is that you don't realize the importance of teeth when you have them! Why should we copy the food of the English, and where do we have the funds to manage that? The most suitable food for us is our simple, cheap and nutritious Bengali food—like that of East Bengal. Imitate their food as much as you like. The more you copy the food of the West, the worse it will be. In the end you will be left with only black lentils and sour fish—neither here nor there. You will become like the people of BankuRa-Birbhum. You have created the trap of sweetmeats and fried food because of which BankuRa has thrown its famous and original popped rice and jaggery into the river Damodar, the black lentils and the *posto bata* (ground poppy seeds) have disappeared. Dhaka and Vikrampur have thrown away their fish and turtles into the water and become "civilized"! You have destroyed yourselves and are now leading the rest of the country in that direction. This is your civilization! Fie on you! And those foolish villagers are picking up all the refuse from Calcutta and will not admit that it is rubbish, although it is causing them dyspepsia! Instead, they keep saying it is the air of Calcutta (saline) which is causing their problems. They want to become "civilized Calcuttans" at any cost, even if it kills them!'

Food Habits of the West

Swamiji's discourse on the food habits of Westerners can even today be a textbook for students of catering colleges. Here are some excerpts.

'The wealthy of Europe and all of America eat mainly meat. Their staple diet is meat and fish, while bread and rice are had in small quantities, like how we have our chutney. In America, almost no bread is eaten. The fish or the meat is eaten by itself, with no accompaniment of any rice or bread. And that is why the dishes get replaced after every course. If there are ten courses, the plates will get changed ten times. For example, if we were to do this, then we would first have only the *shukto* with no rice, and then the plate would be changed; then we would get the dal by itself, and then after another change of plate, we would get the vegetable gravy, then the plate would be changed, and we would get a little rice or two *luchis* etc. The advantage of this is that we get to eat a little bit of many courses, and we do not overfeed ourselves.

'The French start the day with coffee and a piece or two of buttered toast. A moderate quantity of fish or meat is taken at lunch and a large meal at dinner. Italy, Spain and similar countries follow the same practice. Germans eat through the day—five or six mini meals—and each time it consists of a little meat. The British have three meals—breakfast is small, and in between meals they have tea and coffee. Americans have three large excellent meals with a lot of meat.

A Happy Meal in *Sukhasan* (the happy pose in Yoga)

On the subject of having meals seated on the floor, Swamiji says, 'Even until recently we have been having all our meals on an *asana* (a small square mat for a single person's use), seated on the floor, while the rest of world is experimenting with chairs, tables and stools.

'The *arya* (nobleman) used to sit on a wooden seat on the ground, in *sukhasan* (cross-legged posture) and leant back on a similar wooden seat at his back. He would take his food on a single metal plate, placed on a very low stool in front of him. This practice is still followed in Punjab, Rajputana, Maharashtra and Gujarat. In Bengal, Orissa, Telangana/Andhra Pradesh, Kerala, etc., the custom is to sit on the floor and eat off a plantain leaf. Even the maharaja of Mysore does the same. Muslims eat off a cloth spread on the ground while the Burmese and Japanese sit with their knees and feet touching the floor and eat off a plate on the ground. The Chinese sit on chairs and eat at a table using bowls, spoons and wooden chopsticks. In earlier days, the European style was to recline on a couch and use their fingers to eat food, but now they use all kinds of knives, forks and spoons.

'The Chinese style of eating requires skill. Just like our paan vendors use the deftness of their hands to trim the leaves with two thin iron sheets held in their palms like a pair of scissors, similarly the Chinese use two thin wooden chopsticks and, using two fingers and their palm, employ them as tongs to carry the greens up to their mouth. The same two sticks are then held together like a shovel, and the rice is pushed in from a bowl held very close to the mouth.'

Every faith contains injunctions about which food should be eaten and which should not, causing a lot of debates and discussions. Some of these restrictions may not be clearly declared or very well known, but there are hidden ongoing discussions on which foods will lead one to lose one's dharma! Swami Vivekananda elaborates on this in a few paragraphs:

'Eskimos live in the snow, where nothing green ever grows. Their staple food is fish and meat. If they sometimes lose their appetite, they eat a piece of fermented meat and the appetite returns.

'Europeans also do not cook the wild bird or animal meat until it is fermented. They hang up the fresh meat until it turns

putrid and begins to stink. In Calcutta, decayed deer meat is
in great demand and people believe a slightly rotten carp is
much better than a fresh one! In England, the more rotten the
cheese and the more worms in it, the tastier it is considered.
They are happy to even eat the worms running away from the
cheese! Even vegetarians in India enjoy a little onion and garlic.
South Indian Brahmins particularly insist on having them. But
the Hindu shastras closed that path too, saying that eating
onions, garlic, domestic fowl and boar would mean they lose
their Brahmin caste. Hearing this, orthodox Hindus gave up
all of this but started having asafoetida, which has much more
offensive smell than onions or garlic! Similarly, the orthodox
Hindus of the Himalayas discovered and started to have a grass,
which smelled just like garlic. After all, the scriptures have not
said anything against the asafoetida or grass!

'Every religion other than Christianity has a clear set of
rules regarding eating certain food and not eating others. Jains
and Buddhists do not eat fish or meat. Jains do not even eat
anything that grows underground in case the process of digging
kills worms. They do not open their mouths to eat anything
after dark in case insects go in and die.

'Jews do not eat any fish that has no scales, nor do they eat
pork, and they only eat animals which are cloven-footed and
do not ruminate (Whatsoever parteth the hoof, and is cloven-
footed, and cheweth the cud among the beasts, that shall ye
eat. – The Book of Leviticus) Another strange thing with the
Jews—if milk or anything made from milk enters the kitchen
where fish or meat is being cooked, they will throw away all
the fish and meat being cooked there! That is the reason why
an orthodox Jew will not eat anything cooked by someone
belonging to another faith. Again, like some orthodox Hindus,
the Jews too do not eat meat unless it has been offered to God

and is being served as prasad, i.e., it is not "futile meat". In Bengal and Punjab, this offered meat is called *mahaprasad*. The Jews too have only this *mahaprasad*, first offered to God. Therefore, they too, like the Hindus, do not buy meat at any and every shop. The Muslims too follow many rules similar to the Jews, but they are less likely to go to such extremes. They do not have fish and meat in the same meal as milk but do not mind if these items are together in the same room. They do not believe that touching one to the other causes ruin.

'There are a lot of similarities between the Hindu and Jew dietary habits, except that the Jews do not eat wild boar while the Hindus do. In Punjab, because of the extreme hostility between the Hindus and Muslims, it has become a necessary food item for the Hindus! Rajputs hunt the wild boar and treat it as an act of dharma! Non-Brahmins in the South also eat domestic pork. Hindus have wild fowl, not domesticated ones. From Bengal to Nepal and the Himalayas, including Kashmir, they follow similar diet patterns. In these areas, even to this day, Manu's principles are followed. This is particularly true in the region of Kumaon to Kashmir, and less so in Bengal, Bihar, Allahabad or Nepal. For example, Bengalis and Nepalis do not eat hen or hen eggs but they do eat duck eggs. From the Kumaon northwards, even that is not allowed. Kashmiris are happy to eat wild duck eggs but not those of domesticated ones. From Allahabad to all parts of India other than the Himalayas, those who eat goat's meat also eat fowl.'

The middle class of Bengal today does not seem too enamoured of milk, and the habit of adding milk to tea has almost disappeared. Here is what Swamiji has to say about milk:

'Milk is very difficult to digest, particularly when one is suffering from acidity. There have even been cases of death when a glass of milk is gulped down suddenly, without a breath!

Milk should be had the way babies are breastfed mother's milk. If it is sucked or sipped very slowly it is digestible; otherwise, it is not. Being difficult to digest in itself, it becomes doubly difficult when taken with other complex food like meat, which is why Jews are prohibited from having both at the same meal. The foolish, ignorant mother forces milk down her child's throat and in a few months when the baby dies, beats her breast in despair.

'The prescribed quantity of milk even for adults is quarter of a litre at a time, to be had slowly over half an hour! Feeding bottles are the best way to give babies their milk. Normally, the mother is busy with housework and the maid holds the baby down, putting her leg across it to prevent it from getting away, and forces the milk in large gulps down its throat! The baby ends up with liver complaints and does not grow, the milk proving to be its doom. Only those children who are able to withstand this treacherous style of feeding with their innate energy grow up to be strong and healthy adults.

'There were also the atrocities of the confinement room—with hot fomentation and other dangerous treatments. It is only due to the grace of Ma Shashti (the guardian Goddess of little children) that the mothers and the infants of those days were able to survive all this torture and come through safe, sound and healthy! With the blessings of the holy tulsi plant in the courtyard nearby, the mother and newborn managed quite often, to evade the *yam doots* (emissaries of Yama), i.e., the local quacks, and survive!'

The Nomad's Food Worries

Paribrajak is another exceptional book by Swami Vivekananda written in 1899 on board *The Golconda* (a ship) when Swamiji was travelling westward for the second time. Accompanying him were Swami Turiyananda (Tu Bhai) and Sister Nivedita, whom Swamiji considered a daughter.

This book was serialized in the magazine *Udbodhan* (Ramakrishna Mission's monthly publication) over the first two years of the magazine's publication, as *Bilatyatri'r Patra* or *Letters from a Foreign Traveller*

Here are some excerpts in our Swamiji's inimitable style. It is no wonder then that he is considered Bengal's greatest travel writer.

'One day Tu Bhaya said, "Sir! We should offer a goat (sacrifice) to Ma (the Goddess) one of these days." I said, "So be it! Why one day? Let it be daily." The next day he asked me again, "What happened about that?" I didn't respond, but when he asked me again the next day, I showed him the meat on my plate at the dining table. Flabbergasted, he said, "But you are eating that!"

'Then I had to lovingly explain the concept to him through a story. In some place where the Ganges doesn't flow, a young man arrived at his mother-in-law's place. At mealtime he found a large band of festive drummers standing around. His mother-in-law insisted that he have a little milk first. The son-in-law thought perhaps it was the custom of the place. As soon as he sipped the bowl of milk, the drums began to play loudly. Then, his mother-in-law, with happy tears in her eyes, blessed him and said, "You have now done the duty of a son, my dear. You have the water of the Ganges in your stomach and your father-in-law's ashes were powdered and added in your milk. Now your father-in-law has attained salvation by blending with the Ganges water."

'"Therefore, my brother! I am a Calcutta man and the ship is awash with meat. Slowly the meat is entering Ma Ganga, please don't worry!" But brother is such a serious person, I don't know how my speech went down with him!'

* * *

Swamiji tells us how the ship's management and staff are organized for eating and drinking.

'The absolute head of the ship is the captain. In the olden days, the captain was the supreme commander on high seas and he doled out punishment, caught bandits and hanged them, etc. Now his power is a little less, but on board the ship, his word is still law. He has four officers under him, and five engineers report to them. The chief engineer holds an officer's rank and has his meals at the first-class deck. Then, there are four or five *sukanis* who steer the ship in turn; they are also Europeans. All the rest—the servants, the khalasis, the coal man—they are all Indians, all Muslims too. It was only in Bombay on the P&O Company's ship that I met Hindus.

'The servants and khalasis are from Calcutta, the coal man is from East Bengal and the cooks are East Bengal's Catholics. There are also four sanitary workers who remove the dirty water and clean the cabins, the bathing spaces and the toilets.

'The Muslim servants and khalasis do not eat food cooked by the Christian cooks. That does cause a daily uproar on the ship, but they handle it so that it is not obvious. They seem to have no problem eating the bread baked in the ship's kitchen, and the more modern Calcutta servants don't worry about doing anything surreptitiously either! There are three messes for the staff—one for the servants, one for the khalasis and one for the coalmen. The company assigns one *bhandari* or cook and a servant to the fee-mess. The fee-mess is assigned a place for cooking. Some Hindus were going to Colombo from Calcutta.

They would cook their meals and eat in that kitchen after the fee-mess's cooking was done.'

'The servants draw their own drinking water as needed. On both sides of the fee-deck there are two pumps—one for salty water and the other sweet. The Muslims draw the sweet water from there. So for those Hindus who do not mind drinking tap water, it is very convenient to travel on the ship without sacrificing any of their customs and to visit all the countries they want to. There is a kitchen to cook in, and you do not have to drink or even bathe in water touched by anyone else. Rice, dal, greens, vegetables, fish, milk, ghee—everything is available on the ship. Because the workers on these ships are all Indians, there is a daily ration of rice, dal, cauliflower, potatoes, radish, etc., given out.'

Swamiji observes, 'In one word, it is all about money. If you have the money, then even if you travel alone, you can quite easily carry out all your rites and rituals.'

Swamiji tells us a little about the South Indian palate too. 'And then the Tamil, Telugu and Malayalam languages, which even if you hear for six years you will not be able to understand a word of! Which have a factory churning out all the possible "l" and "d" sounds of the world! Where we slurp up the rice with the "mulligatawny" rasam, causing a heart attack with each mouthful because of its sharp spice and sour tamarind; the sweet neem leaves (curry leaves), the tempering with chickpeas and *muger* dal, the curd rice and other such dishes; and fish fried in sesame oil, massaging the body with sesame oil before a bath—without all these things, would it be a Southern region!'

On the evening of 25 October (1900), the world-renowned author of *Paribrajak* reached Vienna by train. The hotel sent its carriage to receive him, and the other passengers and everyone duly arrived at their destination. Now let us read an excerpt from our traveller himself:

'In all hotels of almost all countries of Europe other than England and Germany, the style and fashion are typically French. Like the Hindus, they too eat two major meals in a day—the morning meal is had by twelve noon, while the night meal is finished by eight. Early in the morning, at around eight or nine, they have a little coffee. Other than in England and Russia, tea is not very much in favour. The morning meal is called "*déjeuner*, i.e., breakfast; and the evening meal is called "*diner*", i.e., dinner. Russia drinks a lot of tea, for not only is it very cold, but China is also next door. Chinese tea is of an excellent quality, and most of it goes to Russia. Like the Chinese, the Russians also drink their tea without adding any milk. Tea and coffee become almost poisonous if you add milk to them. The real tea-drinking nations—China, Japan, Russia and Central Asia—all take their tea without milk. Similarly, the original coffee-drinking nations like Turkey take their coffee milk-less. In Russia, however, they take their tea with a slice of lemon and a lump of sugar. The poor share a lump of sugar by placing it in their mouth and drinking their tea over it and then passing it to the next person who does the same!'

Swamiji has written many unflattering things about other faiths. He clarifies though, in *The East and the West*: '... perhaps I am offending many of my friends, who are saying, I suppose, that I am flattering my own countrymen. But let me ask this: what will I gain by flattering my countrymen? If I die of hunger, this lot will not provide a handful of rice to save me. If I beg from others and somehow manage to feed an orphan, they will jump to take a portion of the credit, and if they don't get it, will malign me to the skies. Oh pandits of my country! Such are my countrymen; why should I flatter them?'

And now it is time to wind down. The story of how a jobless, penniless youth, with no financial or even moral support from anyone, managed to overcome all barriers and cross the Atlantic to enthral a strange new world on the other side will always amaze us. The story of how he managed to spread India's immortal song and came to be worshipped by so many people will continue to inspire and astonish millions of Indians for many thousands of years.

Those overwhelmed by Swamiji have been trying for all these decades to understand the thousand facets of his character but have yet to grasp all of them. We have endeavoured to research his love for the weak and hungry and the joy he discovered in feeding others. But even this dry subject, when touched by his grace, has become eternal and infinite. In the acid test of surviving food and fasting, the writer and chef Swamiji has decorated himself with wondrous majesty.

But perhaps every success of the great has its share of thorns! Else why would the controversy arise about what he had ordered in a restaurant in Chicago to satisfy his hunger, directly after his moment of glory? Why would another powerful religious representative from his own city, instead of applauding him, say, 'That brat, who used to beg on streets to eat, wander around all day, has probably done something evil and come away here to escape. He is such an uncultured yokel that he smokes his cheroot even in the presence of ladies!' He further complained that Swamiji had no knowledge of anything!

Swamiji had neither funds nor shelter abroad and lived at the mercy of others. His body was weakened by many ailments and many days of hunger and starvation. He left home at the age of twenty-three, and what followed was a decade of erratic living. He travelled from one end of India to the other and finally left for unknown horizons abroad.

He earned the praise of an entire universe at the Chicago Parliament of Religions and then returned to give up his life at the Ramakrishna Mission's Belur *Math* on 4 July 1902. We have no other example of someone who has achieved so much in spite of a body racked by illnesses. Swamiji fell ill in Cairo while travelling with Madame Calve (Emma Calve, famous French Opera singer). As soon as he became a little better, he decided to take the first ship out to Bombay. On 26 November 1900, he wrote to Miss MacLeod, '*The steamer was late; so I am waiting . . . it will arrive some time in the evening if everything goes right.*'

The ship docked at Bombay on 6 December 1900, and Swamiji boarded a train to Calcutta. Fortunately, he had an unexpected meeting with his friend Manmathanath Bhattacharya, and in the evening of 9 December, he landed up at Belur *Math*, surprising and delighting everyone.

According to the writer of *Yuganayak Vivekananda*, 'The sanyasis of the *Math* were sitting down to the evening meal when the gardener came running. Panting, he said, "A *saheb* (foreign gentleman) has come." Everyone was stunned to then see the gentleman himself striding swiftly towards them.' Swamiji joked, 'As soon as I heard the dinner gong, I realized I had better run or else you would all finish everything and I would get nothing to eat!'

* * *

At midnight on 28 December 1900, Swamiji was in Kathgodam on the way to Mayavati. Feeling slightly feverish, Swamiji rested one night at Kathgodam, reaching Mayavati the next day. Having spent his thirty-eighth birthday at Mayavati, he set out for Calcutta again on the 18 January.

While in Mayavati one day, Swami Birajananda expressed a desire to go out and beg for alms, but Swamiji said, 'Don't kill your body with so much struggle. We have damaged our bodies a lot, and to what avail? Did we see any result? No. We are still trying to recover from that time when we let our bodies break down, when, in fact, it should have been the best time of our lives.'

About the new abode in the Himalayas, Swamiji said, 'I will come here at the end of my life, leaving behind all philanthropic activities, and will spend my days writing books and singing songs.' In the extreme cold, one day the sanyasis of the *Math* brought some water from the lake nearby and made a huge lump of ice cream for their Swamiji.

There are many anecdotes about Swamiji, which Swami Gambhirananda describes as examples of Swamiji's childlike behaviour. At Mayavati once, since the food was not ready on time, Swamiji scolded everyone. Entering the kitchen, he saw Swami Birajananda desperately trying to get the cooking done. After a while, when the food arrived, Swamiji said, 'Take it away! I won't eat!' Swami Birajananda stood there quietly and after a few minutes, his anger evaporated and Swamiji began to eat. As he ate, he commented, like a little boy, 'Now I know why I was so angry earlier.'

Another time in Champavat, Swamiji was with Swami Shivananda, Swami Sadananda and Swami Birajananda. Swami Birajananda had taken on the cooking himself, but the rice was a lot more than the pot could handle, as a result of which the half-cooked rice began to spill over. A hungry Swamiji kept enquiring when the food would be done. Entering the kitchen, he saw what was happening and advised Swami Birajananda to put some ghee in the rice and cover it with a raised lid. With his expert advice, the rice turned out very well that day and everyone enjoyed the 'ghee-rice'.

Another time, at Pilibhit station, dusk was fast approaching when Swamiji realized that his co-traveller Swami Sadananda was missing. A worried Swamiji sent another of his co-travellers, Govind Lal Shah, to search for him. Around half an hour before the train was to leave, Sadananda arrived with a group of people, carrying a large basket full of hot *puris*, all kinds of fried savouries, curries, chutneys and an assortment of sweets!

Returning to Belur *Math* of 24 January 1901, Swamiji heard the sad news of the death of Maharaja Ajit Singh of Khetri. The maharaja was buffeted by strong winds and fell down eighty-six feet to his death.

Now let us look at Swamiji's travels to East Bengal and Assam. On 9 February of the same year, Swamiji arranged to receive the Trust Deed for Belur *Math*, duly signed at the registrar's office. The very next day Swamiji announced Swami Brahmananda as the head of the *Math*.

Swamiji's travel to East Bengal started on 6 March 1901. Let us read some gastronomic stories from *Yuganayak*. Swamiji's co-traveller, the government employee from Allahabad Sri Manmathanath Ganguly, has given us a beautiful portrayal of the steamer journey.

Seeing the fishermen catching fish on the Padma River, Swamiji said, 'I feel like eating the fresh *ilish*.' The co-travellers realized that his real intention was to feed the poor workers on the steamer. It was found that for an anna one could buy six *ilish*. Swamiji immediately wanted to buy *ilish* worth a rupee (16 anna). To everyone's great joy, he also received four bonus fish! Now, when I am writing this in 2017, the price of *ilish* in Calcutta is Rs 1500 per kg, i.e., a rupee of Swamiji's time is worth at least around Rs 30,000 today! Economists will get a fair idea of the inflation rates of Bengal from this.

What goes best with the *ilish* is *pui shak*. The steamer was stopped at a village to procure rice, but there was no sign of any *pui shak*! Finally, a gentleman told Swamiji that his garden had *pui shak* and he would give it to them on the condition that Swamiji himself visited the home. We hear through our sources that Swamiji was so happy to get the *pui shak* and fish that day that before leaving he initiated the owner of the garden!

Those readers who would like to award the first prize in the list of Swamiji's favourite foods to *pui shak* and *ilish* should consider that his mother and grandmother's *shukto* and *mocha* also compete for the gold medal here. Swamiji had announced after eating those dishes that it would be worth taking rebirth in Bengal just to eat them again! Our dear writer Syed Mujtaba Ali has recommended that we take these words seriously because what short-lived persons say about rebirth always comes true!

We have some more interesting anecdotes about the East Bengal travels. Manmathanath tells us about a man, selling boiled chickpeas on the train. Swamiji told his disciple, 'It would be good to have some boiled chickpeas.' The disciple bought chickpeas worth one paisa, but realizing what was in Swamiji's mind, paid the man one *sike* (25 paise) instead. When he came back to his seat, Swamiji asked him, 'How much did you give the man?' When he heard it was just one *sike* he said, 'What good will that do for him? He must be having a wife and children at home. Go on, give him a rupee.' An amazed Manmathanath noted that Swamiji did not eat a single chickpea himself that day.

Swamiji's mother Bhuvaneswari Devi accompanied him on the 26 March on a pilgrimage to Narayanganj. Many people had come to Dhaka to pay their obeisance to Swamiji. A young woman who was suffering from asthma had appealed to Swamiji for some medicines. Swamiji's loving response was,

'My dear, I myself am suffering from asthma and am unable to do anything for myself. If I had the power to heal would I be in this condition myself?' A disciple asked him, 'Swamiji, how did your health break down so badly? Why did you not take better care of yourself?' Swamiji's response was, 'In America I was completely oblivious of my own body's needs.'

Then he travelled to Shillong where his illness increased. In Dhaka itself he was racked by asthma and diabetes. In Shillong when the asthma became severe, he used to collect many pillows and press them down on his chest.

Swamiji returned to Belur *Math* on 12 May 1901. On the eighteenth, he wrote in a letter: 'In Assam's Shillong, my fever, asthma and albumin increased, and my body had swollen up to double my size, but after returning to the *math* I find the symptoms of illness have all disappeared.'

In Calcutta, in response to a question put to him by Sharat Chandra in the book *Swami-Shishya Dialogue*, Swamiji said with a lot of enthusiasm, 'The beauty of the Brahmaputra region is incomparable. The people there are far stronger and able to work harder than our people in Bengal. Perhaps because they have a lot of fish and meat—they do everything in full measure. Of course, they do put a lot of fat in their food, which is not good.'

Swamiji's thoughts have always been focused on various problems that plague our society. Girish Chandra Ghosh once asked him, 'You have studied all the Vedas and Vedanta, but does your knowledge create any solution for all the lamentation, hunger, for the immorality, abortion and various sins being committed in society today? The plight of that housewife, who used to cook and feed fifty people daily, but now has not cooked rice for her own family for the last three days? The antisocial elements who attack and torture poor housewives, the killing of foetuses, gambling, looting all property from widows—is there anything in your Vedas which tells us how to stop these miseries?' Swamiji sat silently and at last walked out of the room, his eyes filled with tears. Girish Babu said (to Swamiji's disciple), 'Your Guruji is not only a great pandit, but also a great lover (of humanity). Your Vedas also do not explain, that *sat-chit-anand* (truth, consciousness and bliss) are all three exactly the same.'

After his return from Shillong, Swamiji's deteriorated state of health distressed and worried all the sanyasis at the *math*. It was unanimously decided that henceforth Swamiji would not be allowed to undertake any physical stress at all. For the next seven months, Swamiji stayed put at the *math*, and many types of treatment were carried out to help him recover. Swami Gambhirananda informs us that during this time he suffered oedema in both legs and found it very difficult to walk. His entire body had become so tired and delicate that the slightest pressure to any part of his hands or legs caused pain.

During this time, a famous *kabiraj* was called to treat Swamiji for diabetes. He ordered a diet of only milk for twenty-one days—with no other food, water or even salt. His disciple Sharat Chandra said, 'You normally drink water four to five times in an hour. It will be intolerable for you to stop drinking water altogether.'

Swamiji responded, 'I will not drink any water as long as I am taking the medicines.' Once that iron willpower was exercised, no drop of water could dare go down his throat!

Swami Gambhirananda also informs us in *Yuganayak* that around five to seven days after the medicines started, one Sunday a big *rui* was delivered to the *Math*. After keeping aside a portion to be offered as *bhog*, Swamiji himself cooked the fish in four or five different Western and continental styles, using milk, vermicelli, curd, etc., ignoring all pleas to stay away from the heat of the fire. 'At mealtime however, he barely touched a drop of the various dishes himself, feeding them all to the others present there.'

Sharat Chandra has given us some very valuable information in his famous book *Swami-Shishya Dialogue*, a book serialized in *Udbodhan* over seven years. Mastermoshai, the author of *Sri Ramakrishna Kathamrita* too, was instrumental in realizing this project.

Swami Turiyananda brought Sharat Chandra to meet Swamiji a few days after Swamiji's return from his first trip to the USA in 1897.

Sharat Chandra has devotedly recorded Swamiji's praise for Americans at the very beginning of their meeting. 'It is impossible to find another race of people who are so large-hearted, warm, kind, hospitable and always keen to receive new ideas.'

As per Narendranath Sen, the editor of *The Mirror*, Swamiji further said, 'With the worldwide spread of Vedantic knowledge, the Western countries will soon have huge respect and empathy for us. In fact, to a large extent, they already do.'

While having his meal, Swamiji once told his disciple Sharat Chandra, 'It is best to avoid eating high fat. *Ruti* is better than *luchi*. *Luchi* will lead to illness. Eat fish, meat, fresh vegetables, and keep the sweets low.' As he was speaking, he asked the disciple, 'How many *rutis* did I eat? Should I eat some more?' Swamiji had no idea how many *rutis* he had eaten!

Sharat Chandra once asked him, 'Sir, what kind of food did you eat abroad?'

Swamiji: 'I ate like they ate—the food of the place. We are sanyasis—we will never lose our caste, whatever we eat.'

The Ramakrishna Mission's campaign against hunger started in 1897 itself. Hearing about Swami Akhandananda's endeavours to provide relief to the famine-stricken caused an overjoyed Swamiji to write to him from Almora on 15 June 1897: 'The detailed reports I am receiving about you are making me more and more delighted. The world can be won over by exactly this sort of work. What do the differences between faiths and opinions matter? Well done! You have all my blessings and a hundred thousand embraces from me! Work! Work! Work! I do not ask for anything else. Work—even unto death! We must be great workers and great champions for those who are feeble and weak. Don't worry about money—it will fly to you from the heavens! . . . If in the effort to bring food to the hungry, our name, possessions and everything is lost, अहो भाग्यमहो भाग्यम्—it is our great fortune!'

In the same vein, Swamiji wrote to Swami Brahmananda on 10 July 1897: 'The kind of work going on in Behrampur is very nice. It is work like this that will make us victorious. Can opinions touch the heart? Work, work—that is life. What do opinions and judgments matter? Philosophy, yoga, austerities, the puja room, rice and vegetables for offering—these are personal religious choices of a man or a country. The greatest universal religion is helping another person. Everyone can understand this religion—men, women, old and young, the outcaste and even animals! Can a religion that is only negative be of any use at all?'

Another time, a saffron-clad turbaned preacher from the *Gow-raksha sabha* (the association for safeguarding cows) met and presented Swamiji with a framed photograph of *Gow Mata* (mother cow). Swamiji asked him, 'What is the objective of your association? What is your source of income?' It was discovered that the merchant community patronized this association and funded them generously. Swamiji then brought up the topic of the severe drought in Central India and said, '(The) Indian government has published the news that nine lakh people have died due to hunger.' He wanted to know whether this association has provided some relief to the affected people and was very annoyed to hear that no help had been provided to the hungry and dying people. He said, 'An association that has no empathy for human beings deserves not the slightest empathy from me!'

The preacher then asked for alms, to which Swamiji replied, 'I am a sanyasi and a fakir myself . . . but if I ever have any funds in my hand, I will first spend it in the service of human beings. Mankind needs saving first—through feeding, educating and bringing into the spiritual fold.'

After the preacher left, Swamiji told his disciple Sharat Chandra, 'Look at what he says—that human beings die out of their own karma, so there's no reason why they should receive any kindness! . . . Did you see where this whole discussion on karma has reached in Hinduism? If a human being's heart does not cry at the misery of another, is he a human being at all?'

The Last Chapter

Now let us skip all minor events and anecdotes and go straight to the last chapter. We will look at the facts leading up to Swamiji's untimely death on 4 July 1902.

Narendranath's father, as we know, was a diabetic who died from heart complications on 23 February 1888, at the age of fifty-two. Many of Swamiji's nine siblings died at an early age. However, in spite of her deep sorrow and troubles, Swamiji's mother survived till the age of seventy when, as per the Corporation records, she died due to 'weakness brought on by senility'.

I have, at one time, researched and written a book about Swamiji's health in an essay entitled 'Sanyasi's Body'. Interested readers can find it in my book *The Monk as Man*.

In Romain Rolland's famous book (*Life of Vivekananda*), he writes that Swamiji was built like a wrestler, strong and powerful. He was tall (five feet, eight and a half inches), with strong arms capable of hard work, square-shouldered, broad-chested, a wonderful voice, with a beautiful body, a full face, wide forehead, strong jawline . . . and so on. His special attraction were his heavy-lidded, magnificent, coal-black eyes.

But Swamiji's weight was never steady. In the early days in America, the reporters estimated Swamiji's weight to be around 225 pounds (approximately 102 kg), and later Romain Rolland estimated him to be 170 pounds (77 kg). Swamiji has sometimes jokingly referred to himself as the fat Swamiji!

Swamiji's biggest problem was getting good sleep. He spent most of his nights tossing and turning on the bed. We have seen how he tried to get some sleep during the solar eclipse, in the hope that he would get it manifold in later years, but even then he could not sleep more than fifteen minutes.

I have tried to narrate the account of Swamiji's passing away in my book *The Monk as Man*. That description, in conjunction with two letters written by Swami Saradananda—the first on 9 August 1902 to Swami Abhedananda and the second on 23 August to Swami Premananda—are excerpted here.

During this sad time, Swami Saradananda and Swami Brahmananda were not in the *math*; they returned to Belur very late in the night on hearing the news.

Swami Saradananda writes in his 9 August letter: 'Some unexpected events led up to Swamiji's demise. Around two months before his death, he had gone to Kashi and fallen seriously ill. When he returned to the *math*, he began *kabiraji* treatment and became much better. After a month of treatment, the swelling of the hands and feet disappeared and so did the bloating of the stomach.' During this time, Swamiji could easily walk two miles without discomfort. 'In recent times his ascetic tendencies had also become very strong. He would take everyone with him to the puja room at four in the morning for meditation and chanting and he would always say, "My work here is done. Now you all look after everything and give me leave." Sometimes he would say, "My death is upon me; I have done enough of work and play."'

I have earlier written the entire schedule of 4 July. Swamiji woke up very early and went to the temple to pray with no sign of any illness. He had his usual breakfast of warm milk, fruits, etc. . . . An *ilish* had been bought from the Ganges—the first of the year. There were a lot of pleasantries on its price with Swami Premananda. Swamiji called an East Bengali and asked, 'I understand that when you get a new *ilish* you do some puja to it? Do whatever puja you have to do now.'

At 11.30 in the morning, instead of eating alone in his room, he had his lunch along with everyone else. With great satisfaction he had the *ilish* gravy, chutney, etc., and said, 'After *ekadashi* (the eleventh day of each lunar phase every month, which is treated as auspicious and when all ascetics and many householders fast and pray) it seems like my hunger has gone up. I have a tough time even sparing the plates and saucers!'

There were a lot of questions raised later about the *ilish*: whether eating excessive *ilish* was the cause of Swamiji's death! But our school friend's research did not yield any information to support this view.

After an hour's rest in the afternoon, Swamiji gathered everyone and took a class in grammar and mathematics. At four in the evening, he had a cup of warm milk and went out for a walk with Baburam Maharaj. Returning after an hour he said, 'Today I am feeling healthier than I have felt for a long time.'

At 6.30 p.m., Swamiji had a cup of tea with the other sanyasis. At 7 p.m., as soon as Brajendra had completed the evening *arati*, he went to his room with two strings of rosary beads and said, 'Do not disturb me till I call.'

At 7.45 p.m. he told his attendant, 'It is very warm, open the windows.' He lay on the bed on the floor and said, 'Please massage my legs.'

At 9 p.m. that evening, his right hand shook for a few seconds, his forehead was covered in beads of sweat. And then there was a cry like a child!

From 9:02 to 9:10, his head shook and fell off the pillow, his eyes were still and his face wore a beautiful light and smile.

At 9:30, Swami Bodhananda held his body and cried. He told someone, 'Rush and bring Dr Mahendra.' The doctor lived in Barahanagar.

At 10:30, both the doctor and Swami Brahmananda reached the *math* at almost the same time.

At midnight, the doctor announced that Swamiji was no more. A sudden heart failure was the cause of death.

Swamiji died at the age of thirty-nine years, five months and twenty-eight days. He had frequently said, 'I will not cross 40.'

Some Incidents Leading up to His Mahasamadhi

On 1 April, Ram Dada's wife had passed way. On 2 April, Japan's famous Okakura (Okakura Kakuzō, Japanese scholar) visited the *math* and had lunch. On 7 April the *kabiraj* came to see Swamiji and advised him to start having fish and fish oil. On 2 June, Swami Shivananda informed us that because of his eye problem Swamiji was unable to read or write. On 19 June, Swamiji went to Calcutta to meet his mother.

A week before his passing Swamiji had requested his dear disciple Shuddhananda to bring a *panjika* (almanac), and he would often look at that almanac, turning the pages.

In 1901, at a meeting in Dhaka, Swamiji had announced, 'I have at the most another year to live.'

Three days before his demise, Swamiji pointed to a spot at the south end of the field and said, 'When I go, do my final rites at that spot.' Two days before he died, he said, 'The spiritual strength and power that has been created here in Belur will last for 1500 years . . . don't think this is my imagination—I can clearly see this in front of my eyes.'

Now a quotation from Sister Nivedita. 'On the Wednesday before his departure Swamiji had told someone, "I am getting ready for death. A feeling of great *tapasya* and meditation is awakening within me. I am preparing myself for death."'

Sister Nivedita further writes, 'That very same Wednesday Swamiji maintained a fast for *ekadashi*—having nothing, not even water. That morning he insisted on serving his dear disciple himself.' Every item, including boiled jackfruit seeds, mashed potatoes, rice and chilled milk, was served by him, with various interesting stories alongside. After the meal was over, he poured water for her to wash her hands and then wiped it with the towel. When the disciple protested, Swamiji said, 'Jesus had washed the feet of his disciples!'

Another letter of Sister Nivedita's about Swamiji lies almost lost in the second volume of the book *Letters of Sister Nivedita*. Written from 16, Bose Para Lane, Baghbazar, at midnight on Sunday, 5 March, it gives us two important pieces of information. It is written to her favourite Miss MacLeod, whom she lovingly addresses as Yum.

'Yesterday (Saturday) at two in the afternoon Swamiji unexpectedly arrived at Baghbazar! I sent word that I will be there for tea. He responded, "Come right away," so I happily did! I found him alone, and he was in very high spirits. He then said, "Come with me to the *math* and have dinner there. Mrs Banerjee has given me the boat for a while." He told Sadananda to bring my hat and I went with him . . . As we spoke, Swamiji said, "Once I have initiated someone, I do not worry about him or her. If any of them want to become a sanyasi, I do not believe it falls within my responsibilities. This has a bad outcome too—if they make any mistakes I have to pay for it. But it also has a convenience, because of all this I too have remained a sanyasi and this is what I want. To remain a natural sanyasi like Ramakrishna Paramahamsa, who has no greed, no desire for riches or property and no thirst for fame. The desire for fame is the worst thing possible.'

After writing a lot more, it was time to discuss the story of the previous Sunday. Nivedita says that the lunch was a 'huge success'. 'It would have been wonderful if you were here to see it. Our Master himself had cooked everything. He had even taken the responsibility to serve us at the table himself. The table had been set on the first-floor veranda. Sarala was able to see Dakshineswar from there. The "geographical" meal reflected almost the entire world!

First: Yankee, fish chowder

Second: Norwegian, fish ball, which "Madam Agneowasan has taught me herself".

"Who is this lady Swamiji? What does she do? She sounds familiar."

"Among many other things she also cooks this fish ball."

Third: Yankee, boarding house hash. He said it has been cooked as per the rules, so it may contain some nails! (Although we did not find anything other than cloves—a few nails would have been good.)

Fourth: Kashmiri mince pie; meat cooked with almond and raisins.

Fifth: Bengali, *rosogolla* and fruits. It was at this mid-day meal that Swamiji had told us to see Dakshineswar on a full moon night, particularly on the night before Thakur's birth anniversary.'

Sister Nivedita's letter gives us an interesting glimpse into our chef Swamiji's endeavours to turn international! One day his researchers will have to discover at what point in his wanderings in search of God and in service to man Swamiji became such an accomplished cook! Sanyasi Vivekananda's becoming Maharaj Vivekananda is a landmark in our 5000-year-old cultural history.

We have no photograph of this world-famous personality's last year. After Thakur's death in Kashipur, his doctor had come forward and donated ten rupees to take a photo. After Swamiji's death however, it was deliberately decided not to take any group photo. The pilgrim spot that was set up to promote the inconsequentiality of death did not deserve a photo of death.

But there are many other memories and many letters and, using them, many books have been written since that fateful date of 4 July 1902. Here are some excerpts from Pramathanath Basu's writings.

'Sometimes, clad only in his loincloth, he would walk all around the *math* or wear a long flowing gown to cover himself and walk around the quiet temple road. . . . Often he would go to the kitchen and examine what was being cooked or even enjoy cooking a few delicious dishes himself.'

After roaming the entire world Swamiji had become interested in baking. 'He would test various yeasts and wheat for making bread.' Just before his death, he baked bread at the *math* and sent some across to his beloved Nivedita at Baghbazar.

'In this chapter of his life, Swamiji was not constrained by any social norms. He would walk around as per his own wish; sometimes with footwear sometimes barefoot; sometimes in a saffron garment, sometimes in his loincloth.'

As per *Kabiraj* Mahananda Sengupta's instructions, he was not allowed any water during his month-long treatment—only milk. 'For the duration of the month he had only milk; no water at all. . . . After two *kabiraji* treatments, from September he walked daily, morning and evening, clad in a gown with a cap over his ears and a strong stick in hand, all the way till Grand Trunk Road. . . . Swamiji's food intake had by then reduced considerably and Nidra Devi, the goddess of sleep, had also long deserted him.'

After Kali Puja one day, he visited the Kalighat temple with his mother. . . . At her bidding, he entered the temple with clothes wet from bathing in the river and offered puja in the temple. He also observed the ritual of rolling on the ground in the front of the Goddess to appease her.

In October, when his health failed seriously, he was taken to the famous Dr Sanders.

* * *

At the time, there were Santhal tribals from the Chhotanagpur area working in the *math*. Swamiji one day asked them, 'Will you eat with us?' Their headman Keshta was unwilling. 'If we eat salt touched by you, we will lose our caste!'

Swamiji immediately said, 'Why should you eat salt? We will cook without any salt.' After feeding them, Swamiji said, 'You are Narayan!' He further added, 'I sometimes wish we could sell off all the *math* and everything and give it all away to these poor Narayans. After all, we can find sustenance even under a tree.'

Swamiji said to his disciple Sharat Chandra, 'This body is born; it will die. Always remember sacrifice is the key to life.'

Swami Brahmananda once said about the ill and irritable Swamiji in Belur *Math*, 'Who has understood him? Who could understand him? . . . These people do not know how difficult it was to live with him, to tolerate him. How many times we have found his rebukes unbearable and decided to leave the *math* altogether!'

Once in Belur *Math*, Raja Maharaj closed the door to his room in sorrow and pride after being shouted at. In a short while, coming to ask forgiveness, Swamiji said, 'What can I do? My mind does not know . . . what my body is saying. Raja, will you do something for me? When their racing horses cannot run any more, they shoot them. I will also arrange for a revolver for you. Will you shoot me? There will be no harm done; after all my work here is completed.'

Racked by innumerable diseases, sleep-deprived, Vivekananda yet did not completely lose his ability to enjoy life, as we can see from several incidents before his passing away.

He wanted to go back to his days of youth and play the role of a *pakoda* seller! (*Pakodas* are fried savouries made of various vegetables dipped in a batter of chickpea flour). He even acted out the part of a *pakoda* seller, making the fries himself and selling them in a mock drama!

On the eve of his departure, he frequently remembered his childhood days. We have a heart-warming scene from the pen of Sharat Chandra. Once, walking along the Ganges in Calcutta, Swami Sharat Chandra saw a beautiful sight. 'A little ahead of me a sanyasi was walking towards Ahiritola ghat. As he neared, I saw this was none other than my own guru, Swami Vivekananda. Swamiji was holding a leaf cone full of a fried mixture of chickpeas, nuts, etc. and like a small child, was happily walking along, enjoying the mixture.' Swamiji told his disciple, 'Here, have some mixture. It has lots of spice and salt—you will like it.' The disciple did not let go of the wonderful opportunity, and the two of them took a boat back to Belur *Math* across the river.

We don't know the exact date of this event, but we do know it was in 1902, not too far from Swamiji's *mahasamadhi*. If this was a serialized historic story, we would have conducted some research into why Swamiji, the great exponent of Vedanta, had this great attraction for all mixtures, fried chickpeas and nuts and created a chapter on the findings. There have been so many incidents revolving around all these fried and boiled nuts and peas in various countries. The same Vivekananda who was so inordinately fond of all these common-man's snacks also told his disciple Sharat Chandra, 'Whenever you get the time, meditate. . . . Be respectful, be true to your dharma, achieve spiritual ability and spend your days in helping others—this is my desire and blessing.'

Earlier Swamiji shared many stories of the old days with Sharat Chandra. 'On some days the situation in the *math* was so dire that there was nothing at all. Rice came as alms but there was no salt. Some days we had just rice and salt but no one was perturbed at all. . . . Those were the days! . . . Because we had seen Thakur's life, we were completely unconcerned about any

sorrow or trouble. Today's boys will not be able to work under these conditions. That is why it is necessary to organize a small place to stay, a handful of rice to eat. If they get some simple rice to eat and simple clothes to wear, they will be able to focus on devotion and chanting and will learn to live in the service of others.'

Food, hunger and deprivation have all come together and walked closely in Swamiji's life. If someone were to record all this faithfully, today's readers would be overwhelmed. He who would raise such a storm at the Chicago conference two days later almost starved to death in the new country. It was very difficult in America—begging was a crime punishable by imprisonment. Mary Louise Burke's deep research has shown us that even after becoming famous, the sanyasi's life was not without problems. In New York, once his disciple Kripananda informed his *dheera mata* ('calm' mother) Mrs Ole Bull, 'In order to spread the word of Vedanta, Swamiji himself rents the home, advertises, prints the pamphlets, etc. In order to pay for all of this, he often goes without food.'

Swamiji's anxiety to put some food in the mouth of the hungry arises from his own nightmares of hunger. Towards the end of his life, he told Sharat Chandra, 'When the money comes, we have to build a giant kitchen. The only sounds will be of a chorus of "Please serve! Please receive! Please eat!" The starch drained from the rice will flow down to the river, whitening the waters of the Ganges. When I see this, then I will know peace.'

Hand in hand with food, hunger and deprivation, some banquets hosted by the wealthy also found their way in Swamiji's overseas life. In my book *The Unfamiliar, Unknown Vivekananda*, I have collected some information about royal feasts. Which states eat when, how frequently they eat, how

they are seated, etc., has been more thoroughly researched by Swamiji than by any Indian in any era.

Arguably one of Swamiji's favourite food items was the ice cream, which he often called 'kulfi'. His brother Mahendranath has described with great enthusiasm the imported ice cream they had as children in the Datta home. We also know how he used to love putting ice and sugar in the tender coconut and eat it chilled. In the USA, his favourite was the chocolate ice cream.

In America's well-to-do families Swamiji's love for ice cream was well known. Mrs Legett as we know, used to tease him by announcing "there is ice cream today" to keep him from jumping up after dinner and going out to smoke his pipe. We have seen how in the coldest of California weathers Swamiji would still order an ice cream at the hotel, and he couldn't bear to be kept waiting for it. He would tell the manager, 'Please don't delay!'

Undeterred by his diabetes, Swamiji also brought the foreign ice cream to India. Sister Nivedita's letter has a very credible description of Swamiji's weakness for ice cream. She writes in 1899 from Baghbazar to Miss MacLeod, 'Tomorrow, Sadananda and I will spend five rupees for "His" ice cream. I know it is rather ostentatious but he wants it.'

And now it is time to end our tale. A new example has been revealed in our times of the age-old story of food and hunger that is running through the world. The delicious taste of the pure white *rosogolla*, that greatest sweet of all times, has been introduced anew in the minds of the young and old. A new door of possibilities has opened, which will continue to unfold over the forthcoming thousands of years. The new sanyasi of our times has given to the planet a new voice for the modern world. Embracing the challenging powers of both food and hunger together, he has commanded, 'Wake up!' And the wise and enlightened one has blessed the people of the world, 'May you be awakened!'

Two years before his passing away (18 April 1900), the sanyasi, plagued with illness, writes from Alameda, California, to his American well-wisher and friend Miss Josephine MacLeod,

'Pray for me Joe that my works stop for ever, and my whole soul be absorbed in Mother. Her works, She knows.'

The eternal friend of the hungry also writes,

'The battles are lost and won, I have bundled my things and am waiting for the great deliverer. Shiva, O Shiva, carry my boat to the other shore.'

To this Vivekananda of feasting, fasting and hungry humanity, we again offer our prayers.

The End

Acknowledgement

I have lost track of how many books I have researched since 1942 and my days at Howrah's Swami Vivekananda Institution to find out about the food habits and culinary interests of our Swami Vivekananda, who has won the hearts and minds of the world. Kananbihari Mukhopadhyay's *Life of Swamiji* was then taught in the eighth standard. In my craving to be ahead of my peers, I read it well before schedule. Then, one by one, from Swamiji's letters to his speeches and writings, I devoured everything.

Once I had bunked school and gone to hear Swamiji's brother Mahendranath Dutta in North Calcutta, on Gourmohan Mukherjee Street. From a distance that day, I couldn't really understand him. Later, reading his most valuable books over and over, I was amazed. I still wonder why those books were never valued as they should have been. If Mahendranath had not, with great dedication, written so many books over the years, we would never have understood or even known Vishwanath, Narendranath or Vivekananda as deeply as we now do. His English and Bengali books about Swami Vivekananda are extremely valuable too.

To understand Maharaj Vivekananda, I have delved into thousands of letters, biographies and research theses by various writers. I convey my respectful pranam to all of them.

Sankar

Bibliography

Bengali Books:

(The titles are translated here for easy understanding of the readers.)

Basu, Dheerendranath. *In Conversation with Sri Mahendranath*.
Basu, Pramathanath. *Swami Vivekananda, Volumes 1 & 2*.
Basu, Rajnarayan. *Those Days and These Days*.
Basu, Sankariprasad. *The Mighty Vivekananda*.
Basu, Sankariprasad. *Vivekananda and Contemporary India*, *Volumes 1–7*. Kolkata: Mondol Book House, 1975.
Bhattacharya, Hiranmay. *Rasik Vivekananda*.
Chakraborty, Sharacchandra. *Swami–Shishya Dialogue*.
Chattopadhyay, Harihar. *Memoirs of Sri Ramakrishna*.
Datta, Mahendranath. *Events in the Life of Srimad Sharadananda Swamiji*.
Datta, Mahendranath. *Events in the Life of Srimad Vivekananda Swamiji, Volumes 1-3*. Calcutta: Mahendra Publishing.
Datta, Mahendranath. *Kolkata's Ancient Story and Customs*.
Datta, Mahendranath. *Reflections of Ajatshatru Srimad Swami Brahmananda Maharaj*.
Datta, Mahendranath. *Reflections of Gurupran Ramchandra*.

Datta, Mahendranath. *Swami Vivekananda in Kashi Dham.*

Datta, Mahendranath. *Swami Vivekananda in London, Volumes 1–3.* Kolkata: Mahendra Publishing Committee.

Datta, Mahendranath. *Swami Vivekananda's Childhood.* Kolkata: Mahendra Publishing.

Datta, Mahendranath. *Thoughts of Sri Sri Ramakrishna.*

Datta, Narendranath, and Sri Baishnabcharan Basak. *Sangeet Kalpataru.*

Datta, Vishwanath. *Sulochana*

Debsharma, Kaleejeeban. *Sri Ramakrishna Parikrama, Volumes 1–2.*

Dutta, Viswanath. *Sulochana.* Edited by Sankar. Kolkata: Sahityam, 2006.

Ghatak, Lakshminarayan. *In Conversation with Sri Mahendranath.*

Mukhopadhyay, Kananbihari. *Swamiji's Biography.*

Mukhopadhyay, Pyaremohan. *An Offering of Memories.*

Sankar. *The Unfamiliar, Unknown Vivekanada.* Kolkata: Sahityam, 2003.

Sankar. *Food Habits of Bengalis* Kolkata: Sahiytam, 2005.

Sankar. *The Original Bengali Kitchen.* Kolkata: Dey's Publishing, 2000.

Sharma, BeniShankar. *A Forgotten Chapter of Swami Vivekananda's Life.*

Sri M. *Sri Sri Ramakrishna Kathamrita.* Kolkata: Udbodhan, 1902.

Swami Abjajananda. *At the Feet of Swamiji.*

Swami Chetanananda. *The Many Forms of Vivekananda.*

Swami Gambhirananda. *Sri Ramakrishna Bhakta-maalika.*

Swami Gambhirananda. *Yug Nayak Vivekananda, Volumes 1–3.* Kolkata: Udbodhan, 1991.

Swami Poornatmananda. *Vivekananda in the Light of Memory.*

Swami Prabhananda. *Sri Ramakrishna's Antaleela, Volumes 1–2.*

Swami Sharadananda. *Sri Sri Ramakrishna Leelaprasanga, Volumes 1–2.*

Swami Vivekananda. *Patrabali.* Kolkata: Udbodhan, 2008.·

Swami Vivekananda. *Speeches and Essays Volumes 1–10.* Birth Centenary Edition. Kolkata: Udbodhan, 1963.

English Books:

Burke, Marie Louise. *Swami Vivekananda in the West, Volumes 1–6.* Kolkata: Advaita Ashram, 1994.

Chaudhuri, Asim. *Swami Vivekananda in America—New Findings.*

Chaudhuri, Asim. *Swami Vivekananda in England and Continental Europe.*

Dhar, S.N. *A Comprehensive Biography of Swami Vivekananda, Volumes 1–3.*

Letters of Sister Nivedita, Volumes 1–2. Kolkata: Advaita Ashram, 2017.

Reminiscences of Swami Vivekananda

Sister Nivedita. *The Master as I Saw Him.*

Stavig, Gopal. *Western Admirers of Sri Ramakrishna.*

Swami Chetanananda. *East Meets West.*

The Complete Works of Swami Vivekananda, Volumes 1–9. Calcutta: Advaita Ashram, 1962.